# A PARADIGM FOR MANAGEMENT INFORMATION SYSTEMS

# A PARADIGM FOR MANAGEMENT INFORMATION SYSTEMS

Phillip Ein-Dor
and
Eli Segev

PRAEGER

PRAEGER SPECIAL STUDIES • PRAEGER SCIENTIFIC

Published in 1981 by Praeger Publishers
CBS Educational and Professional Publishing
A Division of CBS, Inc.
521 Fifth Avenue, New York, New York 10175 U.S.A.

© 1981 by Praeger Publishers

Library of Congress Catalog Card Number: 81-1825

ISBN 0-03-058017-X

123456789   145   987654321

Printed in the United States of America

To Our Children

Ido
Miriam
Aviv
Shai
Noa

# PREFACE

This book is the culmination of a five-year effort; we contemplate its completion with considerable gratification. It began in an attempt to find a model in the literature that could serve as a basis for empirical research into management information systems (MIS). This led, after some search, to the realization that no model existed that we considered completely satisfactory. Finally, we were motivated to devise our own model from the materials prepared for us by others. The outcome of this evolution is presented to you, should you find yourself in a situation similar to ours.

In the process, this study has generated a textbook as well as a number of articles that have appeared in various journals. Each of these papers deals with one of the areas of the study. However, less than one-third of the material included in this book has seen publication, and none of the several attempts to synthesize accumulations of research in specific areas has been published. The work is based on a survey of hundreds of articles and many books. If the organization of this fragmented material into a consistent theory is considered to be its principal contribution, we will rest content; if our own somewhat ambitious goals are realized, the book will also become a common model for the execution and integration of future studies in MIS.

It is with some trepidation that we adopted the use of the word "paradigm" to describe our work. For one thing, some of its dictionary definitions (ideal; standard; paragon) may lay us open to accusations of pretentiousness. Our trepidations increased when one of our colleagues let it be known that he "wouldn't be caught dead using the word"—a reflection of the recent disrepute into which this word has fallen. After much thought, however, we concluded we were striving to formulate a paradigm (in the sense of an example; pattern; mold) that would appear as such to others and that, no matter how hard we tried, we could find no better description for what we were trying to do. So, at the risk of appearing somewhat gauche, paradigm it is.

Throughout the book, we have tried to synthesize all of the significant empirical research into MIS of which we are aware, and to suggest areas in which research is most promising or most urgent. Thus, in presenting the existing state of knowledge it should be of use to students of the field and hopefully will trigger ideas for empirical study. Executives and practitioners may find it useful since it may permit them to assess the current state of the art of MIS and to realize when experts in MIS expound from a solid platform of public knowledge and when, as is sometimes the case, they present their own private intuition or wishful thinking as natural law.

In The Moonstone, by Wilkie Collins, the trusted old house-steward, Gabriel Betteredge, states:

> . . . that such a book as Robinson Crusoe never was written, and never will be written again. . . . When my spirits are bad—Robinson Crusoe. When I want advice—Robinson Crusoe. In past times, when my wife plagued me; in present times when I had a drop too much—Robinson Crusoe.

Although Robinson Crusoe may indeed be a repository of all human wisdom, Defoe required several hundreds of pages to encompass it. Lewis Carroll's Hunting of the Snark is no less a compendium of philosophies to soothe the soul, and all in eight short Fits! As evidence, we supply mottos from the Hunting of the Snark to fit every chapter, except the first, which "was a Boojum, you see."

In conclusion, we wish to acknowledge our debt of gratitude to all those who contributed to the formation and completion of this book. A number of anonymous reviewers contributed encouraging comments and helpful suggestions. This book was completed while we both were on leaves of absence from Tel-Aviv University, enjoying all that California has to offer; during that period, the Naval Postgraduate School and the University of California, Los Angeles provided technical support. Most important, our families lent unlimited patience and strong moral support in those periods when they were most needed.

Los Angeles      Monterey
California      California

# CONTENTS

LIST OF TABLES

# LIST OF FIGURES

# *1*
# INTRODUCTION

> The genuine problem is to show how empirical proposi-
> tions can be made at all about systems that, given cir-
> cumstances, might be quite other than they are.
>> Herbert A. Simon, <u>The Sciences of the Artificial</u>

Many innovations have been made in management in recent
years. Some of these, such as budgeting methods, cost/benefit
analysis, project management techniques, and corporate planning
methods, have had significant effects on the way organizations operate and make decisions. None of these innovations, however, can
begin to compare with management information systems (MIS) in the
rapidity, depth, pervasiveness, and magnitude of effect. This is
because the vast majority of innovations affect one function or one
facet of organizational activity. MIS, on the other hand, influence
all organizational functions and all facets of organizations' activities.
Innovations in MIS affect the very structure and processes of organizations at every level, from operations to strategic planning.

The reason for the effect of MIS lies in their content (information) and their use (decision making). The processing of information
to make decisions is the essence of management; thus, management
information systems are to organizations as central nervous systems
are to living creatures. The nervous system both controls and en-
capsulates the whole system; similarly, MIS mirror and control organizations. This analogy would be complete only for the all-inclusive, fully integrated, and as yet unattainable, total management information system. Given the current state of the art, in which each
organization has a number of more or less integrated MIS, one may
think of each of these systems as analogous to one facet of a biological

1

nervous system. Thus, organizations may have personnel, production, financial, and other MIS that in federation form the organization's total information system, just as the visual, aural, tactile, and motor systems together form the central nervous system. In living things, the integration of the various systems is accomplished by the brain. In organizations, this integration does not yet exist except in the minds of its managers. Thus, an organization's formal management information systems are an incomplete approximation of its managerial processes.

MIS are embedded in, and are part of, managerial processes in organizations. The implementation of a new MIS usually involves changing the information available and the way it is used; thus, the decision parameters frequently change with the availability of information and this in turn changes the decision model or decision rules. The introduction of an MIS is usually accompanied by an improvement in the state of the managerial art. In designing new MIS, managers usually have to redefine the decision problem and the information they need. Implementors of MIS apply their expertness in management science to systematize and improve the decision process, increasing its rationality. The result of this effort, if successfully executed, is often a managerial process quite different from that which it replaces. Thus, the implementation of MIS is usually accompanied by changes in managerial processes.

From the foregoing, it follows that a framework for a theory of MIS should view such systems as a mirror image of the managerial process, rather than as a machine enabling managers to do more of the same things as before more rapidly, while expending less of their own energy. Many textbooks designed to introduce students and managers to the concepts of management information systems do indeed adopt this approach. For example, Davis's widely used text examines in detail the decision-making processes and organizational factors with which MIS are interwoven (Davis 1974). Other examples are Murdick and Ross (1975) and the authors' own text (Ein-Dor and Segev 1978).

Although textbooks on MIS often relate to the topic in this broader context, most empirical research does not. Since significant research calls for well-defined and manageable problems for which consistent data can be collected, most empirical research focuses on a small number of variables out of the large number that affect the design, functioning, success, and failure of MIS. Often, the variables studied are technical in nature, referring to such things as response times, level of accuracy, and degree of aggregation. One sometimes has the feeling that they are chosen for ease of operationalization and measurement, rather than for their real significance in understanding MIS processes.

Irrespective of the variables chosen and their significance, studies dealing only with some small subset of the variables affecting MIS can contribute meaningfully to our knowledge of the area if—and only if—there exists a framework or paradigm to which the findings can be related and into which they can be incorporated. Such a framework should delineate the area, identify the variables relevant to MIS and known relationships between them, and should propose methodologies suitable for research in the field. It would thus provide a filing system into which existing and future research findings can be categorized and accumulated in a systematic manner, leading to an improvement in understanding of the phenomena with each new finding. A paradigm of this sort, by providing a shared frame of reference for all those active in the area, would direct research into areas of greatest significance, highlight the most important findings, and permit that systematic accumulation of knowledge by which science progresses (Kuhn 1972). The intention of this book is to present such a paradigm for management information systems.

## THE PARADIGM

### Definition

It was the original intention of the authors to solve the dilemma of defining an MIS by resorting to the common practice of letting the readers supply their own definitions. In the course of working on this book, however, it became clear that this solution may be impractical. Since the plausibility of the existence of MIS has been brought into question by authorities on the subject (Dearden 1972; Mandell 1975), one cannot reasonably study them without first establishing their existence; one would hate to study the Cheshire cat only to discover that there was no more to it than its grin. Thus, the issue of definition cannot be ignored.

There seem to be two classes of definitions of MIS. One definition calibrates Management Information Systems (upper case) by their degree of integration. An extreme view regards only a completely integrated total model of the organization as being an MIS. This was probably the intention of those who first resorted to the concept of an MIS. In addition to integration, frequently required attributes include data bases, direct access, and decision support. Brief consideration will lead the reader to the conclusion that this is a design-oriented definition, since it defines an MIS in terms of its structure or design attributes. In practice, these attributes prove difficult to achieve. There are numerous examples of organizations that backed away from the idea of a total corporate model in favor of a large number of simplified partial models. This development probably contributed to the scepticism mentioned above concerning the feasibility of MIS.

The second class of definition defines a management information system (lower case) as an information system that serves management, rather than serving operations or process control functions. In this view, management information systems are one of many co-equal types of information systems. Many organizations report having considerable numbers of management information systems (Hanold 1972; Roark 1970; Schwartz 1970). Given this definition, a simple, stand-alone, unintegrated information system serving management is a management information system. This is a use-oriented approach that states that a system is an MIS when it is used by a manager who finds it useful in the performance of that manager's duties.*

Many managers claim that they have management information systems. The fact that information systems often fall into disuse when managers change indicates that what constitutes an MIS for one manager does not for another. A system is an MIS for a given manager with a given problem at a given time (Mason and Mitroff 1973). Thus, it is managers who are the objective test of what constitutes an MIS and the authors must reject the original intention of letting the readers provide their own definitions. The authors argue, therefore, that whether an MIS exists is an empirical, not a theoretical, issue. The question is not "Can MIS exist?" but, rather, "If they exist, how is one to recognize them?" The following definition purports to answer the second question:

> A management information system (MIS) is an assemblage of facilities and personnel for collecting, sorting, retrieving, and processing information that is used, or desired, by one or more managers in the performance of management duties.

-------

*This approach is analogous to the Turing test for artificial intelligence (Turing 1950). This test states that an artifact is intelligent when an intelligent human cannot distinguish its behavior from that of other intelligent humans. As intelligent beings are the touchstone for intelligence, so are managers the touchstone for management information systems.

Should any attributes be found that are common to all MIS, as defined, these could be incorporated into a more general definition that would be independent of any particular manager.*

Methodology

The methodology employed by the authors of this book in building a framework for MIS is similar to that of the earlier work of Mason and Mitroff (1973) and of Lucas (1975), both subsequently discussed in detail; all are based on literature searches. The methodology is also similar to that of Lucas in formulating the model as a set of propositions. There, however, the similarity ends. The dependent variable in this paradigm is the success of MIS, greatly enhancing its normative content when compared with the previous models. The point of departure was not to try to apply existing basic disciplines to MIS on an intuitive basis, but, rather, to identify the elements of MIS and thence to infer the disciplines relevant to their study. This difference is evident in the literature surveyed, which in turn has a significant effect on the resulting model.

The data base on which the framework is constructed comes from a fairly exhaustive survey of data and opinions in the scientific, professional, and trade literatures on data processing, computer science, and management science. As a result of this approach, the list of variables of MIS generated is much more comprehensive than in the previous work. This list contains over 100 variables, compared to 5 in the Mason and Mitroff model and 10 in Lucas's model. Comprehensiveness, together with the structure imposed on it in the form

---

*Having read this definition, the reader may be asking, "What is the difference between Management Information Systems and the Decision Support Systems that one hears about recently?" It is not easy to find a convincing answer to this question. A recent conference on decision support systems (DSS), for example, provided not one specific definition (Carlson 1977). The attributes assigned to DSS look very much like those heretofore assigned to MIS. The only consistent difference seems to be that DSS specialize in supporting unstructured decisions. Thus, we support Carlson's contention that "DSS are a subset of Management Information Systems (MIS), since MIS includes all systems which support any management decision making" (Carlson 1977). As one author on the topic has stated, "Decision Support Systems (DSS) is a buzzword whose time has arrived" (Alter 1979). But why is a new buzzword necessary when a perfectly good one, namely MIS, already exists?

of aggregation into major elements of MIS, and the goal-oriented nature of the propositions are the major contributions claimed for the framework presented in this book. In addition, it has been shown that all the variables can be defined operationally. Appendix 1 contains a list of all the variables and suggested operationalizations.

Following a practice common in the behavioral sciences, the model is presented as a series of propositions. There are 93 of them. Examples of this method of presentation range from March and Simon's classic Organizations (1958) through Price's Organizational Effectiveness (1969) and Lucas's work on MIS (1975). The propositions here take two forms:

Relationship between values of variable x and success/failure of MIS. For example: The higher the value of x, the greater the likelihood of success; and

Relationship between values of variable y and x where variable x appears in a proposition of the first form. For example: The higher y, the lower x.

The vast majority of the propositions are of the first form, since it was the authors' intention, insofar as possible, to simplify the model and to indicate the direct effect of each independent variable on success or failure. In the few cases where this was impossible, the effects are stated in two-stage relationships of the second form.

Success of MIS

Criteria of success that have been identified in the literature include the following:

Profitability (Carlson 1967; Garrity 1963; Powers and Dickson 1973);

Application to major problems of the organization (Garrity 1963);

Quality of decisions or level of performance (Carlson 1967; Lucas 1975b);

User satisfaction (Powers and Dickson 1973); and

Widespread use (Garrity 1963; Swanson 1974).

The authors then define a successful management information system as one that is profitably applied to an area of major concern to the organization, is widely used by one or more satisfied managers, and improves the quality of their performance. Of these criteria, the authors believe that use is the most significant since a manager will use a system intensively only if it meets the other criteria. This criterion is also consistent with the authors' definition of an MIS.

The validity of success/failure as an independent variable depends on the ability either to measure degrees of success or to assign any system to one of the two dichotomous states. In general, there seems to be little difficulty in characterizing any given system as either a success or a failure. This is supported by Garrity's (1963) finding that the difference in accomplishment between lead and average companies (in terms of information system success) was striking; he found no middle accomplishment group. Some weighted average of the criteria mentioned above would probably be a better measure than a purely dichotomous differentiation, but for all practical purposes the success/failure dichotomy seems to be quite satisfactory.

## Elements of the Model

The many variables identified in the literature have been grouped into seven elements, each of which represents a partially detachable subsystem. The elements are defined as follows:

● The environment of MIS. This refers to the situational variables, inside and outside the organization, as they impinge on the information system. This environment is characterized by such variables as prevailing technologies, availability of resources, organizational size and maturity, attitudes toward MIS, and perceptions of MIS.

● Procedural aspects of MIS. These include the organization's strategic plan for developing information systems, hardware and software acquisition strategies, organizational arrangements, and project implementation. Strategic planning variables include the general direction of development, the purposes defined for information systems, priority schemes for ordering projects, and project specifications and documentation.

Hardware acquisition strategies deal with computer capabilities, the selection process, the form of acquisition, and equipment deployment. Software strategy variables include project complexity, programming languages, use of external contractors, risk and reliability estimates, and standardization of software practices. Organizational strategies include the organizational location of MIS, degree of centralization, organization of MIS implementors, the user interface, the steering committee, the study group, the data base administrator, corporate computer staff, and external assistance.

MIS project implementation consists of a number of phases including planning, project module selection and scheduling, project staffing, project development, design control, programming, progress review, operation and maintenance, postimplementation review, and computer center control.

- The structure of MIS. This element describes the physical system that is the end product of the procedures adopted. It includes data characteristics, user interface characteristics, mode of operation, and integration.

- Senior executives. This element refers to the ranks of senior executives involved in MIS and the roles they play in terms of their association with MIS, the functions they perform, their capabilities with respect to MIS, and their relationships with other groups of employees involved in MIS.

- Implementors of MIS. Included in this element are the managers, analysts, programmers, and operators who compose the staff responsible for developing, operating, and maintaining MIS. They can be discussed in terms of their functions, recruitment and turnover, organization, capabilities, and relationships with other relevant personnel.

- Users of MIS. The variables relevant to this element are the ranks of users, their characteristics, capabilities, and education, their behavior as users, and their relationships with other human elements of MIS.

- The fit of an MIS. This element is a synthesis of all the preceding variables and examines their interactions as they are expressed in the two dimensions in which MIS adapt to their environments—the fit of systems to the needs and characteristics of individual users (including the user interface) and the compatibility of systems with the structures and characters of the organizations in which they are embedded.

In the elements referring to executives, implementors, and users, relationships with the other groups have been listed as variables. For some purposes it may be useful to extract this web of relationships in its entirety and to think of it as a separate element. To avoid redundancy, the authors have not done so in this book.

Overview of the Paradigm

The elements of the paradigm coalesce naturally into a number of subsystems, in each of which are strong relationships between the elements included. Although elements can, and do, interact directly across subsystem boundaries, the interactions across

such boundaries tend to be more global and less specific. The subsystems, displayed graphically in Figure 1.1, are the behavioral
subsystem, the procedural subsystem, the structural subsystem,
and the environment. The remaining element, fit, is a conceptual
measure of the mutual adaption of the other elements, and therefore
does not appear explicitly in the diagram.

FIGURE 1.1

Subsystems of MIS

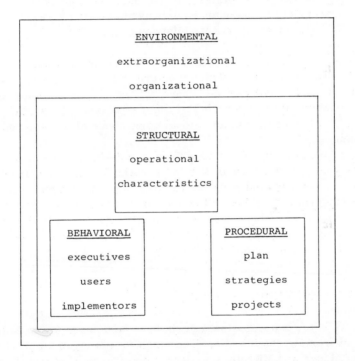

The behavioral subsystem encompasses users, executives,
implementors, and the network of interrelationships between them.
Within this subsystem are worked out the group dynamics and interpersonal relationships that affect the development and success of
MIS.

The planning, strategy, and project variables constitute the
procedural subsystem. These elements describe the procedures
and mechanisms whereby overall organizational goals are successively detailed and operationalized to the point where a system is
finally coded and brought into use.

The behavioral and procedural subsystems both operate within an organizational and extraorganizational environment that determines the limits of what can be done in developing MIS and shapes the form of what actually is done. The relationship between the internal workings of objects and their environments has been stated with admirable simplicity by Simon (1969):

> An artifact can be thought of as a meeting place—an "interface" in today's terms—between an "inner" environment, the substance and organization of the artifact itself and an "outer" environment, the surroundings in which it operates. If the inner environment is appropriate to the outer environment, or vice versa, the artifact will serve its intended purpose.* [p. 7]

In the present context, the MIS is the artifact and its structure is the physical realization. This structure is the interface between the people and activities—the behavioral and procedural subsystems—that are its components, or inner environment, and the organizational and extraorganizational components of its outer environment.

Thus, because of our specific interest—the success and failure of MIS—the structure of MIS is crucial. The external forces of the environment and their interactions with the internal forces of the behavioral and procedural subsystems determine the final form of the structure. The degree to which this structure fits the inner environment and reconciles the inner and outer environments determines the success or failure of the system.

## COMPARISON WITH PREVIOUS WORK

To date, two important efforts have been made to formulate general frameworks for MIS. The pioneering work in the field is that of Mason and Mitroff, who formulated a general model of information systems in organizations based on a review of the literatures in the fields of decision theory, psychology, organizational behavior, and the philosophy of inquiry systems in general and of management information systems specifically (Mason and Mitroff 1973). This

---

*Reprinted by permission of MIT Press from Herbert Simon. The Sciences of the Artificial, copyright © 1969 by the Massachusetts Institute of Technology.

framework has already triggered considerable empirical research that proceeds from their basic model. The second major effort is that of Lucas (1975b). His is a descriptive model of information systems in the context of organizations and is derived from the literature on organizational behavior and information systems and on his own empirical studies.

Having presented the paradigm, it will be useful to briefly examine these two previous efforts in the field. This will indicate the authors' indebtedness to them while illustrating the synthesis and extensions made possible by the paradigm.

Mason and Mitroff (1973)

The Mason and Mitroff definition of an information system explicitly states the variables that they consider relevant to the investigation of such systems (1973):

> An information system consists of at least one PERSON
> of a certain PSYCHOLOGICAL TYPE who faces a PROB-
> LEM within some ORGANIZATIONAL CONTEXT for
> which he needs EVIDENCE to arrive at a solution (i.e.,
> to select some course of action) and that the evidence is
> made available to him through some MODE OF PRE-
> SENTATION.* (Emphasis in the original.) [p. 475]

Following is a very brief elaboration of the dimensions of each of the variables in Mason and Mitroff's model:

Psychological type. The psychological type of an information system user is determined by the combination of modes of information perception and evaluation as defined by Jung; that is, "sensation" and "intuition" as modes of perception combined with "thinking" and "feeling" as modes of evaluation.

Problem types. Information systems are affected by the type of problem in the solution of which they are designed to participate. The basic distinction is between structured and unstructured problems.

---

*Reprinted by permission from Mason, Richard O. and Mitroff, Ian I. "A Program for Research on Management Information Systems," Management Science, Volume 19, Number 5 (January 1973), Copyright (1973) The Institute of Management Sciences.

Organizational context. This describes the hierarchical level in an organization that an information system is intended to support—operational control, management control, or strategic planning.

Evidence. Based on the history of philosophy, five types of evidence generators and guarantors are identified: Lockean, Leibnitzian, Kantian, Hegelian, and Singerian-Churchmanian.

Modes of presentation. Information systems vary according to the degree to which the information they provide is personalistic or impersonalistic.

Lucas (1975b)

Lucas's approach is more empirically oriented and not quite so eclectic as that of Mason and Mitroff. His model is also much more specific in that it attempts not only to describe the variables but also posits the relationships between them. It originates from empirical data and draws on fewer relevant disciplines. Lucas differentiates three main variables in his model, with each of seven more affecting one or more of these or other minor variables. The relationships between the variables are posited by Lucas in 16 propositions not detailed here but exhibited graphically in Figure 1.2.

The major (numbered) and minor (lettered) variables in the figure are as follow:

1. User attitudes and perceptions of information systems and information system staff, affected by:
   a. policies and attitudes of the information services department;
   b. management action; and
   c. user contact and involvement with information system activities.
2. Use of a system, determined by:
   1. user attitudes and perceptions;
   d. technical quality of the system;
   e. decision style;
   3. performance; and
   f. situational and personal factors.
3. Performance, determined by:
   e. decision style;
   f. situational and personal factors; and
   g. user analysis action (the ability of the user to analyze alternatives and to utilize system outputs).

There is some repetition in these lists of variables because some of them affect more than one other variable.

FIGURE 1.2

Descriptive Model of Information Systems in the Context of the Organization

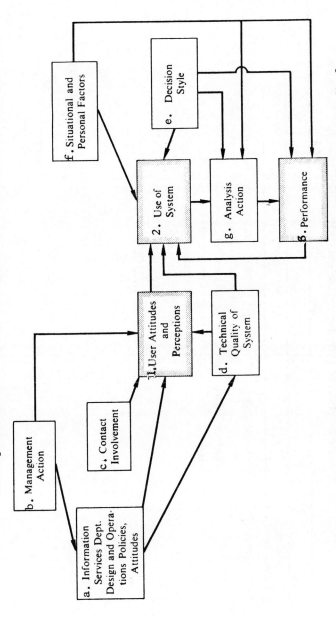

Note: Major and minor variables are identified by digits and letters, respectively.
Source: Henry C. Lucas, Jr. Why Information Systems Fail (New York: Columbia University Press, 1975), p. 20. Reprinted by permission.

13

## TABLE 1.1

### Comparison of Paradigm Elements with Other Models' Variables

| Paradigm MIS Element | Mason and Mitroff | | Lucas | |
|---|---|---|---|---|
| | Variable | Comments | Variable | Comments |
| Environment | Problem type | Mason and Mitroff distinguish between the problem types—structured and unstructured—and organizational context, which characterizes hierarchical levels. In the paradigm, both are subsumed under MIS environment. | User attitudes and perceptions | User attitudes and perceptions are part of the psychological climate toward MIS—one of the variables in MIS environment. |
| | Organizational context | | | |
| Procedure | | — | | |
| planning | | — | Information services design and operations policies | The way in which MIS are designed and implemented is among the variables that determine the project element of the paradigm. |
| strategies | | — | | |
| projects | | | | |
| Senior executives | | — | Management action | In Lucas's model, this variable defines the role played by executive |

14

| | | | | |
|---|---|---|---|---|
| Implementors | | — | | — |
| Users | Psychological type | Mason and Mitroff's psychological type is, in the paradigm, one of the variables describing users—user characteristics. A complete description of users requires additional variables | Situational and personal factors<br><br>Decision style<br><br>Contact involvement | These variables all relate to the characteristics and roles of users of MIS and appear in the user element of the paradigm. |
| Structure | Types of evidence generation | In Mason and Mitroff, this variable refers to the view of the world or general way of looking at data built into an information system. In the paradigm, this is part of the structure element. | Technical quality | This refers to system characteristics and user interface, both subsumed under the structure element of the paradigm. |
| Fit | Modes of presentation | In the Mason and Mitroff scheme, this refers to the degree of personalization of information presentation. This appears in the paradigm under the heading of individual fit of system to users. | | — |

Source: Compiled by the authors.

15

From an analysis of the two models discussed above, and identification of the differences between them, it is evident that neither is complete. Not only is each of these models incomplete, but each of the underlying approaches contains deficiencies that disqualify them as general paradigms. To establish an effective paradigm for studying MIS, a comprehensive synthesis is required, at the least, and some extension is also required.

It may be helpful at this juncture to compare the paradigm with the models of Mason and Mitrofff and of Lucas to highlight the similarities and differences. First, it can be shown that all of the Mason and Mitroff variables are subsumed by the paradigm presented in this book. This is best demonstrated, perhaps, by Table 1.1, in which the elements of the paradigm are presented with the parallel variables from the Mason and Mitroff and Lucas models and accompanied by comments where appropriate.

Of Lucas's ten variables, seven are subsumed in the paradigm. Those that are not are use of system, analysis action, and performance. These are not included in the list of variables embodied in the paradigm because the authors think of them as defining the success or failure of an MIS. This success or failure is the dependent variable in the authors' system, in which only the independent variables are specified. This also points to differences in concept between the three studies discussed. These will be examined later.

Although all the variables of the Mason and Mitroff scheme are clearly included in the paradigm presented in this book, the reverse is not true. Thus, Mason and Mitroff touch primarily on the structure, environment, user, and fit elements of MIS; by the same token they completely ignore the procedural elements, planning, strategy, and projects, and two of the three behavioral elements, namely executives and implementors. Thus, although Mason and Mitroff present a cogent list of variables to be investigated and suggest operationalizations of those variables, their list is far from complete. Furthermore, they suggest no relationships among the variables identified and they suggest only two general and nonspecific propositions. Their model is a basis for partial descriptions of information systems, but suggests little specific research; nor does the model, per se, have any normative implications.

Lucas, with a longer list of variables than have Mason and Mitroff, alludes to more elements of the paradigm, but nevertheless ignores three of them: planning, strategies, and implementors. Thus, these three elements, which have been extensively discussed in the literature, are excluded from both of the studies that preceded this one. Lucas also posits relationships between the variables, and singles out performance as the critical goal variable of his system, introducing a normative flavor. Although Lucas's model is more comprehensive than that of Mason and Mitroff, it proposes a specific and intricate structure that leaves little room for addition or modification. The propositions he puts forward can be empirically tested, but if any are rejected the whole structure would tend to collapse. Thus, the model can be accepted or rejected but cannot provide a framework within which additional findings can be readily incorporated.

The paradigm presented in this book is specifically designed as a comprehensive framework, stated as a series of propositions with minimal interdependence that can be tested and modified, removed, or complemented where necessary without rebuilding the whole structure. These propositions are stated so they have clear normative import.

Conceptual Differences

The preceding discussion of three alternative frameworks for MIS has hinted at some conceptual differences between them that should now be made explicit. Mason and Mitroff presented a number of variables that together determine the structure of an MIS. Their concept may be represented graphically:

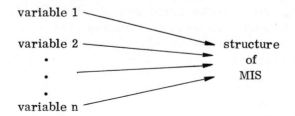

This is essentially an open-ended process in which the states of the independent variables determine the form of the dependent variable, MIS structure, with no feedback considered.

Lucas's concept is that of a feedback system in which some of the variables are both dependent and independent if one thinks of it as a cyclic process in discrete units of time, or as a system of simultaneous equations if one thinks of it as a continuous process. A graphic abstraction of Lucas's model is as follows:

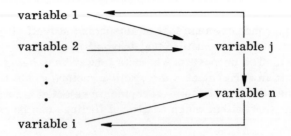

There appear to be no purely dependent variables in Lucas's model and few purely independent ones. The feeling of the authors is that, although this concept may be more realistic than that of Mason and Mitroff, it is rather complex and this complexity inhibits discussion and understanding. A certain degree of simplification, such as that exhibited by Mason and Mitroff, greatly facilitates discourse.

The paradigm presented in this book contains elements of both the preceding concepts, together with some innovations. As in the Mason and Mitroff model, there is a clear dependent variable, but now it is success/failure, rather than structure. In the authors' model, structure becomes another independent variable affecting success. Unlike Mason and Mitroff, however, the authors do not completely ignore the feedback loops; in those cases where the feedback loops are very strong, they are represented by explicit propositions. These feedback propositions, or "interactions" as the authors have labeled them, are a small proportion of the total, and most of the propositions directly relate independent variables to success and failure. This concept may be represented graphically:

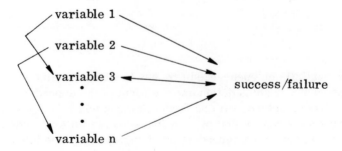

This concept, although not quite as simple as that of Mason and Mitroff, is considerably more realistic, and this realism is achieved at a much smaller cost in complexity than that of Lucas's model. This paradigm, while permitting a description that approximates the richness of the reality of MIS, is easily decomposable and therefore readily permits modification and change when necessary.

## DISCIPLINES RELEVANT TO THE STUDY OF MIS

The decoupling of MIS into a number of subsystems, as in the paradigm presented above, indicates clearly that a number of disciplines are relevant to understanding them, different disciplines being appropriate to each of the subsystems. The remainder of this chapter is devoted to exploring the areas of study relevant to research in MIS and to determining their applicability.

### General Systems Theory

Beginning at the highest level of abstraction, it is clear that, as systems, management information systems are as amenable as any other to the approach of General Systems Theory. Broadly speaking, General Systems Theory deals with four issues: the relationships between objects that compose a system, the relationships between systems and their environments, the division of systems into subsystems and the hierarchical relationships between subsystems, and feedback and control in systems. The paradigm presented in this book deals with three of these four issues. The authors have identified the objects composing MIS and will devote most of the remainder of this book to analyzing the relationships between them. The environment of MIS has been identified and a chapter is devoted to the relationships between that environment and MIS. The objects of which management information systems are composed have been aggregated into subsystems and the hierarchical relationships between them have been established. The only element of systems theory the authors have not employed extensively is that of feedback and control theory—cybernetics. The reasons for abstaining from the use of this element were indicated in the comparison of models of MIS.

Kenneth Boulding (1952), one of the earliest and most enthusiastic proponents of General Systems Theory, has stated:

General Systems Theory is the skeleton of a
science in the sense that it aims to provide a
framework or structure of systems on which to
hang the flesh and blood of particular disciplines

and particular subject matters in an orderly and co-
herent corpus of knowledge.* [p. 208]

This, precisely, is the objective of the authors' paradigm—to provide a framework or structure in which to place the content of the
particular disciplines relevant to the study of MIS. Thus, this study
is a specific application, or microcosm, of General Systems Theory.

Organizational Development

Given the pervasive effect of MIS on organizations, the introduction of such systems into organizations is worth considering as
a case in organizational development. The Organizational Development (OD) approach stems from General Systems Theory and therefore is one level of abstraction below it. This approach recognizes
that an organization is a fabric of tightly interrelated and interde-
pendent subsystems and that the organization interacts with its internal environment, consumes inputs, produces outputs, and is ex-
posed to constraints placed upon it by the environment. Thus, any
organizational change is viewed in the wider context of the organizational system and its environment. This, in two senses, is precisely the approach taken in the paradigm: first, the MIS, as a
microcosm of the organization, is made of the same fabric and has
the same elements as the organization, except that in this case the
organization is the environment; second, the effects of an MIS on an
organization may profitably be studied from the viewpoint of organizational development.
    Beckhard (1969) has defined OD as follows:

    Organizational development is an effort (1) planned,
    (2) organization wide, and (3) managed from the top, to
    (4) increase organization effectiveness and health through
    (5) planned intervention in the organization's "processes"
    using behavioral-science knowledge.⁺ (Emphasis in the
    original.) [p. 9]

_____

*Reprinted by permission from Boulding, Kenneth D. "Gen-
eral Systems Theory: The Skeleton of Science," Management
Science, Volume 2, Number 3 (April 1956), Copyright (1956) The
Institute of Management Sciences.
    ⁺Beckhard, Richard. Organizational Development: Strategies
and Models, © 1969, Addison-Wesley Publishing Company, Inc.,
Adaptation from Chapter V, pages 1-7. Reprinted with permission.

Thus, the introduction or modification of MIS includes all the elements of Organizational Development. When performed consciously, it is a planned effort, the results of which intervene in organizational processes. The purpose of MIS initiation is to increase organizational effectiveness and health, generally expressed in slightly more concrete terms such as profitability, user satisfaction, and performance of key tasks. The MIS effort in an organization is organization wide, even if it is not an integrated system that is under consideration, and it is managed from, or at least requires the approval of, top echelons in the organization.

It is widely accepted that there is more than one modality for introducing change into organizations. A useful typology identifies five models of the change process: research, development, and diffusion; social interaction and diffusion; intervention theory and method; planned change; and action research. These five models, each developed from a different point of view, experience base, and discipline, overlap somewhat, but the last two are most prevalent in Organizational Development. These two are also the most relevant to the MIS effort. Implementation of a new MIS is a typical action research, focused on a study of a specific organizational problem and the use of expertise and knowledge to implement a planned change. Thus, the OD approach can clearly contribute to understanding the procedural subsystem of MIS in that both deal with planned intervention in organizational processes to improve organizational effectiveness, top management playing a significant role in both cases.

Project Management

Project Management is an organizational approach to the nonrecurrent design and implementation of innovative objectives. This approach is based on a concentrated organizational effort to attain a particular target or set of goals fairly independently of other organizational goals or targets. Thus, it usually involves creation of a task force that concentrates on the specific target. Such a task force and its managers are responsible for attaining the target through all the phases of planning, design, implementation, testing, and integration, where relevant.

Thus, the Project Management approach is relevant to studying the procedural subsystem of MIS. Implementation or changes of MIS are specific cases of project management. While the organization carries on with its routine scheduled activities, a special group works to attain the MIS target, within the strategy adopted, from initial analysis through tactical planning to project implementation and initiation of operations.

Organizational Behavior

Having segregated the behavioral elements of MIS into a separate subsystem, it becomes almost tautological to state that behavioral science is the discipline relevant to the study of this aspect of MIS. Behavioral science, however, is a very broad field covering everything from infant learning to sexual behavior and from anthropology to sociology; thus, to be informative, one must be selective. The behavioral discipline most relevant to MIS is clearly Organizational Behavior, given that MIS are subsystems of organizations and that people behave toward MIS primarily in their organizational roles. The areas covered by Organizational Behavior also predict the kinds of issues that arise in the MIS behavioral subsystem. These areas include formal and informal organizational structures, decision making, motivation, participation, conflict, cognitive limitations, and initiation and innovation in organizations (March and Simon 1958). As will be demonstrated in the relevant chapters, many of the behavioral phenomena accompanying MIS might have been inferred from the behavioral literature even before MIS-related behavior was studied specifically.

A Theory of MIS

Disciplines have been proposed that are relevant to the external environment of MIS and to the internal environment and its behavioral and procedural subsystems. Now it only remains to propose a method for studying the structure of an MIS. Here, however, there is no recourse to other disciplines. The structure of an MIS is, as explained previously, the embodiment or essence of the MIS itself. No other discipline has studied this—if it had, it would be a theory of MIS. This, then, is the proper and unique field of study for a theory of management information systems. Significantly, this is the issue that Mason and Mitroff specifically addressed and that Lucas also addressed, although not as specifically or directly. The structure of MIS is the topic of Chapter 6. By the time it is concluded, a framework for the study of this quintessential element of management information systems will have been elucidated.

CONCLUSION

In this chapter the authors have stated the need for a formal framework for the study of MIS to permit the orderly accumulation of knowledge in the field. The frameworks of Mason and Mitroff and of Lucas were described and compared to the general outline of the authors' paradigm. This paradigm views MIS in terms of behavioral and procedural subsystems that are interfaced with organizational and extraorganizational environments by means of a structure. This structure is the physical embodiment of an MIS—the "real" MIS.

The behavioral subsystem consists of executive, user, and implementor elements. The procedural subsystem is composed of planning, strategy, and project elements. Structure is defined in terms of operational characteristics. The interactions of all system components are synthesized in the concept of system fit.

Finally, this chapter presented a number of disciplines relevant to the study of management information systems. These include General System Theory as a means to understanding the system aspects of MIS, Organizational Development as a description of the procedural subsystem in general, Project Management as a guide to the project element, and Organizational Behavior as an illumination of the behavioral subsystem. It was indicated that no theory relevant to the structure of MIS exists and that structure is the subject matter for a theory of MIS.

# 2
## THE ENVIRONMENT OF MIS

> Just the place for a Snark!  I have said it twice:
>   That alone should encourage the crew.
> Just the place for a Snark!  I have said it thrice:
>   What I tell you three times is true.
> Lewis Carroll, <u>The Hunting of the Snark</u>

At the beginning of this book, the concept of MIS structure was introduced as an interface between a system and its environment. There are, however, two levels to the environment in which MIS are embedded.  The first level is the organization of which the MIS are a part.  This is the environment that the organization creates for MIS. From the authors' point of view this is the more significant and interesting aspect of the MIS environment, but discussion of it will be deferred until the other level, outside the organization, has been covered.

### THE EXTRAORGANIZATIONAL ENVIRONMENT

The second level of the MIS environment is outside the organization and constitutes the environment of the organization as a whole.

Proposition 2.1:  The more benevolent the extra-organizational environment, the greater the likelihood of success.

-----

This chapter is an updated and expanded version of material that has been published in Ein-Dor and Segev (1978b).

In most respects, MIS are shielded from direct contact with the external environment of the organizations of which they are a part. Other functions in the organization carry on most of its discourse with the outside world. There is, however, at least one area in which MIS negotiate directly with the extraorganizational environment: the acquisition of MIS resources.

The externally determined states of the art and market conditions in areas relating to MIS define the extent to which the organization can acquire those components of MIS that it does not already possess, including data processing personnel, hardware and software technologies, and decision techniques. Each of these factors has been cited at some time as a factor limiting the development of more sophisticated MIS.

In the early days of computers in the 1950s and early 1960s, hardware capacity frequently limited the ability to construct complex systems. In the late 1960s, case reports began to appear of advanced systems for which the existence of appropriate hardware had been a precondition for successful implementation (Jenkins 1969; Kronenberg 1967; Montijo 1967; Wimbrow 1971). The hardware problem had apparently been largely overcome by that time. Since then, hardware technology seems to have kept pace with developers' needs and the significance of this problem has diminished. It may again become a factor in the future as technology approaches its physical limits and as advanced system designs require capacities difficult to attain.

At about the same time that the hardware constraint was relaxed, a number of articles identified decision techniques as the major constraint on MIS development. Ansoff (1967) and Brady (1967) reported a lag in the development of management technology as the limiting factor on the application of computers to the solution of managerial problems. At the beginning of the 1970s, the blame seems to have shifted to a shortage of good people with adequate training, and "brainpower" was identified as the bottleneck in developing advanced MIS (Alexander 1969; McFarlan 1971; Murdick and Ross 1972). If salaries are any indication of market conditions, the considerable drop in real salaries of most data processing personnel over the last decade would suggest that this, too, is no longer a real problem.*

---

*Consider the following salary data for 1966 and 1978:

The current bottleneck seems to be largely in software, and in recent years considerable effort has been expended in devising software development and control techniques. Structured programming, life cycle software cost estimation, and very high level languages are examples of attempts to improve software development methodology to permit the construction of ever more complex systems.

In addition to this dependency, the external environment can affect MIS indirectly through its effect on the organization. Factors in the external environment that play a part in shaping the organizational environment may thus be filtered through the latter and affect MIS in areas other than resource acquisition. Relationships of this type will be discussed in terms of the internal organizational variable directly affecting MIS, rather than attempting to follow through the chain of interactions. An example of a variable of this type is attitudes toward MIS within the organization, which are partly determined by extraorganizational attitudes.

As with systems in general, and social systems especially, the definition of boundaries is a problem. The general solution, and the one adopted in this book, is to define the boundaries to include those elements that affect most strongly the object of analysis and to exclude those that have a weaker effect. The criteria the authors have adopted for making this distinction are direct involvement with,

| Professional | Smallest Users | | | Largest Users | | |
| Category | $1,000/year | | Increase | $1,000/year | | Increase |
| | 1966 | 1978 | (percent) | 1966 | 1978 | (percent) |
|---|---|---|---|---|---|---|
| Lead systems analysts | 11.0 | 18.2 | 65 | 12.7 | 20.0 | 57 |
| Systems analysts | 8.5 | 17.9 | 111 | 9.6 | 20.2 | 110 |
| Lead programmers | 8.9 | 14.8 | 66 | 10.5 | 26.8 | 155 |
| Programmers | 6.9 | 13.4 | 94 | 8.0 | 14.9 | 86 |

Sources: For 1966: Solomon (1970); for 1978: McLaughlin and Knottek (1978).

These changes occurred in a period when the general price level rose well over 100 percent. This would indicate a drop in real salaries for most data processing professionals, a phenomenon that one would not expect if there were a shortage of persons in these professions.

or responsibility for, MIS. Thus, executives with MIS responsibility, users, and MIS staff are all part of management information systems. Persons who do not use MIS, potential users, and executives with no direct responsibility for MIS form part of the organizational environment.

The authors' measure of success in MIS is use; success implies the transformation of potential into actual users, or absorption by MIS of the people in their organizational environment. Thus, an extremely successful system would be one in which all persons in the organizational environment became absorbed into the system. Such an MIS would permeate the organization and approach the ideal of the total system—no one in the organization would be able to function without it. Until this goal is reached, however, MIS are not synonymous with the organization and the organization may be divided into its MIS and MIS environmental components, the latter being a number of qualitative organizational attributes. These attributes are the structure, decision time frame and maturity of the organization, the availability of organizational resources, the psychological climate toward MIS, the types of problems faced by the organization and, finally, the size of the organization.

STRUCTURE OF THE ORGANIZATION

Proposition 2.2: The likelihood of success in building MIS, at any level of management, is increased when the organization reporting to that level is more centralized and decreased when it is less centralized.

The implications of organizational structure for success in constructing management information systems are probably important, but as yet little understood. Thus, several authorities have indicated this as an area requiring research (Mason and Mitroff 1973; Schultz and Slevin 1975a).

A priori, there is a strong relationship between the degree of centralization of the organization for which a system is intended and the likelihood of success, an assumption that is incorporated in Proposition 2.2. There is also a relationship between the organizational structure and the best degree of centralization for information system resources; this second issue is discussed in a later chapter. The authors' current focus is on organizational structure as an environment for MIS.

In discussing organizational structure there is a tendency to speak of organizations as being "centralized" or "decentralized" as if these were two dichotomous states. This appears to be a misconception. If an organization is centralized from the top down, one may validly speak of it as being centralized. The difficulty in designation begins with organizations that have a decentralized divisional structure at the top level and centralized divisions, or decentralized top and divisional management, and centralized plants. Clearly, each organization must be centralized below some minimal level; above that there is a spectrum of degrees of centralization from complete centralization in which all important decisions are made at the top level, at one extreme, to decentralization of strategic decision making down to the lowest possible level, at the the other extreme. Since MIS may be designed for any level of management, Proposition 2.2 refers to the degree of centralization at the particular level under consideration.

Dearden (1972) has stated that information technology has been of little help in controlling decentralized companies. This is probably related to the finding that decentralization is a source of inconsistency in data, resulting from problems of synchronizing the updating and reporting cycles for units of a decentralized company (Nolan 1973b). Given the paucity of empirical data in this area, one can only hope that more will be made available to permit a more thorough analysis.

ORGANIZATIONAL TIME FRAME

Proposition 2.3: The shorter the organizational time frame, the smaller the likelihood of MIS success.

The decision time frames of organizations differ. Some organizations have relatively stable environments and distant planning horizons that allow considerable time for the construction of systems that may assist in the decision process. Other organizations are characterized by highly volatile environments and close planning horizons, which impose much stricter constraints on the time available for system design and implementation.

Although this proposition is stated in general terms, it is more applicable the higher the level of management for which the system is being built. At the level of operations and operations control, there tends to be a considerable degree of stability, and fairly routine and standardized systems are applicable. But at the highest levels of management, where problems tend to be unique and not recurrent, only a system tailored to the particular problem will be of very much use, and then only if it becomes available within the time frame of the decision process.

The organizational time frame is critical for MIS because, although organizational time frames are in many cases relatively short and tend to become even shorter, the time frame for MIS development is quite long. The length of MIS lead times is caused partly by the length of time required to implement information system projects and partly by the inability of MIS staff to appreciate the exigencies of managerial decision making. Thus, on the one hand, constrained time frames tend to increase the difficulty of system design whereas, on the other hand, the lengthy time frame required for the implementation of management science techniques and management information systems causes managers to bypass them in their searches for problem solutions. In a period when many companies are changing very rapidly, their information systems have difficulty keeping in step (Dearden 1972; Grayson 1973; Hayes and Nolan 1974; Ramsgard 1974; West 1975).

Among factors that may affect the organizational time frame are the culture in which the organization is embedded, the industry in which the organization is engaged, and the size of the organization.

## ORGANIZATIONAL MATURITY

Proposition 2.4: The more mature an organization, the greater its likelihood of successfully implementing MIS.

Mature organizations are those that are formally organized, their processes are well understood and quantifiable, and data are available that are relevant to their management. In light of this definition, old organizations that are organized informally and in which decision making is based on subjective intuition and experience would be considered immature. A new, formally planned organization in which decision making is based on data, rather than on intuitive feelings, may be very mature. There is no necessary connection between the chronological age of an organization and its managerial maturity.

The first attribute of organizational maturity is that the underlying processes of the unit for which an information system is to be built are well understood. This condition is more likely to be met in certain functional areas and in particular industries. Those industries that are technologically mature will tend to be better understood than more innovative technologies. Examples of better understood industries are steel, oil, and food processing. The electronics industry, however, in which the technology is still changing rapidly, would be less amenable to the formalization required for information system development (Hammond 1974). It has also been pointed out that management science applications have been more readily understood and more easily quantified in manufacturing operations; it is more difficult to build systems in areas that are more behaviorally oriented (Hayes and Nolan 1974).

Technologically mature industries and more routine functions are also likely to provide a foundation of historical data of a quantitative nature on which to build sophisticated systems. An empirical study found that the availability of data is often a critical issue in the initial phases of management science implementations and that its criticalness declines as a data base is established and the implementation group matures (Bean et al. 1975).

The second prerequisite for a degree of maturity promoting success is that organizational processes such as budgeting, planning, and control be formally defined and that the definition be quantitative, rather than qualitative (Hammond 1974; Hanold 1972). It is clearly impossible to implement effective management systems if management is not conscious of the processes it directs and if these processes cannot be stated unambiguously. It is not sufficient, however, that the processes be formally stated; they must also operate in accordance with the statement. An interesting illustration of this point is provided by Gibson (1975). While studying the process of deciding on the establishment of new branches in a bank, he received from the analyst involved a description of a rational formal process culminating in the presentation of recommendations on acquisitions. In subsequent discussions with senior executives of the bank, however, he found that action on acquisitions was frequently initiated on the basis of chance opportunities quite unrelated to the analyst's studies. Furthermore, the decision process in such cases was often quite informal and affected by other than rational considerations. Gibson concludes that the existence of such situations predicates a research methodology for implementation in which the researcher is heavily involved in the implementation process; anomalies of the kind described could not be discovered by an outsider examining questionnaires that would detail the officially prescribed formal process. A more detailed description of Gibson's study is included in Chapter 9.

If organizational understanding and formality are sufficient, the remaining prerequisite for maturity is that the data available in such situations also be readily accessible so use can be made of them in managerial systems. The problems that tend to arise in this area are with data that exist but are difficult to extract because they are the jealously guarded preserve of a different organizational function or because they are scattered over a large number of files or are in a form that cannot be processed without considerable prior preparation. In such circumstances, managers will tend to forego use of the information because of the time and effort required for its assembly (Grayson 1973; Hammond 1974).

Because of their complexity, large organizations are motivated in many cases to formalize their procedures and information channels. This formalizing provides a convenient basis for MIS development. In small organizations, however, procedures will often be much less formal, giving rise to a need to institutionalize the way things are done as a precondition to MIS development. This clearly lengthens the development process and increases its difficulty.

Proposition 2.5 (interaction between MIS success and organizational maturity): MIS success and organizational maturity are mutually dependent.

It was proposed above that a high degree of organizational maturity, defined in terms of systematization and data availability, promotes the success of MIS. At the same time, the success of an MIS implementation increases systematization and enhances the availability of data, thus increasing the likelihood of future MIS successes. Little work has been done on this seemingly critical interaction between organizational maturity and MIS success. Research is clearly needed in this area.

RESOURCE ALLOCATION

Proposition 2.6: The budgeting of sufficient resources increases the likelihood of MIS success.

Resource availability problems are a frequent contributor to the failure of management information systems. The MIS function has to compete with other functions in the organization for whatever resources are available. A major difficulty for MIS projects in this regard is that the normal method of justifying budgetary allocations is by financial cost-benefit analysis. In MIS, the benefits are often intangible, arising from improved decision making or greater sensitivity of the organization to internal and external changes. These benefits are usually difficult, often impossible, to estimate in financial terms. Furthermore, the higher the level of management to which a system relates, the greater these benefits are likely to be and the more difficult to estimate. It is not surprising that MIS projects are difficult to justify and that justification often involves understating the difficulty and cost of project development (McFarlan 1972; McKinsey 1968; Ramsgard 1974).

The problem of obtaining budgetary allocations for MIS is further complicated because the information function is not generally perceived to be as important as production, marketing, and finance. Usually, only after the need for information systems has become self-evident and the organization has become aware of their necessity do they achieve a position of significance in the organization's list of priorities.

Some work has been done on the budgets devoted to information-processing resources. The initial study is that of Nolan (1973), who developed a hypothesis relating the growth of expenditures to the developmental stage of the data-processing function; this model has received considerable recognition from practitioners and academics. In its original version, the theory stated, in brief, that there are four phases of the growth of information system budgets and that these phases are related to four levels of system development. In later work, Nolan revised this model to comprise six stages (1979). The stages of development, as proposed in the most recent version, may be summarized as follows:

| Computer Budget Growth | Stage Description |
| --- | --- |
| Stage I | Initiation (computer acquisition) |
| Stage II | Contagion (intense system development) |
| Stage III | Control (proliferation of controls) |
| Stage IV | Integration (user service orientation) |
| Stage V | Data administration (shared data and systems) |
| Stage VI | Maturity (data resource strategic planning) |

Nolan suggested that a plot of budgets against stage of development produces an S-shaped curve over the first four stages, rising slowly in Stage I, accelerating in Stage II, decelerating in Stage III, and largely leveling off in Stage IV. In Stage V there is a renewed acceleration in budget growth, and stabilization on a new plateau in Stage VI. This model is presented as Figure 2.1.

Lucas and Sutton (1977) attempted to validate Nolan's original four-stage hypothesis by correlating budgets with time for 29 counties in California for which data were available for eight years or more. They found that both linear and exponential models provided a better fit for the data than did an S-shaped curve. For most of the counties, the linear model produced a better fit than did the exponential. From this and from discussions with county data-processing managers, they concluded that the data did not support an S-shaped curve as a model of budget growth or as a basis for a stage

FIGURE 2.1

Curves of the Stage Hypotheses

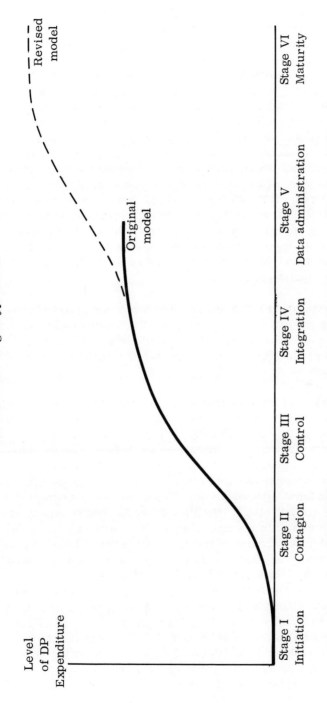

Source: Reprinted by permission of the Harvard Business Review. Exhibit from "Managing the Crises of Data Processing," by Richard L. Nolan (March–April 1979). Copyright © 1979 by the President and Fellows of Harvard College; all rights reserved.

33

theory of system development; budget growth, based on a percentage increase over the previous year's budget, was offered as an alternative hypothesis. Nevertheless, Lucas and Sutton do not reject the stage hypothesis as an explanation of computer system development, merely its link to budget allocations. These inconclusive results clearly call for additional research that could provide normative insights in addition to its descriptive aspects.

The amount of resources required by information systems is a problem for small organizations since there are considerable economies of scale in computer operations. Although this has become less pronounced since the advent of minicomputers, there are still significant indivisibilities in programming and operations that make systems relatively greater burdens in small companies than in large ones. It is almost as difficult to build a complex system for a small firm as for a billion-dollar giant, but the small firm will have to do it with fewer personnel and a smaller computer. Thus, small organizations may run into serious difficulties if they try to build systems at the same level of sophistication as their larger competitors.

> Proposition 2.7 (interaction between resource budgeting and external environment): The more easily an organization can translate its MIS budget into the requisite resources, the greater the likelihood of success.

The point made in this proposition might appear so obvious as to be unnecessary were it not that in practice it is so frequently overlooked. It is not sufficient that an organization budget enough money to finance its MIS operation, but it must also be able to transform the budget into the physical resources—personnel, programs, and machines—with which to achieve the objectives for which the funds were assigned. The ability of an organization to translate its MIS budget into physical resources is dependent on the availability of such resources either internally or externally. As indicated in the section on the extraorganizational environment, the critical resources that are most likely to constrain MIS development at present are managerial skills and software.

The resource drain caused by information systems can seriously affect the financial situation of a small firm, whereas this is unlikely to be the case in larger operations. As a result, smaller organizations may attempt to trim costs by acquiring underpowered hardware or by understaffing. The more complex the systems undertaken, the more severely such corner cutting will affect the outcome. The financial burden may also lead to pressures for quick results that, combined with understaffing and inadequate hardware, can quickly lead to failure (Brady 1967; Farrington 1977; West 1975).

> Proposition 2.8 (interaction between resource alloca-
> tion and success): MIS success and allocation of suffi-
> cient resources are mutually dependent.

The allocation of sufficient resources has been posited above as a condition for MIS success. At the same time, the more successful MIS are, the greater will the readiness be to allocate resources to them, enhancing the prospects for further success. Conversely, MIS failures reduce readiness to allocate resources, further increasing the likelihood of failure. Thus, it would appear that in this area success breeds success and failure breeds failure; this is true of several of the variables that interact with the success or failure of MIS. This may partly explain the observation that MIS tend to be either successes or failures.


THE PSYCHOLOGICAL CLIMATE

Every organization develops its own psychological climate with respect to MIS.* This climate is set by the dominant perceptions of MIS held by members of the organization. It finds its expression in expectations of members of the organization about the future effects of such systems and in their attitudes toward what they perceive MIS to be.

A number of empirical studies have recently examined the effects of attitudes and expectations on management science implementations, but without distinguishing between these two attributes of the psychological environment. The authors feel, however, that they should be differentiated. Expectations are the prior perceptions of people concerning the structure and operation of specific proposed

---

*The following has been offered as a definition of climate: "Climate is a set of properties of the work environment, perceived directly or indirectly by the employees who wor k in this environment and is assumed to be a major force in influencing their behavior on the job. It is an indirect determinant of behavior in that it acts upon attitudes, expectations, states of arousal, which are direct determinants of behavior" (Gibson, Ivancevich, and Donnelly 1973, p. 314).

systems; this is an extroverted or objective evaluation. Attitudes are formed by perceptions of what the systems have done, ex post, and might do in the future, to the individual; this is an introverted or subjective evaluation. The empirical data will be discussed following presentation of propositions on the dimensions of the psychological climate.

> Proposition 2.9: MIS projects will succeed to the extent that expectations are constrained by motivation from below and by reality from above.

Excessive expectations can be self-induced when managers convince themselves that a good information system will solve all their problems, or fostered by experts who sometimes present a list of potential benefits that are unattainable. In both these cases, managers are led to expect much more of information systems than is reasonable. Most surveys of executives convey a feeling that computers have been oversold, or at least overbought, indicating that exaggerated expectations are prevalent (Alexander 1969; Colton 1972-73; Dearden 1972; Hammond 1974b; Heany 1972; Nolan and Knutsen 1974).

Managers sometimes make a different error, however. This occurs when experts, mindful of the dangers of exaggerated expectations and fearful of creating them, play down the possibilities of MIS. The picture drawn may be so uninspiring as to dampen enthusiasm and to deter managers from making demands or even from becoming involved. An additional source of low expectations is horror stories, coming out of other organizations, about MIS failures. Since such failures are rarely reported openly and objectively, uninformed fears feed freely on rampant rumor. People who have had bad experiences with MIS can be very effective in reducing the expectations of their acquaintances (McKinsey 1969).

> Proposition 2.10: Weak preconceptions facilitate the formation of realistic expectations.

Realistic expectations toward information systems can be developed systematically. The task of creating realistic expectations can be affected by preconceptions in the organization concerning such systems. In some cases, executives develop strong preconceptions about what MIS should be like; the existence of such preconceptions can distort the expectations held in the organization about information systems. The weaker the preconceptions held, the better the chances of creating realistic expectations (Hammond 1974b; Nolan and Knutsen 1974).

Proposition 2.11: The generation of positive attitudes increases the likelihood of MIS success.

Expectations and preconceptions play a predominant role in establishing the psychological climate in an organization before the installation of MIS. Once a system has been installed, the climate is also affected by the experience with it. It has been found that attitudes and perceptions of MIS are determined by the quality of the systems. Good experience generates favorable attitudes and encourages widespread use. Bad experience has the opposite effect. Since widespread use is one of the authors' criteria for success, attitudes play an important role in determining success (Lucas 1974b; Manley 1975).

The importance of attitudes and expectations has been recognized widely and has consequently generated more research than most other areas. Some of this research is described below; it vividly demonstrates the need for a paradigm such as that presented in this book. Although the three studies discussed all deal with the same area, inconsistency makes systematic synthesis, or even summary, of the findings extremely difficult.

Lucas (1974b)

One of the first studies on the effects of attitudes was by Lucas. In that study, Lucas attempted to establish relationships between four classes of predictor variables and the use of an information system in a sales organization. The predictor variable classes were situational factors, personal factors, decision style, attitudes, and perceptions. Thus, the study relates primarily to the user variables of MIS and therefore is discussed in greater detail in Chapter 9; it is introduced here briefly because of its attitude aspects.

Notice that the dependent variable in the study was use of the system—this is the authors' criterion for system success. Attitudes toward the system studied were evaluated (on a scale from one to seven) by three variables; namely, quality of output, computer potential, and management computer support. A strong association was found between these three attitude variables and use of the information system. In fact, the relationships between this variable class and use was more consistent than for any of the other variables tested, indicating its importance.

Manley (1975)

Manley's study was intended to verify whether differences in client-group attitudes toward a proposed management science implementation could be detected, and to identify factors affecting those attitudes. A client was defined as "a recipient of an operations research/management science product who does not have any de jure authority to decide whether or not to accept or use it"; such clients are referred to in other studies as computer-dependent workers.

The basic assumption of Manley's model is that "clients are naturally hostile towards technological innovations." He then posits that the level of clients' resistance is dependent on their perception of several external variables that put pressure on them to support the implementation, combined with their attitude toward those external variables. The variables chosen by Manley for his model are exhibited in Table 2.1.

Manley's model is

$$L = 0.5 + \Sigma \overline{(w_i X_i \overline{\sin \Theta_i})} \; i = 1, \ldots, n$$

where:

L     ☐ the dependent variable, is a measure of client behavior, varying between 0 and 1, which can be interpreted as a level of resistance to, or support for, a proposed implementation.

$X_i$     ☐ are the external variables toward which client attitudes are oriented.

$w_i$     ☐ are weighting factors representing individual client value judgments as to the relative importance of each external variable. $\overline{w}_i$ is the expected value of a group of individual client's value judgments.

$\sin \Theta_i$☐ are the intermediate variables registering client's attitude orientations toward the external variables that pressure them into supporting the implementation. $\sin \Theta_i$ is a group attitude orientation toward external factor i.

The clients in Manley's study were schoolteachers who were informed by circular of a proposed OR/MS innovation for optimally computing supplemental pay for extracurricular activities. The circulars were manipulated to project different values of the external variables.

The most important finding of this study was that "very small changes in written communications to clients concerning an OR/MS innovation diffusion project caused significant variations in their

## TABLE 2.1

### External and Intermediate Variables in Manley's Model

| External variable, $X_i$ | Associated intermediate variable, $sin_j$ |
|---|---|
| Level of chief executive support for a specific OR/MS product | Attitude orientation of the client toward what is perceived to be the chief executive's support for the implementation project |
| Priority level assigned to the implementation project by management | Attitude orientation of the client toward perception of the relative urgency placed upon a particular product by management |
| Degree of product relevancy to client's organizational role | Attitude orientation of the client toward perceived relevance of the product to client |
| Level of required client involvement to implement the product | Attitude orientation of the client toward perception of the degree to which client must become involved in the implementation process for a particular product |
| Level of product complexity | Attitude orientation of the client toward perception of the relative simplicity or complexity of a particular product |

Source: Reprinted by permission of the publisher from John H. Manley, "Implementation Attitudes: A Model and A Measurement Methodology," Chapter 8 in Randall L. Schultz and Dennis P. Slevin (eds.). Implementing Operations Research/Management Science, pp. 183-202. Copyright 1975 by Elsevier North Holland, Inc.

observed attitudes toward the project." The attitude orientation
most strongly affected by perceptions of the relevant external variables was that related to the level of chief executive support. This
is also one of the variables for which Lucas found a relationship
between attitudes and use of a system. There is no overlap between
the remaining variables in the two models. Note also that the dependent variable in Manley's model is level of resistance, rather
than use, since, by his definition, clients have no option not to use
the system.

Schultz and Slevin (1975b)

The intention of Schultz and Slevin was to develop an instrument for attitude research in OR/MS implementation. Their work
was directed, therefore, to identifying the relevant variables, which
are now available to other researchers as are the questionnaires
they developed for gathering data on those variables.

Their methodology was, on the basis of a literature search,
to assembly Likert-type statements. These were originally 100 in
number and were refined eventually to 67 by replacement and omis-
sion following field testing. An orthogonal factor analysis performed
on the 67 Likert items yielded seven meaningful factors. The Likert
scale was augmented by 11 semantic differential concepts. The
factors and semantic differential concepts are exhibited in Table 2.2,
where they are compared with Lucas's and Manley's attributes of
implementation attitudes.

The Likert items and semantic differential concepts were
presented to a group of subjects in the context of a specific model
known to them. Five dependent variables were also developed with
the objective of measuring intended use of the system by the subjects. The dependent variables were:

Probability of use of the model by the subject;
Probability of use of the model by other managers;
Probability that the model will be a success;
Evaluation of the worth of the model; and
Level of accuracy the subject expects from the model.

A considerable number of the independent variables correlated significantly with the dependent variables. It appears somewhat un-
fortunate that more thought was not given to the dependent variables.
Apart from the first, which is the generally accepted independent
variable in the studies surveyed, the remaining four are attitudes
or expectations and are therefore independent variables. If this is

the case, it is not surprising to find them highly correlated with other independent variables of a similar nature.

Synthesis

Table 2.2 compares the variables in the three studies discussed above. From this table, it appears that Lucas's and Manley's variables are with one exception all subsumed in Schultz and Slevin's factors and semantic differentials. In terms of this book's propositions, some of these are attitudes based on knowledge on the part of those involved about what has already occurred. The remaining variables are expectations based on estimates of what may happen in the future. This distinction is made in the table. Presumably, expectations are more easily manipulated than are attitudes; hence, the importance of this distinction.

Given the commonly accepted importance of attitudes and expectations for system implementation, and given the limited knowledge provided by the pioneering studies described above, there is room for considerable research in this area. The groundbreaking work already done insures that the area is ripe for such research.

Proposition 2.12 (interaction between extraorganizational situation and psychological climate): Generally favorable attitudes in the external environment foster a benevolent psychological climate, thus enhancing prospects for MIS success.

The psychological climate toward MIS within an organization is affected by attitudes outside the organization toward such systems. The experiences of friends, competitors, clients, and suppliers affect their attitudes and these in turn influence the attitudes and expectations of an organization's employees. On the one hand, when the general attitude toward MIS in the environment is favorable, positive attitudes and expectations will tend to be established within an organization. A generally unfavorable external environment, on the other hand, will foster a negative psychological climate within an organization (Heany 1972; Nolan and Knutsen 1974).

Proposition 2.13 (interaction between success of MIS and the psychological climate): MIS success and psychological climate are mutually dependent.

Expectations and preconceptions play a predominant role in establishing the psychological climate in an organization before the

## TABLE 2.2

### Comparison of Attributes Associated with Implementation Attitudes

| Lucas | Manley | Schultz and Slevin | | |
|---|---|---|---|---|
| | | Factors | Semantic Differentials | Attitude/Expectation |
| | | Goal achievement and congruence | Chance of success using this technique | Expectation |
| | | Client/researcher interface | Confidence in developers of the model | Attitude |
| | | Changes resulting from the model | Changes in executive decision making | Expectation |
| | | | Changes in the communication system | Expectation |
| | | Interpersonal relations | Effects on relationships with others | Expectation |
| | | | The model | Attitude |
| Quality of output | | | | |

| | | | | |
|---|---|---|---|---|
| | Product relevancy to client's organizational role | Effect of model on manager's job performance | Personal importance of this project | Attitude |
| Management computer support | Level of chief executive support | Support for the model | Amount of support being given this project | Attitude |
| | Priority level assigned implementation project by management | Urgency for results | Urgency of this project to the company | Attitude |
| | Level of product complexity | | Technical complexity of this project | Attitude |
| | Level of client involvement required | | Amount of personal participation required | Expectation |
| Computer potential | | | | Expectation |

Source: Compiled by the authors.

installation of MIS. Once systems have been installed, the climate
is also affected by the experience with it, which has a considerable
effect on attitudes. Lucas found that the quality of a system determines attitudes toward it. Good experience with a successful system generates favorable attitudes and encourages continuing widespread use (the authors' criterion of success) (Lucas 1974b).

The importance to successful MIS efforts of a favorable psychological climate in the organization has been brought to light by
almost every survey in this area and has been recognized by many
authorities. Little systematic research has been carried out in this
field, however. Research on this topic promises to contribute
greatly to understanding the successes and failures of MIS and to
the ability of management to establish an organizational environment benevolent to MIS.

## SIZE OF THE ORGANIZATION

The effects of organizational size have been mentioned at
various points throughout this chapter. Since this is an issue that
confronts a very large number of organizations, it may be helpful
to concentrate the relevant material here.

In theory, perhaps, there is no reason that small organizations should have more difficulty with MIS than do large ones. One
might even argue that they should have fewer problems since smaller
organizations are generally less complex than large ones and organizational complexity is one of the major factors inhibiting MIS
development (Dearden 1972; Roark 1970). Although this particular
factor may favor the smaller users of information systems, most
other factors work to their disadvantage. These include the organizational time frame (Proposition 2.3), organizational maturity (Proposition 2.4), and resource availability (Proposition 2.6).

Proposition 2.14: The smaller the organization, the
smaller the likelihood of MIS success.

Because small organizations are often less formally managed
they will tend to be less mature in terms of quantification, data
availability, and general understanding of organizational processes.
This will lead to greater difficulty and longer lead times in building
MIS in smaller organizations.

The project lead time in small firms is further lengthened by
the availability of personnel to work on such projects. The available work force being smaller, there is more difficulty in assigning
the requisite number of people. Budget and cash flow restrictions

may also dictate a slower pace of development in smaller organizations (West 1975). All of the factors mentioned—formalization, personnel, and resource availability—would seem to dictate more protracted development cycles in smaller organizations. This longer lead time will result in greater likelihood of failure because of personnel turnover and changing circumstances in the course of project implementation.

In concluding this discussion of the effects of organizational size on MIS success, it should be noted that the validity of this proposition may be restricted to user-made systems. With the ever-decreasing cost of computer hardware and the increasing availability of applications packages for mini- and microcomputers and even of inexpensive turnkey systems, many of the historical disadvantages of small organizations may be obviated. In the future, small organizations may buy systems off the shelf, rather than build their own, and may become no less successful than their larger counterparts (Phillips and Boockholdt 1977; Render and Stair 1977; Farrington 1977). Smaller organizations will still be at a disadvantage, however, when they undertake construction of MIS on their own, rather than acquiring a finished product, especially because of evidence that would seem to indicate that they would like to have no less information than do their larger counterparts (Senn and Dickson 1974).

CONCLUSION

As an aid to the analysis of environmental variables, the authors have suggested a classification of these variables into uncontrollable and partially controllable (Ein-Dor and Segev 1978b). The uncontrollable variables are the extraorganizational situation, organizational structure, organizational time frame, and organizational size. The partially controllable variables are organizational resources, organizational maturity, and psychological climate. Since the environment is, by definition, external to MIS, none of its variables can be fully controlled by the MIS function, and some cannot be controlled by the organization. However, the organizational design variables—specifically, executive responsibility and the steering committee—are fully controllable by the organization. These controllable variables should be set following an analysis of the uncontrollable factors.

If the uncontrollable environment is hostile, there would seem to be little point in proceeding with MIS before it changes. If the uncontrollable environment is benevolent and the partially controllable environment hostile, efforts are required to modify the latter and to make the environment more benevolent before proceeding with, or in the course of, development. If this is the case, or if both the uncontrollable and partially controllable environments are benevolent, then the fully controllable elements should be designed to insure success. As the fully controllable variables are not, strictly speaking, part of the environment, they are covered in subsequent chapters.

In concluding the discussion of factors in their environment that affect the success and failure of management information systems, it should be pointed out how significant the effects of the environment can be. There are a fairly large number of environmental factors and any of them can have a negative influence. As yet, little research has been done on the critical values of these factors and how they can be modified to increase the likelihood of success.

# 3

## PROCEDURAL ASPECTS OF MIS:
## THE MIS PLAN

> This was charming, no doubt: but they shortly found out
>   That the Captain they trusted so well
> Had only one notion for crossing the ocean,
>   And that was to tingle his bell.
> Lewis Carroll, <u>The Hunting of the Snark</u>

A complete procedure for MIS development begins with the establishment of a strategic plan that provides a framework within which subsequent stages unfold. In general terms, each stage of the process elaborates and solidifies preceding stages, culminating in the technical phases of programming, testing, and, finally, routine operations. The procedural aspects of MIS comprise the conversion of general principles embodied in the highest levels of the strategic plan into completely explicit programs and operations at the conclusion of the process.

The concept of an MIS strategy is derived from Anthony's (1965) definition of strategic planning: the process of choosing objectives and deciding how to achieve them. McLean and Soden (1977) adapted this definition to MIS. Strategic planning for MIS, then, is the definition of objectives for MIS, the process by which they are operationalized, and the plan for achieving the objectives.

---

Some of the material in this chapter has been published previously in Phillip Ein-Dor and Eli Segev, "Strategic Planning for Management Information Systems," Management Science 24 (November 1978): 1631-41.

A strategy for MIS is a collection of strategic decisions in a number of related areas. In addition to the strategic plan, which is the subject of this chapter, strategic decisions are also made concerning computer hardware acquisition, software acquisition and development, and organizational arrangements. All of these decisions are strategic in the sense that they are usually made at high levels of management and generally affect more than one MIS. In certain cases, especially for very large systems, equipment selection, organizational arrangements, etc., may all be internal to the project. In most cases, however, project management faces a given environment of hardware, software, and organizational practices that are common to many MIS in the organization. These additional aspects of an organization's MIS strategy will all be covered in the next chapter. The implementation aspects of MIS are also covered briefly in a separate chapter both for the sake of completeness and, more important, because some relationships are posited between project execution and the success or failure of MIS. Thus, this chapter discusses the strategic plan for MIS; Chapter 4 comprises hardware strategy, software strategy, and organizational strategy; and the discussion of procedural aspects is concluded in Chapter 5. Note that in some of the propositions in these chapters a distinction is made between the success of MIS and the success of MIS projects; this distinction is discussed in Chapter 5.

From the definitions of MIS success and of strategic planning, it follows that strategic planning for MIS must focus on directing the MIS effort to achieve high levels of use by managers, concomitant with favorable cost-benefit ratios. The plan is a mechanism for meshing the characteristics of MIS with the needs of the managers of the organization and of the organization as a whole.

A study of the literature on MIS planning indicates that an MIS plan consists of the following elements:

The development strategy;
The purposes of systems;
Priorities for choosing system functions*;

---

*Functions are often referred to as "applications": payroll applications, inventory applications, etc. The term application is somewhat restrictive, however, in that it implies the application of information system technology to specific management problems. Often, the reference is to more general functions that serve a number of applications: for example, data base management systems, communications systems, statistical packages, or auditing packages. The authors have preferred the more general term, functions,

System functions;
Function goals;
Function requirements; and
Documentation.

These elements (excluding documentation) form a logical sequence
in which the level of abstraction declines and the level of operationalization increases (McLean and Soden 1977):

> It is essential to recognize that there is not a plan but
> a hierarchy of plans, running the gamut from a single
> strategic statement, which is quite conceptual, to de-
> tailed operational plans for individual projects.

The overall philosophy of development, or development strategy, sets the framework within which the process of MIS planning
unfolds. Within the general concept, a unifying purpose of the system provides a sense of direction. This overall purpose plays a
role in determining the priority scheme for choosing between functions that may be included in systems. Goals are then established
for each of the functions and, finally, these goals are operationalized as requirements or specifications. Each of these phases requires the creation of appropriate documentation to direct the following stages of the process and for future reference. Following
specification, systems are ready for implementation, a process described in Chapter 5.

Kriebel (1968) pointed out the responsibility of top management
in developing a computer strategy and stressed the importance of
top management philosophy being expressed in that strategy. The
strategic planning process for MIS may therefore be considered as
beginning when top management includes development of such systems among the goals of the organization. The strategic plan for
MIS is then developed within broad terms of reference defined by
management as consistent with overall aims of the organizations
(Hedberg 1975; McLean and Soden 1977; Soden and Tucker 1976).
When top management is unaware of the need for strategic planning
or is unwilling to invest in it, this function may be taken over by information system management. A good example of this tendency is
Shidal's (1979) advocacy of initiation of DP planning at the information system level. This is a possible cause of MIS pathologies that
is worthy of study.

---

to describe the systems chosen for implementation, most of which
will be applications in the conventional sense and some of which will
be general systems software.

## DEVELOPMENT STRATEGY

An organization's development strategy is its overall approach to implementing information systems. The three dimensions of this variable are the degree of comprehensiveness, the degree of integration, and the propensity to pioneer.

### Degree of Comprehensiveness

> Proposition 3.1: The more structured the organization, the greater the likelihood of success of the more comprehensive approaches.

The degree of comprehensiveness relates to the philosophy underlying the development of information systems in the organization. There are at least five such philosophies, distributed on a continuum between comprehensiveness and modularity. In decreasing order of comprehensiveness and increasing order of modularity, these approaches are:

> Top-down: The information needs of management are first specified within a model of the organization and the system is then designed to meet those needs.
> Inside-out: The computer is exploited, as the opportunity arises, within the organization's planning function in the generation of development plans and later integrated with other functions.
> Parallel or feedback: Operations systems and management systems are developed in parallel and successively stronger feedback loops established between them.
> Bottom-up: Operations modules are designed and built first and then successively integrated into MIS. A bottom-up development executed within the framework of a plan developed top-down has been described as a hybrid approach.
> Evolutionary or modular: Systems are developed as the need arises. This last approach may or may not be accompanied by a road map that describes a final goal and general method for getting there (Ackoff 1967; Ansoff 1967; Aron 1969; Blumenthal 1969; Ein-Dor 1975; Geller 1976; Gershefski 1969; Grossman 1972; Hammond 1974a; Hayes and Nolan 1974; Head 1967; McFarlan 1971, 1976; McKinsey 1968; McLean and Soden 1977; Munro and Davis 1977; PoKempner 1973; Schwartz 1970; Vazsonyi 1973; Zachman 1977; Zani 1970).

Scholars tend to advocate the more comprehensive strategies, but practitioners generally seem to favor the more evolutionary approaches. The comprehensive approach has been successful in particular, structured situations, for example, military command and control systems, whereas in complex, less structured situations, the less comprehensive approaches seem to have been more appropriate (Blumenthal 1969; Gibson et al. 1973; Hansen 1975; Heany 1972; Powers and Dickson 1972; Shults and Bruun 1974; Zani 1970).

Degree of Integration

> Proposition 3.2: The better adapted the degree of integration to the governing technological and economic variables, and to the level of integration of the organization itself, the greater the likelihood of MIS success.

In the past, a trend has been noted toward increasing development of integrated systems, especially among those firms that have been using computers for more than ten years. Aron (1969) suggests that integrated systems are most valuable to large firms, to firms with aggressive growth plans, and to decentralized organizations with geographically dispersed facilities. This view is basically refuted by Schwartz (1970) who advocates a degree of integration commensurate with the personality of the organization; in his view, only monolithic organizations can benefit from total systems, and the wider the range of activities, the looser the integration must be. This view is close to the consensus on the interrelationship between organizational structure and other aspects of MIS and so is adopted in the proposition preceding this section.

Most practitioners seem to think of MIS as collections or federations of more or less integrated subsystems. Proponents of this approach tend to regard it as a necessary compromise, dictated by the practical difficulties encountered in trying to build totally integrated systems. Thus, integration is generally considered desirable, but constrained by technical factors, even more strongly by economic ones, and perhaps even by the human cognitive limitations of managers (Beehler 1976; Dearden 1972; Emery 1973; Hammond 1974b; Powers and Dickson 1973; Roark 1970; Schwartz 1970).

There has been considerable development in recent years in the availability of technologies permitting varying degrees of integration, irrespective of the geographical or functional structure of the user organization. Several years ago, Emery (1973) regarded technological developments as favorable to integration, with the long-term trend tending in that direction. At the same time, Kriebel

(1973) noted that distributed system technology might permit a reduction in the scope of applications without a loss of economies of scale and so might prevent the drift toward increased integration. More recent thinking on this topic tends to suggest a continuum of solutions from which organizations may choose those best suited to their particular needs. The continuum begins with centralized MIS operating on large computers centrally located in the organization and reporting to a high level of management; it continues through varying degrees of distributed MIS, which provide departmental minicomputers in addition to the central facility; the other end of the spectrum consists of dispersed MIS with independent minicomputers deployed by operating departments. It has been suggested that the solution best fitted to an organization will depend on user styles, organizational structure, degree of budget control, management style, size of organization, nature of operations, and level of personnel (Kelsch 1978; Kroeber and Watson 1979; Walsh 1978). The concept of distributed systems is still new and far from mature and the number of such systems is growing rapidly. The effects of distributed system technology on the nature of information systems is one that will undoubtedly generate much interesting research.

Propensity to Pioneer

> Proposition 3.3: The more unique the situation, the greater the likelihood that duplication of an existing system will lead to failure.

The third dimension of a development strategy is the propensity to pioneer. Because of the expense of pioneering new systems technology, and the high cost of failure, there is a tendency to wait for other firms to test innovations. There is another view, however, that each corporation faces a unique set of problems and opportunities and it may be dangerous to attempt to duplicate the successes of others; if this is true, there may be little to be gained by hanging back, especially if one accepts the premise that the true measure of innovations in MIS is contribution to management decision making, rather than technological sophistication (Alexander 1969; Alter 1976; Brady 1967; McFarlan 1971; McKinsey 1968; Nolan and Knutsen 1974).

PURPOSE OF AN MIS

> Proposition 3.4: An explicit statement of purpose enhances the likelihood of MIS success.

The purpose of an MIS is a concise, explicit statement of the role assigned a particular information system in the organization. Four such roles have been identified:

A decision and planning tool;
An analog or model of the organization;
An information bank; and
A problem finding and solving aid.

(Alexander 1969; Alter 1976; Ansoff 1967; Aron 1969; Birkhahn 1976; Burdeau 1974; Carlson 1967; Diebold 1969; Farley et al. 1971; Financial Executive 1974; Geoffrion 1976; Grayson 1973; Grossman 1972; Hamilton and Moses 1974; Hammond 1974a, 1974b; Hanold 1972; Hayes and Nolan 1974; Hodge 1974; Kennedy and Mahapatra 1975; King 1973; King and Cleland 1971, 1973, 1974; Kronenberg 1967; Lanahan 1973; Lieberman and Whinston 1975; Lucas 1975b; Mitroff, Nelson, and Mason 1974; Murdick and Ross 1972; Nolan and Knutsen 1974; PoKempner 1973; Powers and Dickson 1973; Sass 1975; Seaberg and Seaberg 1973; Sprague and Watson 1975; Zani 1970.)

Clearly, there is considerable overlap between the four purposes, and any MIS contains elements of each of them. But it is noteworthy that organizations that define the purpose of MIS seem to single out only one aspect as being of overriding interest (see, for example, Carlson 1967; Kronenberg 1967; Lanahan 1973). Of the large number of case reports considered in this book, only a small minority actually reported the purpose of the MIS discussed. Although this would seem to indicate that the purposes were not defined, the authors assume that the reporters (generally senior EDP men) were either unaware of them or did not consider them important. Also worthy of note is that in spite of the scarcity of statements of purpose in the case reports, more than 30 papers discuss MIS conceptually in terms of one or more of the four purposes defined above. Given the large number of authors who have identified one or more purposes, it is also interesting that only four distinct ones have emerged.

It would appear that the particular purpose chosen is affected by the development strategy. Advocates of the top-down approach think in terms of decision-aid development and modeling (for example, Ackoff 1967), whereas advocates of the bottom-up approach are oriented toward the development of information banks (for example, Blumenthal 1969). This is an area in which additional research might yield interesting results.

PRIORITIES

> Proposition 3.5: The existence of a priority scheme
> for project selection that is in accordance with or-
> ganizational objectives increases the likelihood of
> MIS success.

The sequence in which MIS projects are chosen from the entire list of such projects that are feasible for the organization is
determined by the priority scheme. It has been found necessary to
develop priorities in accordance with organizational objectives.
These are implicit in the statement of purpose and development
strategy, which help shape the priorities. In addition, information
system management should be aware of overall organizational objectives. In a few cases, priority scheme problems have been
quoted as a prime cause of MIS failure (Coe 1974; Colton 1972;
Financial Executive 1974; Hax 1973; Keen 1975; Kriebel 1968;
McFarlan 1971; McLean and Soden 1977; Morgan and Soden 1972;
Soden and Tucker 1976).

FUNCTIONS ASSIGNED TO MIS

> Proposition 3.6: Functions that contribute to MIS suc-
> cess provide benefits to the organization, directly or
> indirectly; are consistent with institutional criteria;
> address major problems of the organization; and are
> consistent with the level of sophistication of the or-
> ganization.

Functions include general purpose systems such as data base
management systems and communications, but, in the present context, refer especially to the applications developed specifically for
use by managers. The range of functions—implemented and potential—is enormous and the full range of possibilities is as yet unde-
fined. This is partly because the application of computers to management has been limited to existing management systems and practices by lack of understanding of managerial processes and by management technology (Ansoff 1967; McFarlan 1971).

A priority scheme serves to put in order those functions that
are feasible. The feasibility of the chosen applications is posited
as a critical factor in the success or failure of MIS. Five criteria
of feasibility are suggested in the literature and conformance with
them is proposed as increasing the likelihood of success. The criteria are:

Direct effect on profitability: Lack of attention to cost effectiveness has been indicated as leading to systems that are not profitable. A study of 150 of the 500 largest corporations found that only one-third of their computer operations were profitable (Gupta 1974).

Indirect effect on profitability and other intangible benefits: The existence of this criterion causes difficulties since it renders simple cost-benefit or rate-of-return criteria inadequate; as a result, there are as yet no realistic cost effectiveness formulas for MIS. A methodology has been suggested for a combined evaluation of technical cost-benefit considerations and managers' perceptions of the potential utility of systems (King and Cleland 1975); evidence is not yet available on the effectiveness of this method.

Institutional criteria: These include consistency with organizational goals, the balance of information system development between units of the organization, and the availability of human and other resources.

Key tasks or assistance with major problems: An important factor regarding system functions is the extent to which they address the major problems or key tasks confronting the organization; this is considered to contribute critically to the success of MIS. However, system developers are sometimes advised to be opportunistic, to implement with minimum delay and to score early victories; such advice can lead them into the trap of attacking trivial problems in their desire to get working systems up quickly.

Organizational sophistication: This criterion has to do with selecting functions consistent with the level of sophistication of the organization. The desire to show quick results may lead implementors to develop simplistic systems based on established procedures and inconsistent with the maturity of the organization and with its level of expectations.

(Argyris 1971; Coe 1974; Colton 1972; Diebold 1969; Emery 1973; Garrity 1963; Geoffrion 1976; Gupta 1974; Hammond 1974a; Hayes and Nolan 1974; Head 1970; Herzlinger 1977; Keen 1975; King and Cleland 1975; Knutsen and Nolan 1974; Kronenberg 1967; Lucas 1973; McFarlan 1971; McKinsey 1968; McLean and Soden 1977; Murdick 1977; Nolan 1973; Nolan and Knutsen 1974; Schaffir 1974; Schwartz 1969; Seaberg and Seaberg 1973; Sihler 1971; Soden and Tucker 1976; Strassman 1976; Watson et al. 1977; Zani 1970.)

FUNCTION GOALS

Proposition 3.7: An explicit statement of function goals facilitates the specification of function require-

ments consistent with organizational needs and so increases the likelihood of success.

Goals broadly define the objectives of a function and are a
first step toward operationalizing the requirements of systems.
Thus, goals play the same role for specific functions as the purpose
does for whole systems. Goal definitions are not precise specifications, but they do indicate which areas are critical for the function
under discussion. Examples of requirements delineated by goal
follow:

Information content, stated as "predetermined information
requirements" and "integrated data";
Response times, stated as "predetermined times," "timely
information," and "information on changes available within a given
time";
Reliability, stated as "accurate information";
Economy;
Service to clients;
Intangible benefits; and
Improved operations.

(Ansoff 1967; Aron 1967; Birkhahn 1976; Burdeau 1974; Carlson
1967; Colton 1972; Diebold 1969; Emery 1973; Garrity 1963; Geisler
1970; Grayson 1973; Hamilton and Moses 1971; Hax 1973; Jenkins
1969; Kenneron 1970; Kronenberg 1967; Lanahan 1973; Lucas 1975b;
McFarlan 1971; McKinsey 1968; Montijo 1967; Murdick and Ross
1972; Nolan 1973b; Nolan and Knutsen 1974; Schwartz 1969; Wimbrow
1971.)


FUNCTION REQUIREMENTS

Proposition 3.8: The better adapted the definition of
function requirements to organizational needs and the
more explicit and complete the statement of requirements, the greater the likelihood of success.

Requirement definition is the final phase of the strategic plan.
The requirements are an operationalization of the more generally
stated goals of functions and are the end product of the strategic
planning process. They constitute the terms of reference for system designers to whom the development process is then delegated.
For completeness, the requirements should also include the budget
and time frame for development and a feedback and control mecha-

nism, including procedures for revising the plan should circumstances dictate. At this point, the direct responsibility for information system development devolves upon the information systems unit, and the implementation phase is entered.

The technical requirements that an organization places on its information systems determine, in part, the characteristics of the systems, or at least set constraints on them. Since organizations differ, the requirements also differ with the personality of the organization. Furthermore, the requirements of each information system will be affected by the level and predelictions of the managers to be served by it. The preciseness of requirements definitions and the degree to which the requirements meet organizational needs have an effect on the success of systems (Birkhahn 1976; Hayes and Nolan 1974; Head 1967; Juergens 1977; Keen 1976; Kronenberg 1967; Lanahan 1976; McFarlan 1976; Roark 1970).

The requirements mentioned in the literature are stated either as specific values (usually in case studies) or in general terms (especially in the conceptual papers). Typical requirements can be classified into a number of major groups:

Quality of information, including accuracy, integrity, timeliness, and input and output characteristics of data;

System operating characteristics such as mode of operation and priority scheduling;

Capacity, in terms of transactions per hour or input rates;

Time constraints, as measured by processing schedules or response times;

System quality, including reliability and software considerations;

Security considerations;

Economy and efficiency;

User interface requirements, including flexibility, modularity and capacity for evolution, responsiveness, and ease of use; and

Sophistication in the form of modern information processing and management science techniques.

(Aron 1967, 1969; Birkhahn 1976; Emery 1969, 1973; Garrity 1963; Head 1967, 1970; Kronenberg 1967; Lucas 1973; McFarlan 1971; McKinsey 1968; Montijo 1967; Morgan and Soden 1973; Sprague and Watson 1975.)

DOCUMENTATION

Proposition 3.9: Formal and complete documentation of the strategic plan for MIS enhances the likelihood of success.

Documentation of the strategic plan is the form in which MIS projects are presented to top management for evaluation and control. Items that should be included in such documentation are:

The development strategy;

The purposes of systems;

Feasibility studies, including major challenges and problems, economic factors (costs, savings, and returns), qualitative or intangible factors, institutional factors, and manpower aspects;

Goals of functions and their consistency with corporate goals and strategy; and

Plans for development and operation, including requirements definitions.

It has been found repeatedly that one of the most significant factors distinguishing companies that are effective information system users from those that are not is the selection of applications on the basis of careful feasibility studies and the quality and content of their written plans (Garrity 1963; Hammond 1974a; Head 1967; Herzlinger 1977; McFarlan 1971; McKinsey 1968; Schwartz 1969; Shafto 1976; Soden and Tucker 1976).

McLean and Soden conducted a survey on long-range planning for information systems as part of a conference on the same topic held at UCLA in 1974. (The survey is reported in Chapter 3 of McLean and Soden 1977.) An initial questionnaire and a follow-up questionnaire were completed by top EDP executives from 20 very large organizations with average annual revenues or budgets over U.S. $1 billion and annual MIS budgets of over U.S. $15 million. The organizations represented a wide range of industries: aerospace, two; airlines, one; business equipment, two; chemicals, two; consumer goods, one; education, two; government, three; insurance, one; medical services, one; petroleum, two; and public utilities, three.

The two questionnaires included questions about the organization, about its DP unit, and, mainly, about the MIS planning effort. The authors identified what they defined as a "novice" group (with only a year or two of MIS planning) whose approach was "reactive" and saw themselves in a service role, and a sophisticated group (with some years of experience in MIS planning) whose approach was "proactive" and saw themselves in a change agent role. The data compare these two groups.

Although it is impossible to reproduce all the data collected in this survey, some are reproduced below, namely long-range planning objectives and their degree of attainment (Figure 3.1), documentation content (Figure 3.2), and planning pitfalls (Figure 3.3).

FIGURE 3.1

Long-Range Planning Objectives and
Their Degree of Attainment

**Planning Objectives**

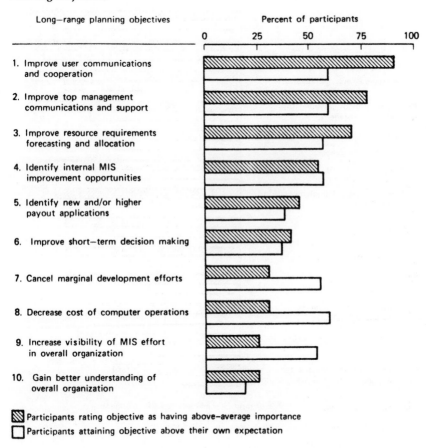

Source: Ephraim R. McLean and John V. Soden, eds.,
Strategic Planning for MIS (New York: John Wiley, 1977), p. 67.
Copyright © (1977) John Wiley & Sons, Inc. Reprinted by permission of John Wiley & Sons, Inc.

FIGURE 3.2

## Long-Range Planning Document Content—
### Ideal versus Actual

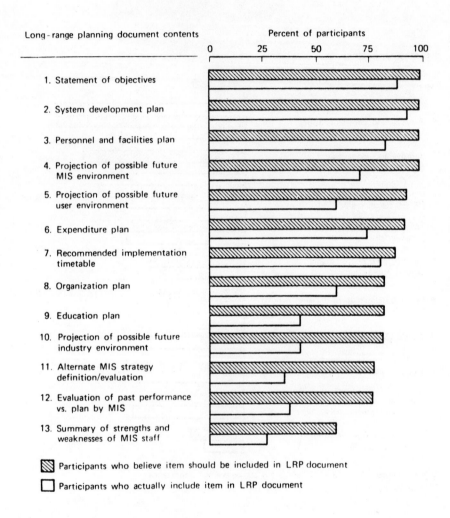

Long-range planning document contents

Percent of participants

Source: Ephraim R. McLean and John V. Soden, eds.,
Strategic Planning for MIS (New York: John Wiley, 1977), p. 69.
Copyright © (1977) John Wiley & Sons, Inc. Reprinted by per-
mission of John Wiley & Sons, Inc.

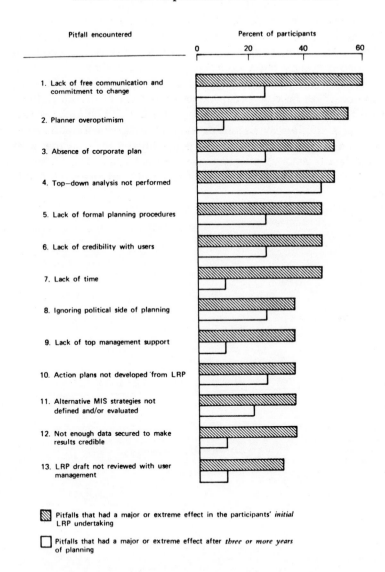

FIGURE 3.3

Long-Range Planning Pitfalls—
Initial versus Experience after Three Years

Source: Ephraim R. McLean and John V. Soden, eds.,
Strategic Planning for MIS (New York: John Wiley, 1977), p. 75.
Copyright © (1977) John Wiley & Sons, Inc. Reprinted by per-
mission of John Wiley & Sons, Inc.

It is important to point out that the organizations surveyed are very large (average size is larger than the average size of the Fortune 500) and the findings are a description of the state of the art and the opinions of top EDP executives, rather than research on planning factors that enhance or diminish MIS success.

The procedural aspects of MIS planning are an extreme exemplification of the authors' contention that much of the theory and practice of MIS is based purely on intuition and personal experience, uninformed by research; a recent paper by the authors on strategic planning for MIS (Ein-Dor and Segev 1978c) contains 103 references, only one of which may be regarded as empirical research in this area (the book by McLean and Soden just cited). The authors are unaware of a single experiment or even of a rigorously planned survey in the area of MIS development procedures except at the most technical levels such as programmer productivity. The higher the level of procedure considered, the less empirical research has been performed.

# 4
## PROCEDURAL ASPECTS OF MIS:
## MIS STRATEGIES

> "That's exactly the method," the Bellman bold
>   In a hasty parenthesis cried,
> "That's exactly the way I have always been told
>   That the capture of Snarks should be tried!"
>       Lewis Carroll, The Hunting of the Snark

As the MIS plan is executed, it calls for the acquisition of hardware and software and for the establishment of appropriate organizational arrangements. The nature of the MIS plan and of the projects undertaken in it affect the decisions made in each of the three areas mentioned. Similarly, if projects are undertaken within the context of existing hardware, software, and organization, these factors must be taken into consideration. Thus, there are strong interactions between the three areas of MIS strategy and the sequential procedure that translates overall organizational objectives into functioning information systems.

### HARDWARE STRATEGY

A hardware strategy for MIS development refers to equipment capabilities, the selection process, the form of acquisition, and the

---

Some of the material in this chapter has been published previously in Phillip Ein-Dor and Eli Segev, "Centralization/Decentralization and Management Information Systems," Information and Management 1 (1978): 162-72, and Phillip Ein-Dor and Eli Segev, "Organizational Arrangements for MIS Units," Information and Management 3 (1980): 19-26.

deployment of computer equipment within the organization. As indicated earlier, these decisions are frequently made for organizations' data processing activities as a whole and are not specific to any particular MIS, although the needs of specific systems may affect the strategy formulation.

## Computer Capabilities

> Proposition 4.1: Sufficient computer capabilities are necessary for the success of MIS and MIS projects.

It has been stated that computer potential is one predictor of high-level information system use; the principle criteria for evaluating potential have been identified as throughput, the instruction set, and upward compatibility. Specific types of equipment are associated with MIS; these include mass random access storage, on-line terminals, and communications networks (Head 1970; Lucas 1975; Nolan and Knutsen 1974).

The argument has been made that choice of hardware is critical for MIS success. Equipment limitations have been found to be extremely critical in surveys of hospital systems. The problems encountered include reliability and machine specifications that were appropriate at the time of order but were insufficient to accomplish the specified tasks at the time of installation. This problem is aggravated because computer configurations are fixed in the short term and may be difficult and expensive to alter. In similar, but happier vein, at least one case report concluded that the computer and peripheral equipment selected was one of two determinants of a successful implementation (Hansen 1975; Montijo 1967; Singer 1969; Zani 1970).

Diametrically opposed conclusions were reached by Garrity (1963) who found not one case of a company that believed that realization of computer potential had been significantly blocked by technical deficiencies in machine design or operation. Nor did the frequency with which companies traded-up their equipment have any bearing on success. Thus, there is major disagreement over the importance of equipment specifications, and little evidence, making this a potentially rewarding area for research.

## The Selection Process

> Proposition 4.2: Computer selection procedures are not critical to the success of MIS; they may affect the success of MIS projects.

A study of the computer selection process in the United States found that computer selection is generally competitive; is based on conventional selection methods; emphasizes objective as opposed to subjective criteria; and that the selection is usually performed in-house, rather than by consultants. A similar study in Israel reported almost identical findings. One study has found it to be irrelevant to success if one or more equipment suppliers are employed, and cases have been reported where preoccupation with equipment decisions seems to have impeded progress by diverting attention from areas that really determine success (Borovits and Ein-Dor 1976; Cooper 1978; Garrity 1963; Schneidewind 1967).

Form of Acquisition

> Proposition 4.3: The form of acquisition of computer hardware has no effect on the success of MIS or MIS projects.

Computer equipment may be purchased, rented, or leased for in-house use, or use may be acquired from service bureaus. Although it has been recommended that alternatives between on-site and off-site service should be carefully analyzed, surveys in which this issue was studied found no relationship between the form of ownership and the degree of success. This may be because outside services are employed largely to insure flexibility in the timing of computer acquisitions and it has been recommended that outside computer time be obtained for early applications. Service bureaus have also been considered a suitable solution for small businesses, but the advent of mini- and microcomputers will probably considerably reduce their role in this area also (Brennan 1975; Colton 1972; Garrity 1963; Nolan and Knutsen 1974; Singer 1969).

Equipment Deployment

> Proposition 4.4: The optimal deployment of computer equipment enhances the likelihood of MIS success but has little effect on the success of MIS projects.

This issue deals with the degree of centralization of computer equipment, as distinct from the centralization of information systems (discussed later in this chapter under "Organizational Strategy"). In 1970, Head identified three possibilities for distributing computing in a geographically dispersed organization, namely a large processor at company headquarters, small processors at regional or plant locations, and terminals in managers' offices connected to either a regional or central computer or both. Today, the authors would add the possibility of combining small remote processors into networks providing both centralized and decentralized capabilities.

Many advantages have been claimed for centralized systems. These include the availability of more powerful hardware and software, which is also more economical in terms of both hardware and personnel economies of scale, allows more rapid growth for single users (with only a small drain on total data processing resources), permits more efficient scheduling and higher use, facilitates maintenance of data and programs, produces less redundant and more consistent data bases, and minimizes development programming and interface problems (Gibson and Nolan 1974; Head 1970; Kalogeras 1977; Kronenberg 1967; Milutinovich and Kanter 1975; Roark 1970; Smith 1977).

There are also disadvantages, however, that include costs for communications in addition to those between computers, system complexity, greater difficulty in management, budgeting and costing, more machine overhead for operating systems, and making the system development effort a bureaucracy (which may tend to stifle user and implementor initiatives) (Head 1970; Kalogeras 1977; Roark 1970; Smith 1977).

Although some authorities consider hardware centralization to be mandatory in the more advanced stages of MIS development, it appears that there is a best balance of advantages and disadvantages that determines the best level of equipment centralization. This leads to an observed tendency to regionalize, rather than to centralize, data processing capacity. An example of this is Ford Motor Company, which pools computer facilities into centers as large as are consistent with good service, regardless of where system development is done (Gibson and Nolan 1974; Head 1967; Roark 1970; Seib 1978).

Garrity (1963) found no correlation between large-scale centralization of business data processing and degree of success. Nor was the centralization of business, engineering, and scientific applications on the same computers found to have any bearing on success.

The recent introduction of distributed data processing systems—small local processors with local files linked between themselves or with a central site—reduces even further the importance of the centralization-decentralization issue. Distributed architecture permits the construction of logically centralized systems composed of geographically dispersed physical components. This implies that systems may be designed for any point in the two-dimensional space defined by degree of hardware centralization (from completely centralized to extreme decentralization) and degree of communication between hardware sites (from none to complete linkage of every site with every other site). Thus, the degree of logical system centralization becomes independent of the physical centralization and decentralization; virtually centralized systems can be implemented on distributed hardware. Proponents of distributed minicomputer networks prefer them to large centralized systems for reasons of economy, flexibility, responsiveness, and high tolerance to failure. The continuity now possible in the spectrum of hardware deployment options lends credence to the recommendation that systems should be configured to conform to the structure of the organization (Burnett and Nolan 1975; Mandell 1975).

## SOFTWARE STRATEGY

A computer system is composed of both hardware and software, but strategy formulation practices have fared very differently in these two areas. The reasons may be partly historical. In the early 1960s, hardware accounted for about 90 percent of the cost of informat ion systems and software for the remaining 10 percent. Currently, the split is estimated at 40 percent hardware and 60 percent software and projections for the 1980s are that software will account for 80 percent. Nevertheless, much more attention is still given to hardware strategies than to software strategies to the point where preoccupation with hardware has been identified as a serious problem in information system development.

An additional reason for this unbalanced approach to the two components of computer systems may lie in a major difference in the length of time for which decisions commit the organization. Major hardware decisions are generally intended to be effective for at least five or six years and often remain in effect for much longer; thus, long-range plans are clearly called for. With software, the situation is somewhat different because changes in software decisions can be implemented almost immediately. As there is no intrinsic long-term commitment to most software decisions beyond the life of a single project, there may appear to be no need for a long-range strategy and most decisions are specific to individual projects.

The effects of the two considerations outlined above are enhanced by the similarity of hardware decisions to any other capital budgeting problems and are reasonably well understood by senior management. Software acquisition problems are much less well understood even by software experts, let alone nontechnical management. All of these factors have led to what appears to be an

overemphasis on hardware strategy, carried over from the period
when hardware was a major cost factor, and a dearth of software
strategies perpetuated into an era when this is the most significant
part of information system costs.

The cost ratios between hardware and software cited earlier
would seem to refute the contention that technological advances in
information systems seem to be taking place more in software than
in hardware, as has been claimed (Gibson and Nolan 1974). Furthermore, software projects are notoriously difficult to control. In
1969 it was stated that "Production of large scale software has become a scare item for management. By reputation it is often an
unprofitable morass, costly and unending" (David 1969). The lack
of progress during the following decade is exemplified by the statement that:

> The data processing landscape is littered with examples
> of major software developments which faltered and then
> expired. That this situation should exist, after almost
> a quarter-century of experience with implementing these
> systems, is one of the enigmas of the rapidly expanding
> data processing industry.*

The enigma is heightened by the paucity of research in this area in
which such large quantities of resources are so consistently wasted.

> A survey of the papers that were categorized as software
> management appearing in the IEEE Transactions on
> Software Engineering reveals that only two . . . have
> appeared. . . . [a] study of the articles cited through-
> out IEEE TSE dealing with this topic [shows they] are
> mainly government reports . . . or derived from these
> reports.†

Given the high costs involved and the high probability of failure, it is surprising to find that there are very few references in
the literature to software decisions at the strategic level. There is
a somewhat larger number of papers relating to software project
management—the operational level of software development. It is,

---

*Richard D. Merwin, "Software Management: We Must Find a
Way—Guest Editorial," IEEE Transactions on Software Engineering
SE-4 (July 1978): 307.

†Merwin, "Software Management," p. 308.

perhaps, this scarcity of strategic level decisions that increases the difficulty of implementing software projects, even more so than their intrinsic complexity.

To the best of the authors' knowledge, there is only one paper that deals consciously with the issue of software strategy (Cooper 1978). Cooper analyzes software management at the corporate level. The elements of such an analysis are, in his view, overall software costs, performance of software to achieve goals of the corporation, advanced planning for software requirements in the future, and anticipating life cycle costs of existing software programs. Cooper identifies two categories of problems associated with corporate-level software management: psychological problems and procedural problems. The psychological obstacles are:

> Lack of computer-related experience by senior executives;
> Lack of computer-related expertise on project staffs;
> Preoccupation with hardware by managers;
> Preoccupation with development by project managers; and
> Inadequate student preparation by academics.

The procedural obstacles and pitfalls are:

> Potential for projects to become overly complex;
> Use of assembly level languages in projects;
> Buying-on a contract by the vendor;
> Lack of adequate risk, cost, and reliability estimating techniques; and
> Lack of uniform software practices. *

The problems categorized by Cooper as psychological obstacles are common to all aspects of MIS and are covered in the chapters in this book devoted to behavioral issues. The procedural obstacles indicate clearly what the content of a software strategy should be; namely, definition of the limits of complexity in MIS projects the organization is willing to undertake, determination of languages to be used, guidelines for employing external contractors in the software area, institutionalization of risk, cost and reliability estimates, and standardization of software practices, including software project management.

---

*Reprinted by permission from John D. Cooper, "Corporate Level Software Management," IEEE Transactions on Software Engineering SE-4 (July 1978): 319-26.

There are extremely few empirical data relating the effects of software strategy alternatives to the success of MIS and MIS projects. The following paragraphs mention the alternatives, reference expositions of them, and present what little evidence there is.

## Project Complexity

Proposition 4.5: The maintenance of project complexity within the bounds of an organization's level of sophistication increases the likelihood of MIS and MIS project success.

The complexity of software projects an organization can successfully complete is dependent on the sophistication and size of its programming staff and on the resources it is prepared to invest. A method for measuring the difficulty of software projects and the amount of programming effort required to overcome a given level of difficulty has been developed by Putnam (1978). A clear definition of levels of complexity acceptable to an organization would probably prevent many of the instances of organizations biting off more than they can chew and then gagging.

## Programming Languages

Proposition 4.6: The use of high-level programming languages has no effect on MIS success but enhances the likelihood of MIS project success.

Many advantages are attributed to high-level programming languages, including increased programmer productivity, greater reliability, increased flexibility, self-documentation, and portability. Nevertheless, it has been noted that even when management dictates the use of high-level languages, it is still a considerable effort to prevent the use of assembly languages—perhaps because of insufficient hard evidence to support the claims made for the higher level languages (Brooks 1975; Cooper 1978; David 1969).

## External Acquisitions

Proposition 4.7: The effect of externally acquired software on the success of MIS and MIS projects depends on the type of software involved.

A distinction should be made between software purchased externally and in-house production of software. In the first case, a decision often faced in the course of system development concerns the use of off-the-shelf program packages versus individually written programs tailored to users' needs and contracted out to be made to order. The situation depends on the type of program involved. Three types of program packages are generally recognized: system control packages, problem-solving packages, and application packages (Head 1970; Miller 1977).

System control packages, or operating systems, are adopted off the shelf in most situations. However, in one briefing on computers in hospitals, it was reported that a manufacturer's operating system was insufficient for real time hospital systems and had to be substantially modified by the user. In spite of such deficiencies, however, users almost invariably prefer purchasing packages, rather than designing or making their own (Head 1970; Singer 1969).

Problem-solving packages such as linear programming and statistical analysis are also often bought ready made. There is, however, more of a tendency for users to write their own packages in this area than is true of operating systems. Some of the most widely marketed problem-solving packages were originally developed by users; good examples are the statistical packages SPSS and BMD. Problem-solving packages have been further classified into computerized decision models, business games, simulation models, and forecasting models (Head 1977; Sass 1975).

Least progress in disseminating off-the-shelf software has been made with application packages. This has been documented particularly for hospital information systems. A number of reasons have been suggested for this situation, including the inability to develop packages on an economic and timely basis; difficulties in developing packages of sufficient generality to satisfy the different needs of a number of organizations; inability to use programs developed for one environment in another; and difficulties in integrating packages, which are generally built to stand alone, with other application packages. Some applications such as payroll, billing, and accounts receivable are highly structured by requirements of outside agencies and are easier to incorporate into packages than are those specific to an organization or industry. Caution regarding the use of program packages may also be explained by the high cost of pioneering a package and that software seems to improve with age; there would seem to be little gained by hurrying to use a new package (Fisher 1969; Hansen 1975; Head 1970; Nolan and Knutsen 1974; Singer 1969).

Cooper (1978) has identified buying-in—a strategy employed by contractors in which they tender uneconomically low bids to

initiate a relationship with a purchaser—as the major problem connected with contracting out software development. Contractors
buy-in either because they anticipate a considerable volume of additional business for which they will not have to compete and on which
they will recoup their loss from buying-in or because they believe
it will be possible to enlarge the project while it is in progress and
cover their costs on the increments. Having bought-in, the con-
tractor will make every effort to escalate the project or, if unsuccessful in this, to minimize outlay on the project by cutting corners
wherever possible.

Risk, Cost, and Reliability Estimates

> Proposition 4.8: Accurate risk, cost, and reliability
> estimates enhance the likelihood of MIS project success.

Much of the organizational energy wasted on unsuccessful
projects could be saved if the estimation of risks, costs, and reliability were accurate  A strategy for software management should
therefore specify the execution of analyses to provide these estimates. Furthermore, the value of such estimates is enhanced when
they are performed in some standard format so over time they acquire more meaning for those working with them. Cooper (1978)
points out that the inability to provide the necessary estimates
accurately contributes largely to the poor image of software held
by senior management. Some empirical research and a theoretical
model of the risk assessment problem for individual projects are
presented in a paper by Alter and Ginzberg (1978), discussed in
length in this book in the section on stages of the MIS project.

Standardization of Software Practices

> Proposition 4.9: The standardization of software prac-
> tices increases the likelihood of MIS project success.

Insufficient standardization of software practices within an
organization has been identified as a major source of software management problems as different practices lead to status reports with
different meanings, different sets of milestones, different types of
controls, and so on (Cooper 1978). A list of software practices that
might be considered for incorporation in a software strategy and
their current levels of use is provided in Table 4.1.

TABLE 4.1

Modern Programming Practices

| Practice | Used (percent) |
|---|---|
| Reviews (Black 1977) | 81 |
| Program manager authority (Black 1977) | 75 |
| Configuration management | 75 |
| Phase testing (Black 1977) | 69 |
| Program modularity (Black 1977) | 67 |
| Naming conventions (Black 1977) | 56 |
| Structured design (Yourdon 1975) | 44 |
| Structured walk-throughs (Weinberg 1971) | 40 |
| Support library and facilities (Black 1977) | 40 |
| Chief programmer teams (Baker 1972) | 38 |
| Design discipline and verification (Black 1977) | 38 |
| Unit development folder (Ingrassia 1976) | 26 |
| Structured analysis (Yourdon 1975) | 17 |
| Structured form (Dijkstra 1969) | 17 |
| HIPO'S (IBM 1975) | 12 |

Source: John H. Lehman, "How Software Projects Are Really Managed," Datamation 25 (January 1979): 119-29. Reprinted With Permission of DATAMATION® magazine, © Copyright by TECHNICAL PUBLISHING COMPANY, A DUN & BRADSTREET COMPANY, 1979—all rights reserved.

Given the potential value of good software strategies and given the obvious need for them demonstrated by large numbers of costly failures, it is surprising that so little has been written on this topic and that there is virtually no research on it. This would seem to be one of the high-payoff areas for research in management information systems.

ORGANIZATIONAL STRATEGY

The final aspect of an organization's strategy for MIS has to do with the long-term organizational arrangements instituted for the management and development of information systems. Experience has shown that a number of organizational problems need to be

solved with respect to MIS and that these have given rise to various
arrangements for their solution. This section lists the more important organizational solutions and presents the various views concerning their effectiveness. Those issues that arise in the literature are the place of the information processing system in the
organization, the degree of centralization, the interface between
users and MIS projects, the organization of implementors, the
staffing and functions of the steering group and study group, the
data base administrator, corporate computer staff, and finally, the
decision whether to acquire external assistance and services
(Sihler 1971).

Location in the Organization

> Proposition 4.10: Autonomous information system
> departments have greater likelihood of successfully
> implementing MIS projects and of producing success-
> ful MIS than do departments subordinate to a functional
> area.

In many cases, the data processing unit is initially located in
the department in which it is first applied and later becomes autonomous when the range of applications is broadened. This may explain
the finding that in most companies the computer is assigned to the
finance-accounting department (Garrity 1963; Gibson and Nolan 1974).

Perhaps the most pragmatic approach to the question of locating information units is that the location should be determined by
the power structure in the specific organization; when the center of
power shifts, the information function should shift with it (Rue 1976).

There are, however, several more doctrinaire approaches to
this issue. One authority distinguishes between accounting and
finance, and strongly advocates locating the information system in
finance because of finance's close relationship to management,
rather than in accounting, because of accounting's inhibiting effects
on the development of systems for management. This is the solution
at Inland Steel, where the information system organization is part of
the finance function. A different argument leading to somewhat
similar conclusions is that, because managers are interested in
profits, computers should be located in profit centers, rather than
in cost centers such as accounting (Ference and Uretsky 1976;
Hanold 1972; Wilson 1976).

Finally, it is argued that the MIS department should be autonomous, reporting to a senior level of management. Evidence indicates

that MIS are in fact becoming recognized as an independent area with considerable organizational autonomy (Emery 1973; Gibson and Nolan 1974).

Degree of Centralization

> Proposition 4.11: The better the degree of centraliza-
> tion of the information system function, the greater the
> likelihood of success of MIS and of MIS projects.

One should distinguish between centralization of the computer resource ("hardware"), and centralization of the development and implementation, or systems resource ("brainware"), which is discussed here. One study distinguishes five possible combinations of hardware and system resource centralization and decentralization, namely: centralized hardware with decentralized system development and programming; centralized hardware and programming with decentralized systems development; decentralized hardware with centralized development and programming; centralized hardware, systems, and programming with directly linked satellite installations; and centralized hardware, systems, and programming with autonomous satellite installations (Milutinovich and Kanter 1975).

It has been stated that the computer resource should be centralized and that it is the organization of the systems resource that is the subject for contention between centralization and decentralization. The following are advantages and disadvantages of centralization and decentralization of the system function (Head 1970; Milutinovich and Kanter 1975; Roark 1970):

Centralization permits uniform reporting systems and company-wide consolidation of operating results;

Centralization can improve coordination of the information system as a functional entity and helps retain well-qualified and well-motivated professionals because of the greater leeway in providing status, promotion, and state-of-the-art technology in larger organizations;

Centralization may provide greater flexibility for the organization by shielding the information function from organizational changes, but at the cost of greater system complexity, higher communication outlays, and losing sight of users' needs through concentration on overall organizational objectives;

Too much centralization may lead to bureaucracy and reduce the responsiveness of the systems organization, a problem compounded by isolating systems from functional management, whereas decentralization heightens familiarity with local problems and promotes rapid response to local needs;

Decentralization can sometimes provide better opportunities for management development;

Decentralization mitigates the "scapegoat function"—the tendency to blame the computer for all problems; and

Decentralization provides greater autonomy and places profit and loss responsibility with the local manager, who is in the best position to evaluate benefits.

Although calls have been made for more centralization of information system planning and others claim such centralization is impossible, the general attitude toward this issue seems to be highly pragmatic.  Roark (1970) notes that from the systems point of view, centralization is invariably called for, but political issues may favor decentralization.  His argument, therefore, is that there is a best degree of centralization in any organization, and his article offers indices of over- and undercentralization.  This approach is supported by the finding that companies generally organize information systems in conformance with their traditional plans of organization; those that do not, experience abnormal difficulties (Dearden 1972; Garrity 1973; McFarlan 1971; Milutinovich and Kanter 1975; Roark 1970).

The tendency to configure information systems in accordance with general corporate philosophy has led to the development of a "hybrid" organization with shared control.  This is the most popular form, as evidenced by a survey that showed the following distribution of organizations by type of control of information systems:  highly centralized, 32.5 percent; hybrid, 46.5 percent; and highly decentralized, 20.0 percent (Kriebel 1973).

Organization of MIS Implementors

Proposition 4.12:  Team organization of project implementors enhances the likelihood of MIS project success.

The two major forms of organization are functional (with each individual assigned a clearly defined function; for example, system analysis, programming) and project team, in which the team is totally responsible for all phases of development and implementation with no hard-and-fast functional definitions.  Both types of organization have been found in companies with successful information systems.  It has been suggested that regardless of the particular form

employed, there should be an open adaptive organization in the development stage and a closed, stable, mechanistic organization in
the production stage (Gibson and Nolan 1974; McKinsey 1968;
Stuart 1968; Wetherbe and Whitehead 1977).

Although system success has not been found to depend on the
organization of MIS projects, the success of MIS projects does seem
to be enhanced by team organization. In 1972, IBM introduced the
concept of the chief programmer/librarian team in conjunction with
structured programming, top-down development, and the development support library. The productivity ratio of such teams over
more conventional forms of organization has been estimated as five
to one. It is suggested that three members is the right team size
for effective communication between team members and promotes
successful system development. There seems to be a distinct
tendency toward such team organization within project groups and
some data are presented in Chapter 8 (Cooke 1976; Scamell and
Baugh 1975; Stuart 1968).

## The User Interface

> Proposition 4.13: The assignment of systems analysts
> to functional areas served by MIS enhances the likeli-
> hood of success.

In decentralized systems, with users at remote sites, it has
been found necessary to assign system-trained people at the remote
site to maintain the local subsystem and to identify and solve the
local problems. In general, it is believed that systems analysts
will become integrated in the functioning of the user's area and
will serve as a communication link between users and the computer
resource. Another alternative that has been suggested to alleviate
remote users' belief that they are being ignored in the production
stage is to communicate to them the service levels provided by the
system for each application (Gibson and Nolan 1974; Lewis 1976;
Milutinovich and Kanter 1975).

## The Steering Committee

> Proposition 4.14: Steering committees composed of
> high-level corporate officers enhance the likelihood
> of MIS and MIS project success.

As organizations become aware of the importance of information systems, they tend to establish steering committees to guide

the MIS effort. Steering committees are composed of senior executives and their functions are:

  Determining information system policies, objectives and priorities;
  Identifying potentially profitable projects; and
  Projecting personnel, hardware, and software requirements and suggesting budgets.

Steering committees have been advocated both as a way of showing management support and as a method of attaining user involvement (Atkins 1976; Coe 1974; Dearden and Nolan 1973; Gibson and Nolan 1974; Knutsen and Nolan 1974; Lucas 1974b; McFarlan 1971; Nolan 1973a; Nolan and Knutsen 1974; Wilson 1976).

## The Study Group

  Proposition 4.15: Study groups composed of qualified operating management, rather than technical personnel, enhance the likelihood of success.

  Operating management should play a strong role in project selection and planning. Appropriately qualified operating managers are likely to be a better source of ideas for profitable changes in operations than are computer professionals (Carlson 1967; Kronenberg 1967; McKinsey 1968).

## The Data Base Administrator

  Proposition 4.16: The appointment of a data base administrator as a high-level staff position independent of data processing enhances the likelihood of success.

  In 1972, it was predicted that the whole issue of MIS would be reduced to that of data base management (Kriebel 1972). The importance of data bases has certainly increased since then and with them the significance and understanding of the role of the data base administrator (DBA). The evolution in the perception of the DBA's role parallels the increasing acceptance of the view that information is a major organizational resource—as the comptroller is responsible for financial resources, so is the DBA for information resources (Yasaki 1977).

There is considerable confusion over the DBA's area of competence. A technically oriented description of the data administration function comprises data base description; control of data access; information enhancement; and systems support, protection, and tuning. A more general description charges the DBA with developing standards and procedures for creating, processing, and upgrading all corporate data. These different perceptions of the DBA's role also give rise to different views on the appropriate organizational arrangement (McFadden and Suver 1978; Ross 1976; Walsh 1978).

The suggestions for appropriate organizational positions run the gamut from somewhere inside the data processing function, through an independent position reporting to the first or second level of data processing management, to a high-level staff support function at the vice president level and independent of departments and divisions. A compromise solution suggests a matrix organization with local DBAs reporting both to local operating management and to a staff level DBA at headquarters (Ross 1976; Severino 1978; Sibley 1977; Yasaki 1977).

Just as the perception of DBA functions colors views on organizational location, so does it affect capability requirements. At one extreme it is seen as a purely technical position with primarily technical qualifications required. Those who see it as an organization-wide function also stress the need for political skills that permit effective promotion of data base activities (Ross 1976; Yasaki 1977). There seems to be little doubt that the importance of data bases will continue to grow and with them the stature and centrality of the DBA function will also increase.

Corporate Computer Staff

> Proposition 4.17: An appropriately qualified corporate computer staff enhances the likelihood of MIS project success.

There are conflicting opinions of whether a corporate staff is necessary to guide the systems effort. On the one hand, it has been suggested that centralizing control of a company's information system in a staff creates insoluble problems and is therefore infeasible. In practice, on the other hand, it has been found especially among decentralized companies that corporate staffs can lead to a higher level of success in MIS projects (Dearden 1972; Garrity 1963; Head 1967).

The functions of the corporate staff have been defined as providing overall strategy as a framework for long-term systems planning, monitoring programs, and evaluating results. Superior technical knowledge and effectiveness in working with nontechnical personnel are the capabilities that have been found to distinguish successful staff groups (Garrity 1963; Head 1967).

### External Assistance

> Proposition 4.18: Larger organizations benefit less from employing consultants and service firms than do smaller ones.

Faced with an information system project, organizations may recruit the external assistance of consultants and computer service firms.

Feelings are mixed on the use of consultants. Some regard them as a useful extension to existing staff, with local managerial resources being used to implement and monitor the consultant's work. Others suggest that outside consultants may be more successful than are internal EDP experts because they normally have direct access to top management. A survey of computer users concluded that the use of outside consulting is limited, that it is more extensive among small users than among large, and that the use of computer vendors as consultants is more widespread among users with administrative applications only (Sass 1975; Schneidewind 1967; Schwartz 1969).

The use of computer service firms is attractive because of the high cost of in-house computers and staff, a scarcity of good programmers, and the inability of management to communicate with computer personnel. Several case reports do, however, attribute success in part to the decision to implement systems in-house, rather than contracting them out (Alexander 1969; Carlson 1967; Kronenberg 1967).

From the preceding propositions, it follows that the organizational strategy adopted for MIS plays a significant role in the success or failure of both MIS and projects that produce them. Although appropriate organizational arrangements cannot of themselves guarantee success, poor solutions to organizational questions contribute considerably to failure. As in so many other areas, it is surprising how little research has been done in an area the significance of which is generally recognized.

# 5

# PROCEDURAL ASPECTS OF MIS:
# PROJECT IMPLEMENTATION

> They sought it with thimbles, they sought it with care;
>   They pursued it with forks and hope;
> They threatened its life with a railway-share;
>   They charmed it with smiles and soap.
>                     Lewis Carroll, The Hunting of the Snark

It was indicated earlier that MIS project implementation occurs within an environment of the MIS strategies adopted by the organization. The responsibility for strategic planning rests properly
with the highest levels of management; responsibility for implementation of specific projects is delegated to the head of information
systems and to project managers. This is one criterion for distinguishing between the processes. As responsibility for systems
moves from one locus to another, the criteria for success also
change. The criteria for the success of a strategy are the same as
for MIS—a strategy is successful when it produces successful MIS.
The criteria for project success are different; a project is successful when it produces a system conforming to specifications and does
so on schedule and within budget. Thus, a project may be eminently
successful in the terms stated here, yet produce an unsuccessful
MIS because, for example, its specifications do not attract users.
Conversely, a project may be plagued by schedule slips and cost
overruns but produce an end product highly desirable to its intended
users and therefore a successful MIS.

A study by Powers and Dickson (1973) attempted to identify
the management factors affecting the success and failure of MIS
projects. Their study was motivated by their observation that all
the "principles" prescribed for MIS are not results of systematic

studies (1969); thus, they doubted the validity of these principles and conducted research to identify "the correlates of MIS project success."

As indicators of successful projects they chose completion on time, at budgeted cost, to user satisfaction, and with favorable effect on the computer operations function. The study included two steps. The first was asking MIS experts attending the Founding Conference of the Society for Management Information System to evaluate the importance of 34 predetermined factors for MIS project success. The result, based on 140 completed questionnaires, was a rank order (according to averaged score) of the relative importance of the factors, reproduced in Table 5.1.

Sixteen factors were chosen for study in depth in the field, based on the factors' places in the rank order, on factor analysis, and on a pilot study. Ten firms in diverse industries and of different sizes were studied, all in the Minneapolis-St. Paul area. Two MIS projects were considered in each firm. The data were collected by interview from the MIS director, implementors (including the project supervisor), and users.

On the basis of an analysis of the data on the 20 projects, the authors reported the factors whose positive or negative associations with one or more success criteria were statistically significant (see Table 5.2).

Of the ten factors found to be significantly related to success criteria, five are items that have been identified above as elements of an MIS strategy—namely, organizational level of executive, documentation standards, programming language, organization of implementors, and size of systems staff.

Although from the name of the article, and its introduction, one might think that "most of these principles have no basis" and are but myths, Powers and Dickson's work did strengthen some of these observed and empirical principles. Since the ten organizations were arbitrarily chosen and do not represent any population, and since the survey instrument is not reported in the paper, it is difficult to assess the degree to which the findings can be generalized. However, it is clear that factors whose associations with MIS project success were found in this study to be not statistically significant should not yet be discarded.

The implementation process is a complex one comprising a considerable number of distinct phases. In this process, management control phases are interwoven with technical execution phases. Although these two aspects are generally discussed separately, the authors have decided to exhibit them simultaneously to indicate what they believe are the correct interrelationships. The rationale for this synthesis is that successes and failures of the implementation

## TABLE 5.1

### Ranking of MIS Project Factors by 140 Professionals

| Rank | Factor | Score |
|------|--------|-------|
| 1 | Participation by operating management in design, formal approval of specifications, and continual review of project.[1] | 4.38 |
| 2 | Measurable project objectives from conception of the project.[1] | 4.29 |
| 3 | Use of a project team composed of MIS staff and user personnel.[1] | 4.25 |
| 4 | Coordinating ability of project leader. | 4.21 |
| 5 | Operating management conducts periodic management audit of MIS function (evaluation of effectiveness of users). | 4.00 |
| 6 | Formal training program set up for user organization. | 3.95 |
| 7 | Organizational level of top computer executive.[1] | 3.94 |
| 8 | Systems experience of project personnel.[1] | 3.90 |
| 9 | Formal project selection process used to determine which projects to develop. | 3.88 |
| 10 | Persuasiveness of project leader (superior's evaluation). | 3.84 |
| 11 | Proficiency of project personnel (as judged by superiors). | 3.79 |
| 12 | Documentation standards used and enforced.[1] | 3.74 |
| 13 | Use of a formal and regular reporting structure on project progress.[1] | 3.68 |
| 14 | Low turnover of project personnel.[1] | 3.56 |
| 15 | Planning and accounting for all resources throughout project development. | 3.50 |
| 16 | Source of origination of project (MIS staff or user).[1] | 3.48 |
| 17 | High centralization or organizational MIS activities.[1] | 3.46 |

continued

Table 5.1, continued

| Rank | Factor | Score |
|------|--------|-------|
| 18 | Program maintenance and review responsibility specified for definite period after implementation. | 3.45 |
| 19 | Number of years of experience for organization with computerized information systems. | 3.43 |
| 20 | Length of experience in the organization of project personnel.[1] | 3.32 |
| 21 | Use of a formal time-scheduling technique, such as PERT, for project development. | 3.25 |
| 22 | High availability of computer time for program testing. | 3.04 |
| 23 | High-level programming language used for project.[1] | 3.00 |
| 24 | Use existing data base instead of constructing or greatly modifying one. | 2.99 |
| 25 | Low turnover rate of MIS staff. | 2.91 |
| 26 | Short-term, minor project versus large, complex project. | 2.89 |
| 27 | Combination analyst/programmer for small projects. | 2.86 |
| 28 | High rates of MIS staff drawn from within the organization. | 2.81 |
| 29 | High average income level of MIS staff. | 2.77 |
| 30 | Low degree of overall organizational change. | 2.72 |
| 31 | High formal education level of project personnel.[1] | 2.71 |
| 32 | Separation of analysts and programmers for large projects.[1] | 2.51 |
| 33 | Overall size of organization systems staff.[1] | 2.50 |
| 34 | Ratio of computer hardware investment to total sales or operating budget.[1] | 2.30 |

[1]Selected for empirical research study.

Source: Richard F. Powers and Gary W. Dickson, "MIS Project Management: Myths, Opinions and Reality," © 1973 by the Regents of the University of California. Reprinted from California Management Review, volume xv, number 3, p. 149, Exhibit 1 by permission of the Regents.

TABLE 5.2

Relationship of Factors to Success Criteria

| Opinion Rank[2] | Factor | Success Criterion[1] | | | |
|---|---|---|---|---|---|
| | | Time | Cost | User Satisfaction | Computer Operations |
| 1 | Participation by operating management in design, formal approval of specifications, and continual review of project. | | | + | |
| 7 | Organization level of top computer executive. | - | | | + |
| 12 | Documentation standards used and enforced. | + | | | |
| 14 | Low turnover of project personnel. | | | + | |
| 16 | Source of origination of project (MIS staff or user). | | | + | |
| 20 | Length of experience in the organization of project personnel. | - | | + | |
| 23 | High level programming language used for project. | - | | | |
| 31 | High formal educational level of project personnel. | | | | + |
| 32 | Separation of analysts and programmers for large projects. | + | | - | |
| 33 | Overall size of organization systems staff. | - | - | + | |

[1]The 0.10 level of significance was used for all statistical tests.
[2]See Table 5.1.

Source: Richard F. Powers and Gary W. Dickson, "MIS Project Management: Myths, Opinions and Reality," © 1973 by the Regents of the University of California. Reprinted from California Management Review, volume XV, number 3, p. 152, Exhibit 4 by permission of the Regents.

process are often, or even primarily, attributed to the efficacy of management control (Aron 1969; Garrity 1963; Gehring and Pooch 1977; Kronenberg 1967; Morgan and Soden 1973; Nolan and Knutsen 1974).

In Table 5.3, the execution phases are exhibited in chronological sequence in the left hand column; the right hand column contains the control phases relevant to each execution phase.

> Proposition 5.1: The more complete the sequence of execution-control cycles, the greater the likelihood of MIS project success.*

Corollary: MIS projects are most susceptible to failure in loosely controlled phases.

One conclusion that can be drawn from a cursory glance at Table 5.3 is the disparity between the amount of attention devoted to execution compared to that given to control, especially in the early stages. Thus, Lehman (1979) found that 17 percent of the projects he surveyed had no project control mechanism at all. This, combined with the common assertion that management control is a vital ingredient of project success, may help to explain why so many projects encounter difficulties. The following discussion focuses briefly on each of the stages of project development to clarify and evaluate the state of the art, rather than to describe techniques, which latter would be an undertaking far beyond the scope of this book.

PLANNING

The complexity of the planning process and a lack of understanding of it have been identified as major weaknesses of information system management. Failures at the planning stage have been attributed to a tendency to define projects that are too large for the abilities of development teams, to bad or unreasonable initial estimates (partly as a result of pressures to attain a measurable return

---

*It is possible to formulate a proposition for each one of the execution and control phases mentioned. These would, however, all be of the same form, intimating a relationship between execution of the phase and the success of MIS projects. For the sake of brevity, all these potential propositions have been encapsulated in Proposition 5.1.

TABLE 5.3

Execution and Control Phases of MIS Projects

| Phases | Execution References | Control Phases | Control References |
|--------|---------------------|----------------|--------------------|
| Planning | Fronk 1978; Garrity 1963; Hax 1973; Head 1969; Henry 1977; Knutson and Scotto 1978; Kronenberg 1967; Lehman 1979; Miller 1978; Putnam 1978; Roark 1970; Schwartz 1969; Singer 1969 | Endorsement, review, modification, and update of plans | Gehring and Pooch 1977; Knutson and Scotto 1978; Lehman 1979; Miller 1978 |
| Project module selection and scheduling | Garrity 1963; Henry 1977; Knutson and Scotto 1978; Lehman 1979; Miller 1978; Nolan and Knutsen 1974 | Project risk evaluation | Alter and Ginzberg 1978; Morgan and Soden 1973 |
| Project staffing | Garrity 1963; Lehman 1979; Miller 1978; Nolan and Knutsen 1974; Rolefson 1978 | | |
| Project development | Aron 1969; Brown 1977; Fisher 1969; Fronk 1978; Henry 1977; Kronenberg 1967; Lehman 1979; Montijo 1967; Putnam 1978; Roark 1970; Schwartz 1969; Singer 1969 | Design control— review and approval of design specifications | Aron 1969; Lehman 1979; Powers and Dickson 1973 |
| Programming | Coe 1974; Fisher 1969; Fronk 1978; Lehman 1979; Montijo 1967; Moore 1979; Putnam 1978 | Progress review, abandonment evaluation, and validation | Brown 1977; Garrity 1963; Hammond 1974a; Miller 1978; Morgan and Soden 1973; Putnam 1978 |
| Implementation and installation | Brown 1977; Fisher 1969; Gehring and Pooch 1977; Henry 1977; Kronenberg 1967; Knutson and Scotto 1978 | | |
| Operation | Coe 1974; Heany 1972; Lucas 1973; Roark 1970; Schwartz 1969 | Postimplementation review and computer center control | Aron 1969; Brown 1977; Carlson 1974; Coe 1974; Dearden and Nolan 1973; Henry 1977; Lucas 1973; Morgan and Soden 1973; Rolefson 1978 |
| Support and maintenance | Fisher 1969; Powers and Dickson 1973; Putnam 1978 | | |

Source: Compiled by the authors.

on investment), to frequent changes in requirements, and to limited authority over resources (Emery 1969; Fronk 1978; Kriebel 1973; Lehman 1979; Morgan and Soden 1973).

A number of project-planning techniques and methodologies have been described in the literature (for example, Gehring and Pooch 1977; Henry 1977; Knutson and Scotto 1978; Miller 1978); the extensiveness of use of various techniques has been reported by Lehman (1979). It is symptomatic of the state of the art that none of the recipes for project management contains all of the phases listed in Table 5.3, so only by trial and error can a project manager develop a complete project development plan. Furthermore, there is a marked tendency in many of the articles on project planning to confuse it (the guidelines for executing a particular project) with strategic planning (the rules for project selection). Many suggestions for project planning begin with a feasibility study, which is surely an element of strategic planning and a basis for assigning priorities to projects (for example, Henry 1977; Fronk 1978). This phenomenon is probably the result of many organizations not having strategic plans for project selection, so feasibility studies are undertaken on an ad hoc basis for each project. By the time planning for a specific project is undertaken, its feasibility should already be well established.

Preparation of a project plan may involve considerable effort so substantial costs can be incurred before the plan is available (Hax 1973; Knutson and Scotto 1978). Lehman (1979) found that project managers and their staffs spent 12.5 percent of their time on planning.

There is some dispute over the degree of detail desirable in plans. Some state a need for firm, explicit objectives for system design, whereas others believe that the plan and cost estimate should be flexible and may be better presented as a broad conceptual scheme, rather than trying to state final objectives in too detailed a form (Carlson 1967; Nolan and Knutsen 1974; Miller 1978; Zani 1970). Some insight into the practice in this area is provided by Lehman's (1979) study that found that, generally, larger projects produced more detailed specifications, but the more detailed the specifications, the greater the need for rewrite before system design. This survey of 57 projects revealed an average of six planning documents per project, with more than nine documents required for the largest systems (two small projects produced no planning documents).

Control of planning—the endorsement review, modification, and update of plans—receives only the most cursory references despite planning being consistently recognized as one of the most troublesome areas in project management and its importance being stated often (see Table 5.3).  Research in causes of and cures for difficulties in project planning might help alleviate this problem considerably.


PROJECT MODULE SELECTION AND SCHEDULING

Many of those writing on project management realize that large projects should be divided into manageable modules and that, whether modular or not, schedules should be established to provide milestones for measuring project progress.  Lehman's survey found that modularization is one of the major methods used by managers for maintaining control over projects; 79 percent of the projects he surveyed included a module design phase (Garrity 1963; Henry 1977; Knutson and Scotto 1978; Lehman 1979; Miller 1978).

Risk evaluation is increasingly recommended, but the method-ology is not well developed.  Failure to perform such evaluations may be compounded by an impatience to get to technical details (Kriebel 1973; Morgan and Soden 1973).  In principle, risk may be evaluated at any point in the development of a project, following modularization and scheduling; however, the next phase involves staffing and the long-term allocation of resources.  Thus, at this point, more information is available than at any previous juncture and no significant commitment of resources has yet been made.  It would therefore appear to be the ideal time to assess the risk in-volved while the project can still be aborted with little damage.

A paper by Alter and Ginzberg (1978) relates risk factors in implementation and strategies for coping with the risk factors to organizational change theory.  Alter and Ginzberg's paper is a syn-thesis of their Ph.D. dissertations at MIT in 1975.

Ginzberg viewed MIS implementation as a case of organiza-tional change.  Thus, he adopted the Kolb/Frohman model of or-ganizational change (based on the Lewin/Shein theory), which con-sisted of seven stages:

1.  Scouting—The user and designer assess each other's needs and abilities to see if there is a match, and an appropriate organi-zational starting point for the project is selected;

2.  Entry—The user and designer develop an initial statement of the project's objectives and commitment to the project is devel-oped.  They develop a trusting relationship and a "contract" for conducting the project;

3.  Diagnosis—The user and designer gather data to refine and sharpen the definition of the problem and its solution.  They assess available resources (including commitment) to determine whether continued effort is feasible;

4. Planning—The user and designer define specific operational objectives and examine alternative ways to meet these objectives. The effects of the proposed solutions on all parts of the organization are examined and an action plan is developed that takes these into account;

5. Action—The user and designer implement the "best" alternative, providing the training necessary for effective use of the system in all affected parts of the organization;

6. Evaluation—The user and designer assess the degree to which the goals (specified during the diagnosis and planning stages) were met and decide whether to work further on the system (evolve) or to cease active work (terminate); and

7. Termination—The user and designer insure that "ownership" of and effective control over the new system rest with those who must use and maintain it and that necessary new patterns of behavior have become a stable part of the user's routine.*

Extrapolating from this model, Ginzberg hypothesized that success in implementation is positively correlated with the quality of the implementation process, and developed a questionnaire to measure the relation of success or failure of the implementation effort to the specific stages of the model. Data collected by a survey that included 29 computer-based systems (users and designers) yield the findings exhibited in Table 5.4. The data in Table 5.4 indicate that successful projects tend to conform more with the model's seven stages than do unsuccessful projects.

Alter's exploratory study involved 56 systems on which case studies were developed based on interviews with users and implementors. Rather than testing hypotheses, Alter looked for "implementation risk factors" and strategies dealing with these factors. He identified eight risk factors and 16 strategies, presented in Table 5.5. (Inhibiting strategy aimed at preventing occurrence of a risk factor; compensating strategy to cope with it once it exists.)

A synthesis of both studies indicates that all eight risk factors appeared during the four early stages of project implementation/organizational change—accounting, entry, diagnosis, and planning—thus putting the onus for success on these stages.

---

*Reprinted from "Managing Uncertainty in MIS Implementation" by Steven Alter and Michael Ginzberg, SLOAN MANAGEMENT REVIEW, Vol. 20, No. 1 (Fall 1978), p. 24 by permission of the publisher.

Ginzberg's study empirically strengthens the long-current notion that MIS projects should be considered as specific cases of organizational change; it does not appear, however, to have direct practical implications. On the other hand, although Alter's analysis of the project implementation data lacks theoretical foundation, his identification and classification of risk factors does provide practitioners with contingency guidelines. Alter and Ginzberg recognized the limitations of each of the studies and tried to overcome them by "juxtaposing" both. It is hoped that future joint research, referred to in the paper, will strengthen their contribution.

TABLE 5.4

Average Implementation Process Scores of Successful and Unsuccessful Users at Each Stage of Implementation

| Stage | Median Stage Score[1] | | Probability[2] |
| | Success (n = 25) | Failure (n = 13) | |
|---|---|---|---|
| Scouting | 0.60 | 0.40 | <0.05 |
| Entry | 0.33 | 0.17 | <0.025 |
| Diagnosis | 0.60 | 0.30 | <0.05 |
| Planning | 0.57 | 0.25 | <0.035 |
| Action | 0.18 | 0.0 | <0.0007 |
| Evaluation | 0.50 | 0.25 | <0.085 |
| Termination | 0.67 | 0.08 | <0.00003 |

[1]Scores can range between +1.0 and −1.0. A score of +1.0 indicates that all of the problems presented by that stage appeared to have been favorably resolved; a score of −1.0 indicates that none of the problems of that stage appeared to have been properly resolved.

[2]Mann-Whitney U test (1 tail) for difference between distributions of successes and failures.

TABLE 5.5

Risk-Reducing Strategies

| | Risk Factor | | | | | | | |
| Strategy | Designer Lacking Experience | Nonexistent or Unwilling User | Multiple Users or Designers | Turnover | Lack of Support | Unspecified Purpose or Usage Patterns | Unpredictable Effect | Technical and Cost-Effectiveness Problems |
|---|---|---|---|---|---|---|---|---|
| Use prototypes | C | | | | | C | I | I |
| Use evolutionary approach | C | | | | | C | I | I |
| Use modular approach | C | | | | | C | | I |
| Keep the system simple | C | | | | | | | I |
| Hide complexity | | C* | | | | | | |
| Avoid change | | C** | | | | | | |
| Obtain user participation | | I | C*** | | I | I | I | |
| Obtain user commitment | | I | C | | I | | | |
| Obtain management support | | C | C | C | I | | C | |
| Sell the system | | I* | | | I | | C* | |

92

Provide training
programs      C    C    C

Provide ongoing
assistance      C    C

Insist on
mandatory use      C**

Permit voluntary
use***      C    C    C

Rely on diffusion
and exposure***      C    C    C

Tailor system to
people's capabilities      C    C

C = compensating strategy      I = inhibiting strategy

*Inconsistent with general requirements      *Can backfire if system is oversold.
of participative approach to development.

   **A strategy of last resort, violating the basic tenets of
the participative model.

**May imply inability to develop important,    ***These are not really actively pursued strategies; they
interesting systems.      represent resignation in the face of difficulties.

***Very difficult to practice.

Source: Reprinted from "Managing Uncertainty in MIS Implementation," by Steven Alter and Michael Ginzberg, SLOAN MANAGEMENT REVIEW, Vol. 20, No. 1 (Fall 1978), p. 29 by permission of the publisher. Copyright © 1978 by the Sloan Management Review Association. All rights reserved.

PROJECT STAFFING

A major problem in staffing is knowing the correct number of personnel needed during the project life cycle. It is now generally recognized that there is a limit to the number of people who can effectively be employed on any project at any time; the tendency to attempt to make up for schedule slips by increasing the staff often turns out to be counterproductive. Conversely, many large projects suffer from an inability to acquire personnel at the rate planned. Finally, the reduction of personnel should be carefully planned to avoid employment of personnel who are no longer required on that project (Brooks 1975; Putnam 1978). Staffing MIS projects is covered in detail in Chapter 8, "Implementors of MIS."

Noteworthy at this point is that this is the only major phase of project development for which no control procedures have been recommended in the literature. Apparently, staffing is recognized as the prerogative of the MIS chief or of project managers and no external management controls are instituted. The importance of good choice of managers is therefore paramount; many failures have been attributed to errors in this choice (Morgan and Soden 1973; Rolefson 1978).


PROJECT DEVELOPMENT

There seems to have been a considerable increase in sophistication in the approach to the project development phase of system development over the last decade. In the late 1960s, the phase between module selection and coding was included under one heading: system analysis or system design. As the level of understanding of, or experience with, this process increased, the number of subphases mentioned also increased. The most detailed approaches list three elements: functional specification, preliminary or system design, and detailed design. This development is exhibited in Table 5.6, in which the descriptions of the subphases are in the words of the authors cited.

There are many early references in the literature to systems with unacceptable performance characteristics attributed to failures in design resulting from a lack of understanding of the importance of the design process. These failures, coupled with increasing experience, seem to have spurred increasing refinement of design procedures to the current level. It is conceivable that additional experience and the demands of ever more complex systems will add more elements in the future (Alexander 1969; Carlson 1967; Lucas 1973; Morgan and Soden 1973).

TABLE 5.6

Elements of System Design

| Author | Element 1 | Element 2 | Element 3 |
|---|---|---|---|
| One element | | | |
| Kronenberg (1967) | System design | | |
| Aron (1969) | System analysis | | |
| Fisher (1969) | System design | | |
| Fronk (1978) | Detailed design | | |
| | | | |
| Two elements | | | |
| Henry (1977) | System analysis | System design | |
| Putnam (1978) | Functional specification | Design | |
| Gehring and Pooch (1977) | Requirement definition | Analysis/design | |
| | | | |
| Three elements | | | |
| Brown (1977) | Functional specification | System specification | Detail design |
| Lehman (1977) | Requirement specification | Preliminary design | Detailed design |

Source: Compiled by the authors.

DESIGN CONTROL

Given the importance of good design to the success of systems, it is not surprising that some authors stress the importance of this phase; what is surprising is how few do so. Some authors express the opinion that design review is a continuing process because changes need to be made in the course of constructing a system (Aron 1969; Rolefson 1978). Powers and Dickson (1973) found that the participation of operating management in design, formal approval of specifications, and continued review of projects was the factor ranked highest in its effect on success and contributed greatly to user satisfaction (see Tables 5.1 and 5.2).

Lehman's (1979) survey of project management practices found that most projects used formal reviews at some stages of project design; in fact, of 57 projects, he found only 2 with no formal reviews held. The number of design reviews was usually between three and five, the number of reviews tending to increase with the cost of the project. The percentage of projects formally reviewed at various stages were as follows: systems requirement review, 58 percent; systems design review, 68 percent; preliminary design review, 83 percent; and critical design review, 81 percent.

PROGRAMMING

There is an interesting and perhaps costly dichotomy in the literature between MIS project management and the management of programming projects, which are an integral part of MIS project development. Few of the articles that deal with MIS project management even refer to the programming phase (see Table 5.3) and seem to regard the programs as deus ex machina. As software development is rapidly becoming an ever more dominant cost factor in system development, it is strange to find it ignored.

The few papers on software project management that do appear tend to be published in the technical journals devoted to programming technology. A brief list of some recent papers of this type includes Cave and Salisbury (1978), Chrysler (1978), Cooper (1978), Daly (1977), Jones (1978), and Putnam (1978). Occasional reviews of programming management techniques appear in the literature for information system managers; for example, Gehring and Pooch (1977) and Oliver (1978). This dichotomy may help to explain the finding by Lehman (1979) that the application of new software development techniques seems to have peaked; projects in the survey starting in 1977 showed no more use of modern programming practices than did those starting in 1968.

The dangers of relegating software management to technical experts is suggested in recent research by Moore (1979), one of the few empirical studies in the field of MIS project management. He posited that developing MIS-related software is unique and different from other software development projects. He presented a framework for software development that differentiated between what he defined as management support systems (MSS) and computer support systems (CSS) (the primary purpose of a CSS is to facilitate the execution of programs). This framework is presented in Table 5.7.

TABLE 5.7

Framework for Software Development

| Software Attribute | MSS | CSS |
|---|---|---|
| Technological sophistication | Low | High |
| Interactions with end users | Many | Few |
| System specifications known in advance | Rarely | Usually |
| Project management | Decentralized | Centralized |
| Language level utilized | High | Low |
| Software productivity | High | Low |
| Development cost | Low | High |
| Development time | Short | Long |
| Number of end users | Few | Many |
| Importance of operational efficiency | Low | High |
| Implementation problems | Usually | Rarely |

Source: Reprinted by special permission from the MIS Quarterly, from "A Framework for MIS Software Development Projects," by J. Moore, in Volume 3, Number 1, published in 1979. Copyright 1979 by the Society for Management Information Systems and the Management Information Systems Research Center.

Moore claimed that if such differences really exist, then pre-scriptions related to successful project management based on gen-eralizations about performance norms and development practices in software development projects are invalid and may mislead. Seven hypotheses, derived from the above framework, were formu-lated to test its validity.

The empirical data in Moore's study were collected by a ques-tionnaire completed by managers of departments responsible for software development. The response rate was a relatively small 32 percent out of a random sample of 76 organizations in computer programming and other software services (SIC 7372 in Standard and Poor's [1973] and Who's Who in Computer and Data Processing [1972]). The organizations that responded included software houses, six; computer vendors, four; management consulting firms, three; governmental agencies, two; research laboratories, two; manufac-turers, two; energy companies, two; transportation companies, two; and one university computer center.

The data were grouped into MSS and CSS categories. Means of answers (for open questions) and percentages (for closed ques-tions) were calculated for each group. The analysis focused on de-partmental characteristics, successful projects, and unsuccessful projects. Basically, all differences between the two categories of software development projects were consistent with the framework; for example, Table 5.8, which deals with successful projects (for other statistics and significance levels refer to Moore's paper).

Based on these findings, Moore concluded that a theory of development projects for MIS-related software should differ from a theory dealing with other software. Some of his inferences are: MIS software project failures are attributable to managerial, rather than technical, problems; MIS overhead costs other than program-ming costs are substantial; and frequent managerial reporting and a department managed by a generalist manager, rather than a pro-grammer, are associated with success.

Even with the bias possibly caused by the low response rate and some subjectivity in interpretation of responses, Moore's study clearly indicates the danger in leaving the programming aspects of MIS project management to technical experts.


IMPLEMENTATION AND INSTALLATION

The implementation and installation phase of project develop-ment has been defined as "continued acceptance of the outputs of the system by the user" (Fisher 1969 [emphasis in the original]). In-cluded in this phase are system test and acceptance, user training,

## TABLE 5.8

### Statistics for Successfully Implemented Projects

| Implementation Attribute | MSS (n = 12) | CSS (n = 8) | R |
|---|---|---|---|
| Mean number of programmer man-months committed | 62.8 | 12.5 | 0.05 |
| Mean number of years developmental experience per programmer | 5.27 | 6.67 | 0.10 |
| Mean duration of project in months | 14.9 | 29.1 | 0.01 |
| Mean due-date slippage in months | 1.83 | 5.38 | 0.10 |
| Language used | | | |
| Percent using high level | 92 | 55 | 0.02 |
| Percent using assembler | 8 | 45 | 0.02 |
| Manager drawn from development group (percent) | | | |
| Yes | 61 | 90 | 0.07 |
| No | 39 | 10 | |
| Managerial progress reports submitted at least monthly (percent) | | | |
| Yes | 85 | 40 | 0.02 |
| No | 15 | 60 | |

Source: Reprinted by special permission from the MIS Quarterly, from "A Framework for MIS Software Development Projects," by J. Moore, in Volume 3, Number 1, published in 1979. Copyright 1979 by the Society for Management Information Systems and the Management Information Systems Research Center.

document and manual preparation, and data file conversion. There are no empirical data on the relationship of this phase to system success, but this relationship is implicit in the definition given above.

PROGRESS REVIEW

One of the most frustrating aspects of software project management, and one that causes great difficulties, is the inability of project managers to accurately determine what portion of a project has been completed and how much remains to be done. Project management systems have been advocated to alleviate the wastefulness experienced by organizations with uncontrolled computer projects. Surveys and case histories have attributed success in project management to rigid and complete project control systems that pinpoint potential problems for immediate management attention. The most common technique is that of milestones, or phasing projects between a series of subgoals with periodic progress reports. This forces management to compare progress to plans and to decide how to deal with deviations. This kind of step-by-step control has been found necessary even in organizations in which the computer systems group is organized as a profit center (Aron 1969; Dearden and Nolan 1973; Garrity 1963; Lehman 1979; Montijo 1967). The relative use of various project planning systems as reported by Lehman is exhibited in Table 5.9; there are no reports on relative effectiveness of the various systems.

TABLE 5.9

Use of Project Control Systems

| System | Percent Use |
| --- | --- |
| Milestone tracking | 72 |
| Work breakdown structure code | 62 |
| Workloading charts | 37 |
| Gantt charts | 33 |
| Modified PERT | 28 |
| PERT | 9 |
| Other | 9 |
| No systems used | 17 |

Source: John H. Lehman, "How Software Projects Are Really Managed," Datamation, 25 (January, 1979): 119-129.
Reprinted With Permission of DATAMATION®magazine, ©
Copyright by TECHNICAL PUBLISHING COMPANY, A DUN & BRADSTREET COMPANY, 1979 - all rights reserved.

Even with good project control techniques, there is frequently considerable delay in cutting back unsuccessful projects because of a lack of project-abandonment evaluation techniques. The ability to abandon projects that run into insurmountable difficulties is of importance because of the large sums that can be wasted if such projects are permitted to drag on. This is what is known as the 90 percent complete syndrome—the phenomenon of projects continuously reported 90 percent complete for two to three times their scheduled duration (Emery 1973; Head 1967, 1970; Kriebel 1973; Morgan and Soden 1973; Singer 1969).

## OPERATION AND MAINTENANCE

Following completion of a project and implementation of the system, a phase of routine operation and maintenance is entered. Once this stage has been reached, the project may be considered to be complete. Success of the system may still depend, however, on the operations policy and the degree to which it meets user needs and permits the system to achieve its potential (Lucas 1973).

## POSTIMPLEMENTATION REVIEW AND COMPUTER CENTER CONTROL

With a system in place, two types of postimplementation review are called for: review of the project itself to ascertain how the organization may better manage such projects in the future, and a review of the system to ascertain the extent to which it is meeting its goals (Aron 1969; Brown 1978; Rolefson 1978).

A postimplementation review of projects is needed because many projects exceed their budgets and schedules. Thus, Lehman's (1979) survey found that 54 percent of the projects involved were on schedule and 46 percent were delayed for an average of 7 months, or a mean delay of 33 percent, with a range of delay from 1 to 24 months. Cost performance was even less impressive, with 59 percent of the projects reporting cost overruns. The major cause of schedule slips and cost overruns were reported to be, in order of importance: bad initial estimates, changes in requirements, and limited authority over resources.

Postimplementation system reviews are intended to indicate to what extent new systems meet their original goals and, perhaps more important, to indicate changes needed. Thus, system review is not a single occurrence but should be repeated periodically to determine when a system needs to be upgraded or replaced and to provide the data necessary for planning and designing the change. System reviews are the basis for projects to replace old systems, initiating a new cycle of project implementation. Techniques for the evaluation of working systems include event logging, attitude surveys, system measurement, system analysis, and cost-benefit analysis (Aron 1969; Carlson 1974; Financial Executive 1974; Rolefson 1978).

A final area requiring constant monitoring after implementation is the technical efficiency of the computer center in which the system is installed. The operations policy may have an effect on the success of a system because it may either encourage or deter use and because operating efficiency determines the cost side of the cost-benefit equation. Although the design of evaluation measures for the operations department has advanced farther than in other areas, there is still a dearth of control tools on operations at the level of computer center efficiency (Coe 1974; Lucas 1973; Morgan and Soden 1973).

PROCEDURAL ASPECTS OF MIS: CONCLUSION

The last three chapters summarize the vast number of issues pertaining to the procedural aspects of MIS implementation. Because the hardware and software technologies associated with MIS are still changing rapidly and the size and complexity of systems continue to increase, it is not likely that there will be in the near future the kind of stability that might permit consolidation of the experience accumulated so far. There is a need to understand the relationships between the procedural and behavioral aspects of MIS as well as a need for more powerful means of controlling MIS projects. Both of these needs provide broad areas for research.

# 6

## THE STRUCTURE OF MIS

It next will be right
  To describe each particular batch:
Distinguishing those that have feathers, and bite,
  From those that have whiskers, and scratch.
          Lewis Carroll, <u>The Hunting of the Snark</u>

      The structure of an MIS is determined by the technical data processing characteristics of the implementation. These may be summarized as data characteristics, processing capabilities, data base characteristics, user interface characteristics, and degree of integration.

      There are close relationships between several of the aspects of MIS structure. Data characteristics are dependent on the processing capabilities of a system—the ability of a system to process data must have some reflection in the nature of the data it processes. Similarly, the character of a data base is dependent on the characteristics of the data it contains and on the capabilities of the processing system that manipulates it. The nature of the user interface, too, is dependent on the existence and characteristics of the data base and on the processing capabilities of the system. As with any other complex system, division into subsystems is essential if discussion is to be meaningful. The reader should always bear in mind that although discussion of any variable focuses on the relevant subsystem, variable characteristics are determined by the framework of the whole system.

## DATA CHARACTERISTICS

There is a considerable amount of research devoted jointly to data characteristics and to processing capabilities. Presentation of most of this research is deferred until after a discussion of both variables.

Proposition 6.1: Appropriate data characteristics enhance the likelihood of MIS success.

A number of attributes that characterize data have been suggested in the literature. The attributes most commonly mentioned are content or relevance, accuracy, recency or information delay, and frequency.

Many problems have been identified concerning the data content of MIS. These problems range from content being too restricted because of exclusion of nonquantitative, nonverbal, and external information to the collection of large amounts of data irrelevant to the decisions that need to be made. Added to the tendency to collect too much of the wrong kinds of data and not enough of the right kind is the general difficulty in defining what kinds of data are really necessary, because of the dependence of data requirements on personal decision styles. This last problem is discussed at greater length in Chapter 9 under the heading "User Requirements" (Adcock et al. 1968; Colton 1972-73; Miller 1964; Mintzberg 1975b; Mock 1973).

Surprisingly, there seems to have been no empirical research in the effect of data accuracy on the success of MIS; this may be because it is assumed that a high level of accuracy is essential. There have been suggestions, however, that accuracy is less important than timeliness in MIS. Because there is a trade-off between these characteristics, and because accuracy is costly, it would be very helpful to understand to what extent systems are sensitive or insensitive to various levels of accuracy (Adcock et al. 1968; Mintzberg 1975b; Mock 1973; Montijo 1967).

It is generally agreed that data should be kept current, implying that they should be continuously updated to reflect recent occurrences. It has already been pointed out that some consider freshness of information to be more important than accuracy. In an experiment with information structures, Mock (1973) found that the value of more timely data was greater than originally hypothesized. Attaining high levels of accuracy is time consuming, leading to the already mentioned need for trade-off between accuracy and recency. Problems have been noted when processing schedules are not met and data become obsolete by the time they are made available. This may be the result of problems in data acquisition, exaggerated accuracy requirements, or computer systems that are deficient in capacity or reliability (Adcock et al. 1968; Colton 1972-73; Lucas 1973; Mintzberg 1972, 1975b; Mock 1973; Montijo 1967; Sihler 1971; Sprague and Watson 1975). Closely related to this characteristic is feedback time—the time elapsing between implementation of a decision and receipt of a report on the effect the decision has on the environment (Adcock et al. 1968).

The general opinion seems to be that information should be supplied only when action is possible and necessary; or, put differently, that any form of analysis or data should be provided when requested, rather than according to some predetermined schedule. This is contrary to much current practice, which provides reports in constant cycles whether requested or not. There are many cases of successful systems with such predetermined report schedules so the significance of this factor is not clear (Adcock et al. 1968; Kronenberg 1967; Miller 1964).

The information characteristics of a particular system have been studied by Neumann and Segev (1979). A questionnaire was administered to branch managers of a large Israeli bank. The branch managers were asked to evaluate on a five-point scale four data characteristics of the system. The characteristics examined were accuracy, content, frequency, and recency for each of the seven major areas of the bank's activities and for the bank as a whole.

Eighty-one of 148 branch managers completed questionnaires. These questionnaires were analyzed to test two hypotheses:

Users of information have a holistic perception of the information made available to them by an information system; that is, they do not differentiate accurately between the various characteristics of the system.

Content is a dominant information characteristic and the assessment of this characteristic affects other valuations; that is, there is a spillover effect by which evaluation of content causes evaluations of other characteristics to be similar.

Guttman's correlation coefficients of weak monotonicity ( $\mu_2$) among the evaluations of the information characteristics were computed for each area of the bank's activities such as demand deposits, time deposits, and loans. Although all correlations were positive and relatively high, no holistic perception was found; there was clear variability in the correlation structures, depending on the area of bank activity.

When means of correlations for each line of the matrix related to a specific area of activity in the bank were rank ordered, there was a clear pattern in all eight matrices—the mean of the correlations of content evaluation with other characteristics was the highest (for an example, see Table 6.1). Thus, content is a dominant characteristic, with a spillover effect on other characteristics.

This study was done in the context of a report-oriented system, rather than a query-oriented OLRT environment; thus, the findings cannot be applied to OLRT systems where content may not be the dominant characteristic.

PROCESSING CAPABILITIES

Proposition 6.2: The more highly developed and the more flexible the processing capabilities of an MIS, the greater the likelihood of success.

Processing capabilities comprise the data manipulation, data reduction, and analytical powers of an MIS. Systems with limited processing capabilities tend to produce massive amounts of output that are largely unused. Disuse in these cases has been attributed to managers' cognitive limitations, which, in situations of information overload, lead to less and less information being used as more and more is provided (Adcock et al. 1968; Carlson 1967; Lucas 1973; Mintzberg 1975a).

Much of the considerable empirical research on data characteristics and processing capabilities has originated at the University of Minnesota and has, therefore, been named the Minnesota Experiments (Dickson, Senn, and Chervany 1977). It may be useful, before proceeding further, to summarize and synthesize the Minnesota Experiments and to examine their relationships with other research in this area. Four of these experiments are first described in brief and then an attempt is made to identify some general results. The experiments are described in chronological order of publication, presumably the order in which they were performed.

Chervany and Dickson (1974)

This study proceeded from the suggestion that "information overload," defined as an overabundance of unfiltered or uncondensed data, is a common problem in information system use. Chervany and Dickson hypothesized that the form in which information is presented, in terms of degree of aggregation, has an effect on the

TABLE 6.1

Correlations among the Evaluations of Information Characteristics:
Data Relating to Demand Deposits

| Information Characteristic | Accuracy | Content | Frequency | Recency | Mean $\mu_2$ of Line | Rank Order of Mean $\mu_2$ |
|---|---|---|---|---|---|---|
| Accuracy | — | 0.801 | 0.689 | 0.587 | 0.692 | 2 |
| Content | 0.801 | — | 0.729 | 0.583 | 0.704 | 1 |
| Frequency | 0.689 | 0.729 | — | 0.461 | 0.626 | 3 |
| Recency | 0.587 | 0.583 | 0.461 | — | 0.543 | 4 |

Source: Seev Neumann and Eli Segev, "User Evaluation of Information Characteristics," Management Informatics 2 (December 1979): 271–78.

average quality of management decisions, on the average time taken to make them, and on subjects' average confidence in them.

Twenty-two graduate students of business administration served as subjects in the experiment. They were randomly assigned to two matched groups on the basis of their scores in the Admission Test for Graduate Study in Business. After a familiarization session, all the subjects used a computerized operations management simulator and made a series of ten weekly decisions concerning production, inventory, and work force levels, the objective being to operate a plant at minimum cost. Steps were taken to control extraneous variables such as peer pressure, end playing, and time pressure. After each decision, the time taken to make it was recorded and the subject's confidence in the decision was rated by the subject on a seven-point scale.

Following receipt of beginning conditions and parameters, all subjects were provided with reports on costs, production, inventory, and labor. One of the two groups received Raw Data (RD) reports in typical managerial report form, with 1,040 data items. The other group received Statistically Summarized Data (SSD) reports containing 449 data items that presented the same information as the RD reports summarized by arithmetic mean, coefficient of variation, maximum value, and range.

Statistical analysis was performed on observations for weeks three through ten, t-tests being applied to paired differences for the treatment averages and F-tests to the ratios of treatment variances. It was found that SSD subjects had lower average total costs but took longer to make each decision and also had lower confidence than the RD subjects. Variability in average confidence was much higher for SSD subjects. There was more variance among RD subjects in total costs. Thus, the analysis supports the contention that the use of descriptive statistics can "improve performance and make it more predictable," but there are potentially undesirable consequences.

Chervany and Dickson found evidence to support the hypothesis that RD subjects had more difficulty either identifying a key problem (stockouts) or solving it once identified, perhaps because they did not, or could not, transform the data into SSD form. The RD subjects found the results on decision time and confidence "troublesome," with its implication that the SSD subjects did not realize that they had a grasp of the problem; thus, they doubt whether a user would prefer SSD reports over RD reports. This experiment and its findings are restricted to the specific decision environment—highly systematic, structured, and repetitious decisions. The authors would add that the results are probably also specific to the particular group of subjects; namely, graduate students with recent exposure to statistical techniques.

Senn and Dickson (1974)

The vehicle for Senn and Dickson's experiment relating system characteristics to the effectiveness of decisions was a Procurement Decision Simulator (PRODECS). This, they write, "provides an environment which enables examination of several information system structures in an industrial purchasing setting" (Senn and Dickson 1974). Each of the 33 subjects selected at random from a chapter of the National Association of Purchasing Management was assigned to one of three kinds of treatments of information system structure. Assignments were controlled according to the size of the organization in which they were employed. The three treatments were detailed information contained in hard-copy reports, summary statistics in hard-copy reports, and summary statistics presented by CRT.

The three experimental factors, or independent variables, were organizational size (small or large), mode of presentation (hard-copy or CRT), and form of information or degree of aggregation (detailed or summarized). To test the hypotheses, four indicators of the effectiveness of decisions were measured as dependent variables; namely, the amount of information requested by subjects, costs incurred in implementing the purchasing decision, length of time to make a decision, and subjects' confidence in their decisions.

The following list summarizes nine hypotheses stated by Senn and Dickson at various points in their paper:*

1. Decision makers from large organizations will require more information and more detail than decision makers from small organizations, will incur lower total purchasing costs, and will require more time to formulate decisions.

2. Purchasing agents using hard-copy presentation media will request more information than will agents using the CRT medium; will develop more effective decisions, whatever the report form; will require more time to formulate decisions; and will be more confident in their decisions.

3. Decision makers using detailed information will be more confident in their decisions than will decision makers using summarized information and will take less time to formulate decisions.

---

*Adopted by permission from Senn, James and Dickson, Gary W. "Information System Structure and Purchasing Decision Effectiveness." Journal of Purchasing 10 (August 1974): 52-64.

Results from 28 subjects for whom complete information was available strengthen only a few of these hypotheses, as exhibited in Table 6.2.

TABLE 6.2

Summary of Experimental Findings: Response Measures

| Experimental Factor | Report Use | Cost Performance | Decision Time | Confidence |
|---|---|---|---|---|
| Organization size | - | - | - | - |
| Presentation medium | + | - | + | - |
| Information form | - | - | + | - |

+ signifies that the factor in question contributed to variation of the level of the response measure.

- signifies that there was not a significant relation between the factor level and the response measure.

Source: James A. Senn and Gary W. Dickson, "Information System Structure and Purchasing Decision Effectiveness," Journal of Purchasing 10 (August 1974): 62. Reprinted by permission.

Schroeder and Benbasat (1975)

Schroeder and Benbasat focused on the way the characteristics desired of information to be used in decision making are affected by uncertainty in the decision environment. As did all the Minnesota Experiments, this study employed a business game as its environment—in this case, an inventory simulator. Fifty-one undergraduate students participated as subjects, their task being to minimize total inventory management costs. Decisions were required of participants on order point and quantity, the next decision point, and a backorder policy for a simulated period of 150 days.

The independent variable controlled by the experimenters, the degree of uncertainty in the decision environment, was operationalized in three treatments differentiated by the magnitude of the standard deviation of the demand distribution. The dependent variables were decision confidence, inventory operating costs, the amount and degree of aggregation of information selected, and the frequency of information requests. The hypothesis related to these dependent variables.

The results of this experiment were summarized by the authors as follows:

1. The frequency of decision making (and information buying) was not significantly different for the three treatments;
2. Total report usage increased significantly when going from the low to the middle variance group, then decreased significantly when going from the middle to the high variance group;
3. Intra-group variance in report requests increased significantly as the variability of the external environment increased;
4. There were significant differences in preferences for the report types as follows:
   a. Low variance group: preferred summary-short history
   b. Middle variance group: preferred detail-long history
   c. High variance group: preferred detail-short history;
5. There was a very weak relationship between the amount of information requested and effectiveness, frequency of review and effectiveness, and the amount of information requested and confidence.*

Findings 1 and 4 would seem to indicate that, subjectively at least, information content is more important than frequency, although there may be a natural decision rhythm to any problem so large deviations in frequency from this rhythm might have adverse effects. It may have been possible to learn more from this experiment if report frequency had been controlled for some of the subjects. Also worthy of note is the generally weak relationship between information and performance, and one wonders whether this might not be an artifact of the decision problem or of the subject population, the latter deficiency having been noted by the researchers.

---

*Reprinted by permission from Schroeder, Roger G. and Benbasat, Izak. "An Experimental Evaluation of the Relationship of Uncertainty in the Environment to Information Used by Decision Makers." Decision Sciences 6 (July 1975): 556-567.

Benbasat and Schroeder (1977)

A second experiment by Benbasat and Schroeder dealt with the primary effects of certain variables and their interactions. The independent variables were chosen to include both human and information system attributes as follows:

Form of report presentation (tabular versus graphic data);
Decision-making aids (available versus unavailable);
Exception reporting (available versus unavailable, for exceptions greater than 10 percent);
Number of reports available ("overload" versus "necessary");
Decision-making style (high analytic versus low analytic, based on a 17-item multiple choice test); and
Knowledge of functional area (high versus low, based on a 14-item multiple choice test).

The dependent variables observed were cost performance, time performance, and number of reports requested.

The subjects in this experiment were 32 students in an operations research course at the University of Minnesota. The vehicle was a computer simulation of a firm that bought a raw material and manufactured a product that it sold to retailers. There were ten decision points, the objective being to minimize total cost to the firm. A monetary incentive was provided.

Subjects were provided with information systems comprising different combinations of the independent variables. A one-half fractional factorial experimental design was employed, with each factor at two levels. Analysis of variance was performed on the data collected. Benbasat and Schroeder also analyzed interaction effects, but because the experimental design inherently assumes no interrelationships the authors of this book refer to the main effects only. The significant findings are exhibited in Table 6.3. Benbasat and Schroeder concluded from these findings that some type of processing capability (graphic presentation and/or decision aids) should be provided for this kind of decision making and that MIS designers should consider the users' functional knowledge and analytical ability in planning a system.

Synthesis

Since the Minnesota Experiments were all performed in the same academic environment, with a common approach to the description and design of MIS, and all employed computer simulations

TABLE 6.3

Design Variables: The Main Effects

| Independent Variable | Dependent Variable | Level of Significance | Results |
|---|---|---|---|
| Decision aids | Cost performance | 0.033 | Subjects with decision aids had lower cost than subjects with no decision aids. |
| Form of presentation | Cost performance | 0.148 | Subjects with graphic reports had a lower cost than did subjects with listed tabular reports. |
| Decision aids | Time performance | 0.018 | Subjects with decision aids took longer to make decisions than did subjects with no decision aids. |
| Form of presentation | Number of reports requested | 0.076 | Subjects with graphic reports requested fewer reports than did subjects with listed tabular reports. |
| Functional area knowledge | Number of reports requested | 0.070 | Subjects with a high functional area knowledge requested fewer reports than did subjects with a low functional area knowledge. |
| Number of reports available | Number of reports requested | 0.007 | Subjects with the overload set of reports requested more reports than did the subjects with the necessary set of reports. |

Source: Reprinted by special permission from the MIS Quarterly, from "An Experimental Investigation of Some MIS Design Variables," by I. Benbasat and R. Schroeder, in Volume 1, Number 1, published in 1977. Copyright 1977 by The Society for Management Information Systems and the Management Information Systems Research Center.

as the experimental vehicle, it is of interest to compare the results and to attempt to produce a synthesis. The findings of the four studies that relate system characteristics to performance measures are exhibited in Table 6.4.

The only finding consistent throughout is that decision time is significantly dependent on system characteristics. There is also near consensus on a relationship between characteristics of a system and the degree to which it is used. No clear pattern emerges regarding a relationship between effectiveness, or decision quality, and system characteristics. The authors find it hard to believe that the effectiveness of a system is determined independently of its characteristics, so the conclusion must be that this finding is an unidentified artifact of the experiments. The situation of the remaining dependent variable, decision confidence, is also interesting; the one other experiment that measured this variable did not replicate the findings of Chervany and Dickson. The number of experiments is too small to allow any conclusions to be drawn concerning the decision confidence and decision-quality variables and additional research is clearly in order.

The inconsistency of the findings may be partly because there was no uniformity in defining the independent variables. Consider, for example, the degree of aggregation. First, each of these experiments relates to aggregation as a dichotomous variable with values high and low; however, there is a continuum of varying degrees of aggregation and there is no reason to assume that the degrees of aggregation defined as high and low were identical in all the experiments. Second, Mintzberg (1975a) has hypothesized that there are limits to the usefulness of aggregation; he stated that formal systems tend to aggregate data to the point where the information produced is too general for managers. Perhaps some of the experiments exceeded the optimum level of aggregation, if such indeed exists. Third, whereas Chervany and Dickson found a strong relationship between aggregation and performance but Senn and Dickson did not, an earlier study by Mock (1973) found the one remaining possibility: that subjects who received more detailed feedback information performed better than did those with summary information. A possible explanation lies in Aron's (1969) contention that most users have grown up in an environment with limited data processing power and so have learned to cope with detailed reports; this renders suspect those of the Minnesota Experiments in which the subjects were not practicing managers and had not undergone the learning process suggested by Aron. It is by no means clear that the behavior of these subjects—nearly all students—is similar to that of managers in organizations. Age, experience, environment, and recency of exposure to the theory of decision making and to decision-making tools may all bias the outcomes.

TABLE 6.4

The Minnesota Experiments: Relationships between System
Characteristics and Measures of Performance

| Independent Variables: System Characteristics | Study | Dependent Variables: Performance Measures | | | |
|---|---|---|---|---|---|
| | | Use of System | Decision Confidence | Decision Time | Decision Quality |
| Degree of aggregation | Chervany and Dickson | - | + | + | + |
| | Senn and Dickson | | - | + | - |
| Method of presentation | Senn and Dickson | + | - | + | - |
| | Benbasat and Schroeder | + | | | + |
| Frequency | Schroeder and Benbasat | | | | - |
| Decision aids | Benbasat and Schroeder | | | + | + |
| Report availability | Benbasat and Schroeder | + | | | |

+ signifies strong relationship.
- signifies weak or nonexistent relationship.
Source: Compiled by the authors.

In concluding this discussion of the Minnesota Experiments, great credit is due to them for the attempt to produce a number of empirical studies with a fairly consistent approach that permits comparison of the results. Some consistent relationships do seem to begin to emerge, but in other areas there is no clear direction to the results. In any case, the information and experience accumulated in these experiments is an excellent foundation for further research.

DATA BASE CHARACTERISTICS

A data base may be defined as a collection of logical data and a data management system applied to the data collection (Severance n.d.):

> [the] data base system is a mechanism which stores physical representations of one or more logical sets of data. It
> 1. maintains the integrity of the representation as the logical data sets change over time, and
> 2. retrieves extracts from the data base when requested by users.

Three aspects of data bases are discussed here: their necessity, capabilities, and content.

> Proposition 6.3: The existence of a data base is critical to the success of MIS.

It is generally agreed that the usefulness of an MIS depends critically on the quality and accessibility of the data base with which it is associated. It has been stated that the real obstacle to developing MIS in most firms is the structure of the data files and the means of accessing them, coupled with a failure to recognize the importance and complexity of data management. This point of view is supported by a number of case reports that have documented the importance of data bases in particular instances. The opinion has even been expressed that the whole problem of MIS will in time be reduced to a problem of data bases (Carlson 1967; Emery 1969, 1973; Hanold 1972; Head 1970; Kriebel 1972; Montijo 1967; Shults and Bruun 1974). Data bases must be considered an indispensible component of MIS for a number of reasons. Among these reasons are data integrity, responsiveness, data independence, and decision support.

When data for each application are on separate files, redundancy, lack of standardization, and updating problems results. A data base assists in data integrity: keeping data current, minimizing redundancy, and reducing lack of data element standardization as a reason for bad or misunderstood reports (Carlson 1967; Lucas 1973; Nolan 1973c; Roark 1970; Sprague and Watson 1975).

As a means of structuring data, a data base maximizes accessibility of data and facilitates response to ad hoc management requests with reasonable dispatch and efficiency. This use of data bases to produce specific information on request is seen as reducing the tendency to prepare, whether necessary or not, complete sets of structured reports periodically (Lieberman and Whinston 1975; Mintzberg 1975a; Nolan 1973c; Roark 1970; Sprague and Watson 1975).

The concentration of data in a corporate data base permits the separation of data from specific applications and the sharing of data by different programs. Data independence, therefore, is a partial solution to the problem of decision models that fall into disuse because they require special collection of new data for each run; with the data generally available in a data base, use is encouraged (Nolan 1973c; Sprague and Watson 1975).

Data bases are seen as supporting the development of decision models by providing historical data necessary for recognizing relationships between variables and for deriving system parameters (Sprague and Watson 1975).

Proposition 6.4: Appropriate data base capabilities are essential to the success of an MIS.

The capabilities required of a data base management system are:

file design and creation;
file maintenance and update;
report generation;
information retrieval; and
on-line inquiry.

These capabilities are embodied in various hardware and software elements. Data acquisition and inquiry require a physical communications network in addition to the computer and storage device hardware. Software elements include data base organization methods, languages for information retrieval, and software for accessing and manipulating the data base. It has been suggested that purchasing data management software is quicker and cheaper than local development; this is also the universal practice (Aron 1969; Head 1967; King 1973; Nolan 1973c; Shults and Bruun 1974; Sprague and Watson 1975).

Proposition 6.5: The likelihood of success of an MIS is enhanced by correct decisions on data to be included and excluded from the data base.

The problem of data base content arises from the difficulty in determining users' information requirements, discussed at length in Chapter 9. Nolan (1973c) suggests that all of a company's data must be structured in a flexible data base that should not be so large that it collapses under its own weight. Theoretically, the solution is to store all data elements that may be required; this solution is unrealistic because of the excessive storage capacity and retrieval times imposed.

One consideration in reducing the size of a data base is caution about amassing data whose useful life is shorter than the collection period. Others suggest that only frequently used data elements should be stored; the rest will be external to the computer system, which may, however, be designed to expedite search for answers to unexpected questions. In spite of research on the best search strategies, effectiveness still depends largely on designers' abilities to anticipate the pattern of information requests. Thus, in their attempts to include as much relevant data as possible in data bases without losing accessibility and flexibility, designers are seen as compromising between prestructuring data (to save storage and for ease and rapidness of retrieval) and redundancy and minimal structure (to facilitate unanticipated forms of search) (Hayes and Nolan 1974; Head 1970; Martin 1975; Mintzberg 1975b).

The content of information in a data base may be classified by use (in operations, planning, or control), time reference (historic or future oriented) and origin (internal or external to the organization). It has been argued that to achieve the full power of an MIS, especially for top management, company operating information needs to be augmented by introducing environmental information into the system (Head 1970; Sprague and Watson 1975).

USER INTERFACE CHARACTERISTICS

The user interface consists of two factors: input/output characteristics (the user-report interface) and the mode of operation (the user-machine interface).

Proposition 6.6 (input/output characteristics): Suitable output symbols, formats, and contexts enhance the likelihood of MIS success.

It is generally agreed that input and output should be simple and expressed in familiar forms that are easily understood. From the viewpoint of MIS, output characteristics are probably more important than those of input since most management-level users will be recipients of output but will not be concerned, except in special cases, with providing input. It has been noted that systems are often designed so users do not understand much of the output they receive; one survey found poor design of forms and reports to be a frequent source of system failure (Colton 1972-73; Hammond 1974a; Kronenberg 1967; Miller 1964).

An unsuitable symbol set is one factor in poor reports. Bad reports have been attributed to extensive use of codes instead of English titles in output. Thus, English titles are recommended instead of mathematical symbols. The English should be of standard usage because managers are repelled by jargon (Carlson 1967; Grayson 1973; Hammond 1974a).

Unsuitable formats are a second ingredient of unsatisfactory reports. Most managers do not know information formatting, nor do they really understand what a computer system can and cannot provide them. Thus, managers often agree to report formats at the design stage only to find later that their requirements have changed and implementors are unwilling or unable to adapt reports accordingly. This problem is exacerbated when persons who will not use a system are involved in supervising its construction. It seems that managers cannot delegate the design of reports to system staff and must be personally involved. In one case report, success was attributed in large part to output capabilities tailored to requests made by managers (Caldwell 1975; Carlson 1967).

Two problems with information system contexts are their realism and cognitive attractiveness. It has been noted that if too much of a problem is stripped away with simplifying assumptions, the remainder of the problem and its solution may bear little resemblance to the reality with which the manager must deal. Data presentation that attracts the attention and interest of users has, therefore, been advocated (Grayson 1973; Kneitel 1975a). One approach suggested for making information systems more realistic and interesting is to provide dialectical responses rich in contextual information. This approach has been the subject of two sets of experiments, one by Mitroff, Nelson, and Mason (1974) and the other by Cosier, Ruble, and Aplin (1978).

Mitroff, Nelson, and Mason (1974)*

In their paper, Mitroff, Nelson, and Mason laid the philo-
sophical foundation for the development of Management Myth-
Information Systems (MMIS), which are a subset of Management
Information Systems in general and are differentiated from other
MIS by a story-telling manner of presentation. In an MMIS, an
objective datum by itself is not information:

> Information is information if and only if it is tied to an
> appropriate story or myth that has meaning to the indi-
> vidual who needs the information, the organization in
> which he is located, and the type of problem that he
> faces. (Emphasis in the original.) [p. 371]

In discussing the nature of mythology, Mitroff, Nelson, and
Mason state that there are universal motifs and narrative forms
that give it its primeval appeal and ageless meaningfulness. These
can be analyzed to provide a theoretical structure for designing an
MMIS. The assumption is that material presented in story form
speaks to a basic psychic need that is not met by nonmythic information.

The experiment performed within this context involved 30
subjects playing two games with a computer: "Beat the Computer"
and "Freud." The first was a number game in which the computer,
posing as two different characters, presented two diametrically opposed strategies; each character urged the player to follow that
character's advice. Subsequently, a third character presented a
third, synthesizing strategy while pointing out the disadvantages of
adhering to an extreme view and explaining the value of dialectical
thinking. The second game involved the player answering several
questions and being rated on how close the player came to the ideal
of "two-way thinking."

The statistical evidence provided in the paper is a correlated
t-test performed on a 14-item attitude questionnaire pertaining to
dialectical thinking and the value of MMIS. All subjects completed
the questionnaire prior to, during, and after participation in "Freud."

---

*All quotes reprinted by permission from Mitroff, Ian I.,
Nelson, John and Mason, Richard O., "On Management Myth-
Information Systems," Management Science Volume 21, Number 4
(December 1974): 371-382, Copyright (1974) The Institute of Man-
agement Sciences.

Seven of the 14 items showed significant shifts in favor of the dialectical approach; examples of such items are:

> An intense argument between two strongly opposing
> sides of an issue is useful in clarifying points [;] good
> teachers make you unsure of your way of looking at
> things [;] and paintings are as real and as good a means
> of representation as are photographs. [P. 379]

Six other items showed positive, but not significant, shifts. Mitroff, Nelson, and Mason concluded that the results of the analysis indicated that "the subjects left the game with a better appreciation for dialectical thinking and for anecdotal information than when they started." [P. 379]

The researchers stated that these studies were preliminary and that they were primarily laying a foundation for future investigation. Computer technology is having a profound and often traumatic effect on society and the usually impersonal nature of human interaction with computers can antagonize and alienate users; thus, it is commendable that the researchers are striving to incorporate the human element into MIS design. Even as a philosophical foundation, however, Mitroff, Nelson, and Mason present a rather weak, oversimplified, and somewhat muddled case. Particularly troublesome is the lack of a control group in the experiment. Thus, it is not at all certain that subjects responded positively to the dialectical approach rather than to the gaming situation with which it was identified. It is as plausible to hypothesize that the subjects enjoyed the experiment because it was competitive and goal oriented as it is to assert that they enjoyed it because the proceedings had the emotional potency of a myth. A much more closely reasoned approach seems to be needed if there is to be success in meshing the seemingly antithetical scientific method and intuitive, emotional problem solving—in itself an application of dialectics.

Mason (1969) and Mitroff, Barabba, and Kilman (1977) have also conducted case studies of dialectical inquiry systems from which they concluded that this type of system is more effective. Case studies, however, are even less controlled than the experiment just described and so many plausible explanations are possible for the results observed that one hesitates to draw conclusions from them.

## Cosier, Ruble, and Aplin (1978)

Cosier, Ruble, and Aplin report two empirical studies on the effectiveness of Dialectical Inquiry Systems (DIS) relative to other

kinds of MIS. Their point of departure is the suggestion by Churchman (1971), based on Hegelian dialectics, that also motivated Mitroff,
Nelson, and Mason (1974). Churchman's suggestion is that systems
might present two views of the same situation: a plan and a counterplan. In the experiments, two approaches were applied to the evaluation of DIS: Social Judgment Theory and a simulation of a business
situation (for a detailed discussion of the Social Judgment Theory
paradigm see Brehmer [1976]).

In the first experiment, 84 MBA students were asked to predict variable values based on data about three cues. Each subject
was presented with predictions of two other decision makers; in one
treatment (low cognitive conflict) the predictions were in general
agreement; in the second treatment (dialectical) the predictions were
in direct conflict. The results showed no significant differences between the two groups in the effectiveness of the subjects' predictions,
but subjects in the high cognitive conflict treatment evaluated the
additional data as more helpful than did those in the second group.

In the second experiment, 108 undergraduate students of business participated in a game simulating a small business. They
were asked to make a few decisions on price, product mix, adver-
tising, and sales promotion, the goal being to maximize profit. Un-
knowingly, the subjects were operating in three markets, each of
which had different conditions. Subjects received information in
three different structures: DIS (plan and counterplan), devil's advocate (plan and critique), and expert (one plan); a control group received no information. After a few trials, all groups performed at
essentially the same level although immediately after presentation
of the data for the first time the devil's advocate structure was associated with higher performance.

These two experiments by Cosier, Ruble, and Aplin strengthen
doubts on the relative effectiveness of DIS. More important, they
raise serious questions about the whole approach to research in system characteristics. The general hypothesis has been that certain
system characteristics directly improve performance. But the experiments just described and most of the Minnesota Experiments
seem to suggest that performance is virtually independent of system
characteristics. The positive results of Mitroff, Nelson, and Mason
(1974) suggest that subjects prefer certain types of system characteristics to others, but it is necessary to distinguish between what
subjects like and what produces more effective performance. The
evidence available seems to indicate that a subject may prefer one
system to another, without the subject's performance being significantly different if one system is available rather than the other.
Thus, research needs to be directed toward answering two questions:
What effects do variations in system characteristics have on perfor-

mance and how is user motivation affected by system characteristics? It may transpire that within fairly broad ranges the main effect of changes in system characteristics is to change user motivation to use a system, rather than to improve performance.

## MODE OF OPERATION

A sharp dividing line is recognized between two basic modes of operation: batch processing, which produces information on a deferred basis (usually as printed reports) and on-line real-time processing, which provides immediate response (generally by means of terminals placed where users are located). The dichotomy is expressed in effectiveness, technical specifications, user behavior, and in modes of user-system communication (Aron 1967, 1969; Head 1970; Singer 1969).

### Effectiveness

Proposition 6.7 (mode of operation): Direct access to a system by means of an on-line real-time mode of operation enhances management use and increases the likelihood of success.

There has been a steady increase in the number of applications performed by real-time processing and in the size of computer systems devoted to them. On-line real-time capabilities are sometimes considered mandatory in numerous applications such as industrial process control, military and police command and control systems, interactive problem solving, service-oriented business processes such as banking and airline reservations, data acquisition, and management information systems. Frequently, second generation information systems are on-line real-time versions of first generation batch systems (Aron 1967; Head 1974; Montijo 1967).

In problem-solving situations it has been found that time sharing leads to a more effective solution and to faster problem solving. It has also been claimed that time-shared problem solving provides economical solutions. There is, however, some doubt on this point because basic problems in handling OLRT features of systems have proved more complex than originally anticipated and the operating costs of such systems are high. It has also been suggested that a distinction should be made between OLRT data processing and OLRT decision making—there may be situations in which data processing needs to be in on-line real-time mode, whereas decisions may more effectively be batched. Since batch processing provides the advantage of exception reports, which are superior in the problem-finding stage, and OLRT breaks the constraints of fixed report cycles, hybrid batch and on-line systems have been proposed (Kennedy 1974; Kennedy and Hoffer 1978; Lieberman and Whinston 1975; Martin 1975; Sackman 1971; Seaberg and Seaberg 1973; Singer 1969).

It has been stated that an investigation of the managers' machine interface may provide a solution to the information overload problem. Interactive systems may provide managers with direct access at a speed and convenience congruent with the decision-making process. In the past, this interaction was almost exclusively through the mediation of programmers, but this has been changing for some time. In one case it was found that payoffs to computer-based models were increased when functional management could execute them directly to assist in their decision processes. In 1970, Head reported that of 600 respondents to a questionnaire, 350 replied that their organization had installed some kind of terminal device connected to an on-line system for use by management-level personnel (Guthrie 1974; Nolan 1973; Seaberg and Seaberg 1973; Sprague and Watson 1975).

Technical Specifications

> Proposition 6.8 (mode of operation): Technical specifications with a human engineering orientation enhance the likelihood of MIS success.

The technical specifications of a system determine the operating characteristics realized at the terminal device employed for input/output. User reactions to system specifications have been found to depend on response time, verbosity or terseness of outputs, the extent to which users are isolated from fellow users, and the degree of computer knowledge required to interact with the system. An average system response time of three to five seconds has been suggested as desirable from a human factors point of view. One case study reports that a change in hardware from an independent system to a nonintelligent terminal was of major concern to some users, even though resources at their disposal were increased. Thus, the human engineering factors built into system responses and terminal devices may be critical to success (Head 1974; Holt and Stevenson 1978; Milutinovich and Kanter 1975; Singer 1967).

Behavior

The behavior of problem solvers in time-sharing environments and in comparison with batch-processing environments has been studied relatively extensively. Some indication of the importance attached to this topic is the publication of a methodology for modeling the behavior of man-machine information systems (Meldman 1977).

> Proposition 6.9 (mode of operation): The use of on-line real-time or time-sharing systems improves users' problem-solving performance and increases the likelihood of MIS success.

The results of six studies comparing time sharing with batch processing (Erikson 1966; Gold 1967; Grant and Sackman 1967; Schatzoff, Tsao, and Wiig 1967; Smith 1967) were synthesized by Sackman (1971), thus summarizing much of the work in this field. Remarkable uniformity of observed user response times was observed, ranging from 9 to 13 seconds, and indicating that most user interactions occur at essentially a conversational pace. This was interpreted as indicating that users do their thinking away from the terminal and, therefore, not in conjunction with the computer. This is further supported by the finding that users generally use terminals for only one session daily.

Sackman also concluded that there is a 20 percent man-hour advantage in favor of time sharing while 40 percent more computer time is used in time sharing than in batch mode. Thus, one trades off one's own time for computer time. When only computer time and man-hours were taken into account, the trade-off was balanced and neither mode was more economical than the other; it should be remembered, however, that this finding was published in 1971 and the cost factors have changed considerably since then in favor of time sharing.

Variations in user effectiveness are not clear. Whereas Gold (1967) found that time-sharing users performed better than batch-processing users, Senn and Dickson (1974) found little connection between information form (CRT or printed report) and effectiveness (see Table 6.2).

In terms of user preferences, Sackman reported a time-sharing bandwagon effect; this was qualified, however, by the observation that the experiments he summarized were conducted at institutions that pioneered in time sharing and where there was a strong bias in favor of that mode. This interpretation is supported by a study of the effect of terminal use on the motivation of bank tellers (Lawrie et al. 1974), although these are clerical, not managerial, personnel. The study by Lawrie et al. found that the use of terminals had no effect on absenteeism or feelings about the job. On the other hand, use of terminals was associated with more positive feelings about coworkers and responsibility for quality work. There was no change in feeling about the work itself and a moderate decrease in sense of accomplishment.

In Sackman's opinion, the main behavioral result of on-line/ off-line studies is the existence of very large differences in human performance—differences that are typically an order of magnitude larger than computer-related differences. Cost effectiveness thus lies more in human factors than in machine or system configuration variables. This conclusion is supported in the experimental findings reported by Cohen and Van Horn (1972). In a scheduling decision problem it was found that participants possessed information-processing and decision-making capabilities to achieve better performance, but used them only in special circumstances. Note that in this case there was no evidence of information overload or cognitive limitation. The imposition of a different decision rule produced a major change in participant scheduling behavior and improved performance considerably despite an apparently firm and genuine belief of participants that no major change was possible. Since all other parameters of the experiment were unchanged, the difference can be attributed to behavioral factors only.

An additional significant behavioral finding reported by Sackman is that users spend most of their time away from the terminal. Human-computer problem solving consists mainly of introspection or person-to-person communication, and major insights were observed to occur away from the terminal. Problem solving is a human-directed process with the user as a central source of strategic intelligence and the computer as a tactical aid. It is misleading to refer, as many authors do, to human-machine symbiosis in time-shared problem solving.

## Mode of Communication

The mode of communication, or medium of discourse, is a final aspect of the user interface that seems to be significant.

Proposition 6.10 (mode of operation): The implementation of communication modes that are favored by managers enhanced the likelihood of MIS success.

Ochsman and Chapanis (1974) studied the effects of communication modes on the effectiveness of cooperative team problem solving. Ten communication modes were studied: typewriting, handwriting, handwriting and typewriting, typewriting and video, handwriting and video, voice, voice and typewriting, voice and handwriting, voice and video, and all modes (communication rich).

One hundred and twenty undergraduate males from Johns Hopkins University were offered remuneration to participate in the experiment. They were randomly assigned to two-person teams, one of the ten communication modes, and one of three problem-solving tasks. One member of each team was defined as a "seeker," having to solve the problem, and the other as a "source," having related information. They had to cooperate to solve the problem. Accuracy of solution was emphasized as more important than speed of solution. All but two teams solved the problem correctly. Each of the experimenters observed one of the members of each team, who were in separate rooms. Subject behavior was recorded every five seconds on 21 predetermined behavioral categories. Total problem time for a team was defined as the sum of open channel times for each of the two members.

Figure 6.1 exhibits the mean problem solution time for the ten modes of communication. The data tend to fall into two groups, the faster five involving the use of voice communication. Voice communication is excluded in the five slower modes. Ochsman and Chapanis concluded that "there is a sharp dichotomy between modes of communication involving voice, and modes of communication that do not."

There is considerable evidence that managers favor verbal channels as a means of supplementing and even replacing formal sources of information. It has been predicted that the human-machine interface will improve significantly as direct interrogation of computers is made through improved keyboard or voice input; some go so far as to state that this is essential. At present, however, only a few systems permit voice communication. As the problem-solving power of computer systems increases, additional research in the means of making this power available to managers by the most effective means of communication can be expected (Mintzberg 1975a; Murdick and Ross 1972; Sass 1975).


INTEGRATION

Proposition 6.11: The greater the degree of system integration, the greater the likelihood of MIS success.

FIGURE 6.1

Mean Problem-Solution Times for Ten Modes
of Communication

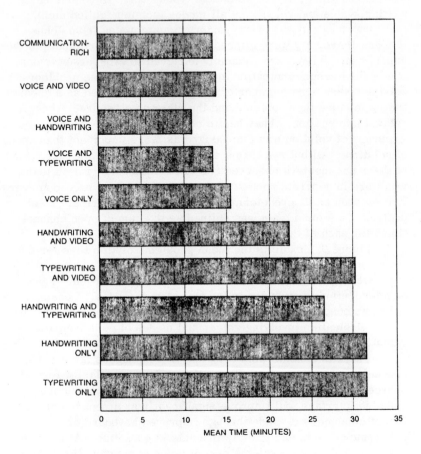

Source: Alphonse Chapanis, "Interactive Human Communication," Scientific American, 232 (March 1975): 41.


    The final structural variable to be discussed is the degree of
integration, a characteristic frequently mentioned in the context of
MIS. Sometimes it is regarded as absolutely essential, or at least
a prime motivation, for the construction of MIS. Although widely
used, the concept of integration is far from well defined and at
least five different dimensions of integration have been discussed
in the literature. Briefly, these are as follows:

Semantic integration at the individual level: Mitroff, Nelson, and Mason (1974) note a behavioral need to blend separate pieces of data into a single coordinated image. This is the basis for their theory of information systems in mythical contexts that was discussed earlier.

Integration of data from different areas of the organization by means of a data base: It has been noted that data bases can combine several data sources horizontally and can also integrate operations, tactical, and strategic data vertically. This permits the data base to accommodate various levels of inquirers so it can be useful to all major organizational levels and components. Use of such integration is facilitated by time-shared models. It has also been noted that technological considerations dictate a decision-support data base distinct from the body of transaction data and other internal and external data sources. It is anticipated that as data base management software develops, all data in an organization will eventually form a unified pool to which all users and data contributors will have direct access (Head 1967; Murdick and Ross 1972; Roark 1970; Seaberg and Seaberg 1973; Sprague and Watson 1975).

Integration of models: Sprague and Watson (1975) mention integration of tactical and strategic models, the output of one model being mapped into, or becoming input to, another.

Integration of models with a data base: This integration is implemented as the models draw the majority of their inputs from a data base and place their outputs back into it. This output is then available to other models as a source of inputs and so decreases suboptimization, redundant data preparation, and overly narrow use of output data (Sprague and Watson 1975).

Output integration: King and Cleland (1974) see integration in use, rather than in process; they believe that integration should be achieved by having compatibility between the outputs of various subsystems so they can be integrated in use as the need arises.


CONCLUSION

The structure of an MIS is the collection of attributes that determine the operating characteristics of the system. These are embodied in the hardware, software, and data base, which together form the physical data processing system.

System characteristics are the principal concern of system designers. A good understanding of the way these characteristics motivate use and improve performance would be a major step toward permitting the routine design of effective MIS. However, the research performed in this area has proved quite inconclusive and could hardly be regarded as providing guidelines for system design. This research does provide a useful basis of operationalization of variables and initial results that may, with additional experimentation and replication, become a foundation for normative statements on MIS design. As recommendations concerning characteristics are probably more easily implemented than are recommendations in behavioral areas, the practical effect of this research would be considerable.

# 7

## SENIOR EXECUTIVES AND MIS

> He was thoughtful and grave—but the orders he gave
>   Were enough to bewilder a crew.
> When he cried, "Steer to starboard, but keep her head
>   larboard! "
> What on earth was the helmsman to do ?
>                   Lewis Carroll, The Hunting of the Snark

Previous chapters contain discussions of the environmental, procedural, and structural subsystems of MIS; this chapter and the next two are devoted to the behavioral subsystem, which comprises senior executives, implementors, and users. Especially useful is to clearly distinguish between two types of management-MIS relationships: one is the relationship of senior executives who are assigned, or adopt, the responsibility for MIS in the broader context of the organization; the second is the relationship of executives in their roles as actual or potential users of MIS. This chapter discusses the first executive role; the second role, indistinguishable from that of users in general, is discussed in Chapter 9. Thus, the decomposition of the behavioral subsystem is functional, not personal. An individual may belong in more than one of these functional categories—an executive may also be a user, the highest level of implementors may attain executive status, and implementors have been known to use MIS.

---

Some of the material in this chapter has been published previously in Phillip Ein-Dor and Eli Segev, "Information-System Responsibility," MSU Business Topics 25 (Autumn 1977): 33-40.

In perusing the literature on this topic, one cannot help but
notice the discrepancy between the lip service paid to it and the
amount of actual study. Beginning with the inception of the MIS
concept, a large number of authors have stressed the importance
of top management's role in the successful implementation of information systems; the amount of research devoted to this role is
virtually nil. This is especially striking because as early as 1970
the "people problem" was recognized as "the major difficulty firms
encounter when they attempt to design, develop, and implement information systems" (Dickson and Simmons 1970). In the paper
from which this passage is taken, Dickson and Simmons identified
four classes of personnel: operating personnel, operating management, technical staff, and top management. These categories
conform with that of the slightly different nomenclature used in this
book: computer-dependent workers, users, implementors, and
executives. For these groups, Dickson and Simmons identified
interactions with MIS, probable types of dysfunctional behavior
(Table 7.1), and reasons for the resistance generated (Table 7.2).
From these tables, their hypothesis is that top management is generally unaffected by, and unconcerned about, MIS and tends to
avoid involvement with them. The reasons for this behavior are
posited to be primarily feelings of insecurity accompanied by role
ambiguity, uncertainty, and increased job complexity. The widespread recognition of the importance of executive participation
renders the lack of research so striking.

Because there is so little research in this particular subject,
the following discussion on the relationship of executive management
to the success and failure of MIS is based almost entirely on the
informed opinions of experts writing in the field, supported by a
small number of surveys. Unfortunately, most of these surveys
are rather old and their findings may no longer reflect the current
state of affairs. Thus, Dickson and Simmons's (1970) contention
that top managers are unaffected by MIS and tend to avoid them may
have been rendered obsolete by the development of more sophisticated systems and better informed management. In spite of these
shortcomings, the topic cannot be avoided and the most must be
made of whatever evidence is available. The variables relevant to
the relationship between senior executives and the success or failure of MIS are the degree of association of these executives with
MIS and their rank, functions, and capabilities.

# TABLE 7.1

Work Groups, MIS Interaction, and Probable Types
of Dysfunctional Behavior

| Organizational Subgroup | Relation to MIS | Probable Dysfunctional Behavior |
|---|---|---|
| Operating personnel | | |
| Nonclerical | Provide system inputs. | Aggression |
| Clerical | Particularly affected by clerical systems; job eliminated, job patterns changed. | Projection |
| Operating management | Controlled from above by information systems; job content modified by information-decision systems and programmed systems. | Aggression, avoidance, and projection |
| Technical staff | Systems designers and agents of systems change. | None |
| Top management | Generally unaffected and unconcerned with systems. | Avoidance |

Source: G. W. Dickson and John K. Simmons, "The Behavioral Side of MIS," Business Horizons 13 (August 1970): 63. Copyright, 1970, by the Foundation for the School of Business at Indiana University. Reprinted by permission.

TABLE 7.2

Reasons for Resistance to MIS
(by working group)

| | Operating (nonclerical) | Operating (clerical) | Operating Management | Top Management |
|---|---|---|---|---|
| Threats to economic security | | X | X | |
| Threats to status or power | | X | XX | |
| Increased job complexity | X | | X | X |
| Uncertainty or unfamiliarity | X | X | X | X |
| Changed interpersonal relations or work patterns | | XX | X | |
| Changed superior-subordinate relationships | | XX | X | |
| Increased rigidity or time pressure | X | X | X | |
| Role ambiguity | | X | XX | X |
| Feelings of insecurity | | X | XX | XX |

X signifies the reason is possibly the cause of resistance to MIS development.
XX signifies the reason has a strong possibility of being the cause of resistance.

Source: G. W. Dickson and John K. Simmons, "The Behavioral Side of MIS," Business Horizons 13 (August 1970): 68. Copyright, 1970, by the Foundation for the School of Business at Indiana University. Reprinted by permission.

ASSOCIATION WITH MIS

Proposition 7.1: High levels of top management association with MIS increase the likelihood of success.

Some years ago it had become somewhat trite to state that top management association contributes, or may even be essential, to the success of MIS. This had been found in a number of surveys and reported in individual cases. Conversely, a lack of top management association had been diagnosed as contributing to poor MIS performance. The types of relationship considered beneficial are exhibited in Table 7.3. This list of desirable relationships was synthesized from 23 articles that mentioned the subject, many of which used more than one descriptor (Aron 1969; Berkowitz and Munro 1969; Brady 1967; Carlson 1967; Colton 1972; Diebold 1969; Farley et al. 1971; Garrity 1963; Hammond 1974a; Hanold 1972; Hayes and Nolan 1974; Holland et al. 1974; Lucas 1973, 1975; McKinsey 1968; Murdick and Ross 1972; Myers 1975; Nolan and Knutsen 1974; Sass 1975; Schwartz 1969; Singer 1969; Willoughby and Pye 1977).

TABLE 7.3

Descriptors of Desirable Executive Association with MIS

| Descriptor | Number of Articles Mentioning Descriptor |
|---|---|
| Involvement | 10 |
| Support | 8 |
| Commitment | 3 |
| Appreciation | 2 |
| Champion | 2 |
| Understanding | 2 |
| Belief | 1 |
| Concern | 1 |
| Participation | 1 |
| Vested interest | 1 |

Source: Compiled by the authors.

A glance at the dates of the references of this section discloses that very little has been written on the subject in recent years and that most of the empirical studies were done some years ago. This implies, perhaps, an intuitive recognition that this area is no longer the problem it once was. Some evidence to support this contention is provided by Willoughby and Pye (1977). Their study consisted of a 20-question survey submitted to the chief executive officers and information system directors of 60 firms selected randomly from a comprehensive list of firms with sales over U.S. $100 million. From the 120 questionnaires sent 50 responses were received; 26 of the responses were from presidents, 23 from information system directors, and 1 was unidentified.

The questionnaire was designed to test two hypotheses: "1. The attitudes of IS managers are more positive than those of top managers. 2. Where top management is more involved, the IS function is more successful." The questions and response indices are exhibited in Table 7.4. Willoughby and Pye concluded that the data strengthen the second hypothesis—that the IS function is more successful when management is involved. But the data on attitudes exhibit no significant differences between the attitudes of executive officers and those of information system managers. This supports our supposition that senior executives may no longer be so distant and uninvolved as the literature tends to suggest.

Proposition 7.2: The level of involvement of top management is dependent on their appreciation, understanding, motivation, and perceptions of MIS.

Swanson (1974) developed operational indices of appreciation and involvement and established in the laboratory that appreciation of MIS and involvement with MIS are coproduced; therefore, managers who are involved will be appreciative and those who are uninvolved will be unappreciative. He regards understanding as an intervening variable through which involvement is transformed into appreciation.

One factor considered as leading to management underinvolvement is a lack of appreciation of MIS or a misunderstanding of the benefits and problems involved. An additional hypothesis is that managers perceive MIS as a threat to their decision-making functions and prerogatives of exercising managerial judgment; this, together with a lack of understanding, can generate feelings of insecurity that lead to avoidance. The threshold of motivation necessary for active involvement may be further raised by the amount of time required for such involvement to be effective—a consideration that will become clear following the discussion of the numerous

TABLE 7.4

Response Indices for Presidents and
Information Systems Executives

| | Question | Presidents | IS Executives | Total |
|---|---|---|---|---|
| 1 | Computer use increases the value and importance of organizational planning. [1] | 3.8 | 3.9 | 3.9 |
| 2 | There are significant cost savings involved with computer systems. [2] | 3.7 | 3.8 | 3.7 |
| 3 | New techniques of analysis made easier by the computer have been tried. [2] | 4.2 | 4.3 | 4.2 |
| 4 | There is a higher level of satisfaction among employees since the computers have become operational. [2] | 2.8 | 3.0 | 2.9 |
| 5 | Reports and procedures have been improved since the computers have been installed. [2] | 4.3 | 4.3 | 4.3 |
| 6 | Information from the computer is more accurate and timely when compared to previous methods. [2] | 4.5 | 4.6 | 4.5 |
| 7 | I question the decisions made by my EDP people. [1] | 2.7 | 3.4 | 3.0 |
| 8 | Computers are an asset to the company's growth. [1] | 4.5 | 4.8 | 4.7 |
| 9 | I have a complete understanding of what the computers do in my company and what they are capable of. [3] | 3.3 | 4.6 | 3.9 |
| 10 | I participate actively in any major decision made by the data processing department. [3] | 3.6 | 4.4 | 4.0 |
| 11 | I helped in establishing the objectives of the computer system. [3] | 3.6 | 4.1 | 3.9 |

(continued)

Table 7.4, continued

|  | | Presidents | IS Executives | Total |
|---|---|---|---|---|
| 12 | I contributed to the evaluation of the system after it was installed.[3] | 3.4 | 4.1 | 3.7 |
| 13 | I meet regularly with the heads of the data processing department to discuss what management believes is needed.[3] | 3.5 | 4.3 | 3.9 |
| 14 | The highest computer executive reports to top management.[3] | 4.4 | 4.5 | 4.5 |
| 15 | I like what the computer has done to the operation of the business.[1] | 4.3 | 4.7 | 4.4 |
| 16 | The budget allocation to data processing is considerable.[2] | 4.5 | 4.7 | 4.6 |
| 17 | Personnel are given time off or paid to further their data processing knowledge.[2] | 4.0 | 3.6 | 3.8 |
| 18 | The data processing department is relatively autonomous when compared to other departments in the company.[3] | 3.0 | 2.9 | 3.0 |
| 19 | The personnel in data processing actively seek new projects that will benefit the company.[2] | 3.5 | 4.0 | 3.7 |
| 20 | I receive operating reports from the data processing department.[3] | 3.8 | 4.9 | 4.5 |

[1]An attitude statement.
[2]An action statement.
[3]A performance statement.

Source: T. C. Willoughby and Richard A. Pye, "Top Management's Computer Role." Reprinted by permission from the Journal of Systems Management 28 (September 1977), p. 12.

activities implied by such involvement (Brady 1967; Carlson 1967; Dickson and Simmons 1970; Holland et al. 1974).

More specific knowledge is necessary. It has been noted that people may retard or even sabotage the implementation of MIS in spite of top management support and blessing. On the other hand, a field survey found that 16 percent of 33 systems surveyed were implemented in spite of top management opposition.* Thus, top management support may not be absolutely essential for MIS implementation. Note, however, that the dependent variable here is implementation, rather than MIS success; it would be interesting to know what proportion of MIS implemented in the face of executive opposition eventually function with success (Heany 1972; Holland et al. 1974).

This area is certainly of sufficient importance to warrant some research to determine whether involvement by senior executives has reached satisfactory levels and what forms of involvement are most beneficial.

Proposition 7.3: High levels of manager-MIS association promote mutually favorable perceptions between information system staff and users and commonly favorable perceptions of information systems.

A new dimension to top management association with MIS was added by Lucas, who pointed out perception of high-level management support as a predictor of high levels of information system use. He hypothesized a mechanism whereby high levels of management support and participation are translated into effective MIS; a high level of management involvement promotes favorable attitudes, and perceptions of information service staff toward their jobs and users. Similarly, it promotes favorable attitudes and perceptions of users toward information systems and information system staff. Thus, not only is a high level of management association necessary, it must also be perceived as such in the organization. Lucas suggests that the appointment of a steering committee is a good method of demonstrating management support and gaining user involvement (Lucas 1973, 1974a, 1975b). Lucas's approach is supported by earlier findings that in companies leading in information system use, top management had specifically spelled out to operating executives

---

*This 16 percent cannot be derived directly from the sample size of 33 and should be considered only an order of magnitude. Whether the inconsistency is a result of round-off error or because of no response from some of those interviewed is not clear.

the corporate commitment to the computer effort, its objectives, and operating management's responsibility for achieving the anticipated benefits (Garrity 1963).

## RANK OF RESPONSIBLE EXECUTIVE

> Proposition 7.4: The likelihood of a successful MIS effort declines rapidly the lower the rank of the responsible executive, and is virtually negligible more than two levels below the chief officer of the particular organization the MIS serves.

Proposition 7.4 refers to the question of how senior the executives involved in MIS should be for the association to promote success. Many writers are suggestive, rather than specific, on this issue; there is only a narrow range suggested by those who are explicit.

Many authors recommend that decisions on computers be kept at the highest level and that the corporate manager or chief executive become directly involved in the configuration and use of MIS. One widely cited example of this approach is the Pillsbury Company. Responsibility for information systems was explicitly assigned by corporate policy to the general manager at the plant level and to the executive officer at the corporate level (Financial Executive 1974; Gibson and Nolan 1974; Gupta 1974; Hanold 1972; McFarlan 1971; McKinsey 1968; Sass 1975; Townsend 1970).

A survey by Colton (1972) found that in successful police department information systems, the chief or the chief's top assistant was deeply involved in the operation. The "involvement and quality of leadership at the top" is the first variable mentioned by Colton in a list of variables accounting for the success and failure of police information systems. That this involvement should begin with the inception of planning for computer systems is suggested by the data in Table 7.5, which show that in 50 percent of the police forces in the survey the chief of police was the initiator and in 70 percent it was the chief or assistant chief.

Some authors suggest that a respected vice president can act as a bridge between senior management and MIS staff. In some organizations (apparently their number is increasing) there are titles such as vice president for information systems. Administration vice president has also been suggested as the level to which the computer and systems group should report (Dearden 1972; Financial Executive 1974; Gibson and Nolan 1974; Hammond 1974; Nolan 1973a).

TABLE 7.5

Origin of Initial Proposal for Using a Computer

| Person Proposing Use | Number Indicating Proposing | Percent of Total Number Responding |
|---|---|---|
| Chief of Police | 60 | 50.8 |
| Assistant chief or chief's direct staff | 23 | 19.5 |
| Data processing manager | 11 | 9.3 |
| Planning, research director | 15 | 12.7 |
| Other administrative officer | 12 | 10.2 |
| Office of mayor or city manager | 24 | 20.3 |
| Outside consultant | 9 | 7.6 |

Source: Reprinted from "Computers and Police: Patterns of Success and Failure," by Kent W. Colton, SLOAN MANAGEMENT REVIEW, Vol. 14, No. 2 (Winter 1972-3), p. 93, by permission of the publisher. Copyright © 1972 by the Sloan Management Review. All rights reserved.

Additional studies indicate that the computer system effort can succeed if the computer executive is within two levels of the chief executive (Dean 1968; Garrity 1963; McFarlan 1971). As information systems become more sophisticated and more closely enmeshed in fundamental organizational structures, the need for top executive involvement will probably increase, rather than decrease. It would be of considerable interest and utility if more data were available both on current practice and on the relationships between ranks of officers involved and success, especially as these develop over time.

FUNCTIONS OF TOP MANAGEMENT

Proposition 7.5: The level of association of top management with MIS is related to the amount of time devoted and to the number of functions performed.

A large number of functions have been suggested for top management exercising its responsibility toward MIS. Table 7.6 is an attempt to order these by major categories. The main areas of management responsibility are, not surprisingly, similar to those of other functional areas, namely: policy formulation, planning, evaluation, organization, institution building, implementation, and control. As measured by the number of authors referring to them, the functions most heavily stressed are establishing priorities and follow through to see that planned results are actually achieved. These may be clues to the major problem areas executive management needs to address.

## CAPABILITIES OF TOP MANAGEMENT

Not only must top management assume responsibility for the MIS effort, it must also be qualified to exercise that responsibility. In practice, management seems to face considerable difficulty in performing some of the functions detailed in the preceding section.

> Proposition 7.6: For a given level of top management association, the degree of MIS success is related to the level of skills acquired by the management involved.

One study found that in successful companies, top management had a balanced view of the potential of computers and the demands made by them. In average companies, either the potential of computers was underrated or their technical requirements overrated (Garrity 1963). In this context of the difficulty in making correct assessments, it has been pointed out that managers often do not understand the technology and are unable to evaluate information systems (Head 1967; Lucas 1973). Experimental work by MacCrimmon (1974) suggests that the inability to evaluate information systems may be the result of cognitive limitations; this is also the rationale for Dearden's (1972) contention that the total MIS is unattainable.

At the level of information requirements, a hesitancy has been noted on the part of some top managers to formally identify decision criteria. Others do not believe that many top managers know what information they need or how to use it if they had it (Ackoff 1967; Alexander 1969; Brady 1967).

An additional managerial deficiency is manifested in the area of control of MIS. Lack of a set of standards against which corporate management and MIS executives can evaluate their own control procedures has been identified as one cause of this deficiency (Morgan and Soden 1973).

TABLE 7.6

References for Top-Management Functions

| Function | Reference |
|---|---|
| Policy formulation | |
| Set goals | Brandon 1970; Diebold 1969 |
| Establish realistic personnel policy | Brandon 1970 |
| Appraise objectives | McKinsey 1968; Myers 1975 |
| Appraise criteria | Gibson and Nolan 1974; McKinsey 1968; Nolan 1973c; O'Toole and O'Toole 1966 |
| Appraise direction | Myers 1975 |
| Planning | |
| Long-range planning | Brandon 1970; Dinter 1971 |
| Guiding and supporting research and planning | Schwartz 1969 |
| Reviewing plans and programs | Garrity 1963; Dinter 1971 |
| Insisting that detailed plans are made an integral part of operating plans and budgets | McKinsey 1968 |
| Planning for equipment | Brandon 1970 |
| Evaluation | |
| Evaluate project proposals | Gibson and Nolan 1974 |
| Require cost/benefit analysis | Dinter 1971 |
| Organization | |
| Decide on organizational arrangements | McKinsey 1968 |
| Recognize organizational implications | Brandon 1970 |
| Establish DP function | Brandon 1970 |
| Place IS at highest level in organization | Dinter 1971 |
| Obtain competent DP managers | Brandon 1970; Dinter 1971 |

(continued)

Table 7.6, continued

| Function | Reference |
|---|---|
| Institutional | |
| Understand the process | Brandon 1970 |
| Provide management support | Brandon 1970 |
| Emphasize organizational commitment | Dinter 1971 |
| Assign responsibility to line and functional executives | McKinsey 1968 |
| Get user departments involved | Dinter 1971 |
| Implementation | |
| Allocate resources | Myers 1975 |
| Initiate design process and be involved in it | Zani 1970 |
| Define information and processing requirements | Hanold 1972; Zani 1970 |
| Support user training | Brandon 1970 |
| Communicate desires on documentation | Schwartz 1969 |
| Control | |
| Verify exercise of responsibility by line and functional management | McKinsey 1968 |
| Establish controls | Brandon 1970 |
| Control the design process | Hanold 1972 |
| Control operations | Hanold 1972; Zani 1970 |
| Follow through to see planned results achieved | Brandon 1970; Garrity 1963; McKinsey 1968; Myers 1975; Schwartz 1969 |

Source: Compiled by the authors.

144

From the preceding catalog of problems, may be deduced that among the characteristics required of senior executives are the abilities to correctly assess the potential of systems and to evaluate their performance, to specify information requirements and decision rules, and to control complex systems. Additional capabilities mentioned in the literature are strong administrative skills, ability to prepare plans and stick to budgets, ability to seek out significant projects, and knowledge of the language of computer personnel, at least to the extent necessary to evaluate project proposals. The manager should be a generalist who understands the need to bring the diverse elements of the organization together as a system (Gibson and Nolan 1974; Murdick and Ross 1972).

CONCLUSION

The MIS literature has done little more than indicate the importance of top management's role to the success and failure of MIS and identify some of the dimensions of this element. If the importance of this factor is accepted, research concerning the most useful areas and forms of top management association with, and direction of, MIS is clearly called for.

# 8

## IMPLEMENTORS OF MIS

> The crew was complete: it included a Boots—
> A maker of Bonnets and Hoods—
> A Barrister, brought to arrange their disputes—
> And a Broker, to value their goods.
> Lewis Carroll, The Hunting of the Snark

System implementors are those who manage or execute the design, construction, and operation of MIS. There are no standard job descriptions or professional categories in MIS, but different authors seem to have fairly consistent models in mind. Table 8.1 compares job categories listed in three different sources. Although the levels of detail vary, it appears clearly that the major functional areas are supervision, analysis, and programming. Expertness in specific technical areas such as data base management and data communications, highly specialized spinoffs of the analysis and operations functions, are rapidly developing. In discussions of data processing professionals, the operations function is sometimes included and sometimes not, depending on the purpose of the analysis; generally, however, operators are not considered to be in that category.

The variables considered relevant to the performance of each of these groups, therefore relating them to the success and failure of MIS, are their functions, recruitment, turnover, capabilities, organization, and relationships with executives and users. Since implementors are engaged mainly in constructing new systems, their effect is mainly on the success of MIS projects, rather than on MIS operation. The propositions in this chapter, therefore, are also related primarily to the success of MIS projects.

# TABLE 8.1

### Professional Categories Related to Information Systems

| McLaughlin and Knottek[1] | Roark | Willoughby |
|---|---|---|
| Corporate staff<br>Division or departmental staff | Supervisory | Supervisor<br>System project leader |
| Systems analysis | System analyst OR analyst | System analyst |
| Systems analysis/ programming | Analyst/ programmer | Programmer/ analyst |
| Applications programming<br>Operating systems programming | Programmer | Programmer |
| Data base administration<br>Data communications/ telecommunication | Technical specialist | |
| Computer operations<br>Production control<br>Data entry | | |
| Other | Trainee<br>Other | |

[1]Include lead, senior, professional and/or staff assistance, and trainee levels in most functional categories.

Sources: R. A. McLaughlin and Nancy Knottek. "DP Salary Survey." Datamation 24 (November 1, 1978): 87-95. Mayford L. Roark, "Information system education: what industry thinks." DM 14 (June 1976): 24-28. Theodore C. Willoughby. "Staffing the MIS Function." Computing Surveys 4 (December 1972): 241-259.

## FUNCTIONS OF SYSTEM IMPLEMENTORS

> Proposition 8.1: Implementors will be more suc-
> cessful in translating management goals into work-
> ing systems the more specifically the goals are
> defined.

> Proposition 8.2: Implementors will be more suc-
> cessful in building working systems the broader the
> definition of their functions.

The basic function of system implementors is to translate
user needs into technically feasible system designs and to develop
them on time and within budget. Most discussions of the functions
of system implementors, especially at the levels of supervision
and analysis, relate to how broadly or narrowly their function
should be defined (Gibson and Nolan 1974; Morgan and Soden
1973).

The general belief is that the responsibilities of implementors
should not extend to the determination of the goals of information
systems or the definition of their requirements. Thus, several
authorities attribute poor choice of applications to a tendency on the
part of top management to relegate the determination of computer
system goals to data processing professionals. The opposite opinion
has also been expressed however: Managers are incapable of knowing their requirements and these should be determined for them by
technicians. This last attitude is not widely supported (Ackoff 1967;
Aron 1969; Diebold 1969; Edwards 1974; Gibson and Nolan 1974;
McKinsey 1968).

It is believed that, within the limits set by externally dictated
goals and user requirements, implementors should be given broad
terms of reference. One reason is that computer technology, modes
of operation, and organizations change continuously, so MIS managers must be heavily involved in planning for the future. In fact,
in Lehman's (1979) survey, more comments from respondents were
received on planning than on any other management function, the
gist being that more effort should be expended on formulating and
revising plans as development proceeds. The definition of project
managers' responsibilities revealed by that survey nearly always
included technical aspects, but were more limited with respect to
hiring, firing, and resource allocation. Lehman's data are exhibited in Table 8.2.

TABLE 8.2

Project Managers' Responsibilities

| Responsibilities | Percent of Respondents |
|---|---|
| Technical quality | 96 |
| Hire and fire assigned personnel (within firm's policy) | 40 |
| Evaluate performance of individual personnel | 81 |
| Administration, budget, etc. | 73 |
| Allocating computer resources | 75 |
| Allocating noncomputer resources | 69 |
| Meeting schedule commitments | 98 |
| Negotiating specification changes with customer | 87 |
| Making a profit (operating within budget) | 44 |

Source: John H. Lehman, "How Software Projects Are Really Managed," Datamation 25 (January 1979): 121. Reprinted with permission of DATAMATION® magazine © Copyright by TECHNICAL PUBLISHING COMPANY, A DUN & BRADSTREET COMPANY, 1979—all rights reserved.

RECRUITMENT OF IMPLEMENTORS

It has been stated that almost all MIS failures are failures of MIS management and personnel and that the appointment of the right MIS executive can be a vital contribution of top management to systems development. The key questions concern where MIS implementors are to be recruited, how they are to be recruited, and which professional categories are to be employed (McKinsey 1968; Morgan and Soden 1973).

Proposition 8.3: MIS projects are more likely to succeed when the characteristics of MIS implementors are consistent with the nature of the implementation problem.

A major problem is that expertness with computers and an understanding of the problems of the particular organization are both necessary and difficult to find in a single individual (Alexander 1969; Hayes and Nolan 1974). The extent of this problem is documented in Lehman's (1979) study in which he found that the typical project manager had 10 years experience in data processing and 7.7 years in the field of the project; nevertheless, all but one of the 57 managers found it necessary to obtain further training prior to or early in the project. The types of training required are exhibited in Table 8.3.

TABLE 8.3

Extra Project Manager Training

| Field | Managers (percent) |
|---|---|
| Project management | 58 |
| Project field | 53 |
| General management | 47 |
| General DP | 44 |
| Modern programming techniques | 30 |
| A programming language | 28 |
| Other | 7 |

Source: John H. Lehman, "How Software Projects Are Really Managed," Datamation 25 (January 1969): 121. Reprinted with permission of DATAMATION® magazine © Copyright by TECHNICAL PUBLISHING COMPANY, A DUN & BRADSTREET COMPANY, 1979—all rights reserved.

This gives rise to the question of whether MIS personnel should be recruited from inside or outside the organization. One solution suggested is to teach information technology to the firm's functional experts; it has been suggested that this is simpler than teaching computer technicians the details of an operation in sufficient depth. An alternative solution is to recruit staff from consulting firms (Dearden 1972; Hayes and Nolan 1974; Murdick and Ross 1972).

The advantages and disadvantages of recruiting systems staff from inside and outside the organization have been discussed by a number of authors. It has been suggested, in line with the authors' proposition, that the recruiting strategy should be based on an evaluation of the relative importance of company versus MIS experience. Garrity's (1963) study, however, found that the internal or external recruitment of systems staff was not a predictor of success (Dearden 1972; Garrity 1963; Gibson and Nolan 1974; Hayes and Nolan 1974; Shults and Bruun 1974; Willoughby 1972).

> Proposition 8.4: Development of implementor selection methods will enhance the effectiveness of the selection process and increase the likelihood of MIS project success.

Testing is widely used in recruiting MIS personnel, especially programmers. In spite of their widespread use, however, even the best tests seem to be rather ineffective. Staffing problems have been attributed to the very short experience in evaluating, selecting, and training key MIS personnel; the higher the level of the position, the worse the problems seem to be. Morgan and Soden (1973) have stated that the screening of candidate executives is particularly ineffective, to the point where "it is said that the key factor for success for anyone in the MIS area is the ability to write good resumes."

Some work on the MIS personnel selection problem was done by Wetherbe and Dock (1976), who discussed the limitations of job descriptions for EDP personnel selection and for affirmative action requirements. They propose a quasi-quantitative selection technique to overcome the limitations of job descriptions. The proposed technique is composed of seven steps:

1. Appointment of a selection committee;
2. Determination of attributes;
3. Deciding on relative weights for attributes;
4. Scoring the applicants;
5. Analysis of scores;
6. Verification of scores; and
7. Interview.

To test this approach they tried it for six different positions over an 18-month period. Table 8.4 exhibits the results for the six selection exercises.

Wetherbe and Dock's evaluation of the proposed method is based on the amount of human resources required, achievement of consensus on top candidates, and the acceptibility of the documentation for discrimination audits. Based on these exercises, their conclusions were that the total man-hours invested in the selection

TABLE 8.4

Tabulation of Field Test Results for Six Selection Exercises

| | 1 | 2 | 3 | 4 | 5 | 6 |
|---|---|---|---|---|---|---|
| Title of Position | Number of Candidates | Committee Size | Average Time Required per Committee Member (hours) | Total Person-Hours Required | Average Time per Candidate per Committee Member[1] | Consensus on Top Candidate(s) |
| Manager of administrative systems | 34 | 5 | 2.5 | 12.5 | 4.4 | Yes |
| Systems analyst | 9 | 4 | 1.5 | 6.0 | 10.0 | Yes |
| Data control clerk | 5 | 3 | 1.0 | 3.0 | 12.0 | Yes |
| Manager of systems operations | 4 | 4 | 1.0 | 4.0 | 15.0 | Yes |
| Keypunch supervisor | 3 | 3 | 0.5 | 1.5 | 15.0 | Yes |
| Computer operator | 9 | 4 | 1.0 | 4.0 | 6.7 | Yes |

[1]Excluding interview.

Source: J. C. Wetherbe and V. T. Dock, "Breaking the Description Dilemma: Personnel Selection by Group Analysis," Data Management 14 (December 1976): 19. Copyright DATA MANAGEMENT magazine. Data Processing Management Association. ALL RIGHTS RESERVED.

152

process were surprisingly low. In all six cases a consensus on the top applicants was reached, and the documentation (reviewed by the organizations' affirmative action officer and a representative of the Department of Labor) was found to be more than adequate.

This method is, of course, highly dependent on the composition of the committee. Different committees may require different attributes and have different weights for them. An experiment with two or more committees selecting for the same positions might contribute to the evaluation of the effectiveness of this method. Another test of this method might involve criterion setting by one committee and scoring of the candidates, on the criteria selected, by another committee; this would indicate whether consensus is achieved even if the evaluators are not involved in criterion setting.

> Proposition 8.5: Mixed teams are more likely to be successful in MIS projects.

It has been suggested that three kinds of people need to be involved in system development; namely, people with related technical knowledge, users, and people who are sensitive to the factors evoking human commitment and alienation in the development and maintenance of management systems. Similar suggestions are for mixed teams of experts and users from different departments for the development of MIS. At least one case report attributes success, among other things, to putting line managers in charge of planning, development, and implementation (Kronenberg 1967; Laverdiere and Smith 1975; Myers 1975).

Surveys have shown that the reinforcement of technical staff by management science personnel is a factor leading to MIS success. Furthermore, successful companies either assign a talented individual with experience in each of the major functions of the business to corporate computer staff or temporarily transfer personnel from operations to serve on project development teams (Garrity 1963; McKinsey 1968). Two studies, one by Argyris and the other by Boland, have focused on the behavior of mixed teams of implementors and users.

## Argyris (1971)

Argyris's work was based on the premise that team organization has become the norm for development projects and it is, therefore, of interest to understand the behavior of such groups. He further assumed that, in the future, MIS may perform critical managerial functions with a consequent rise in the level of organizational rationality. Thus, it was hypothesized that if such MIS appear, they will:

Reduce managers' space of free movement;
Cause psychological failure and double bind;
Emphasize leadership based more on competence than on power;
Decrease feelings of essentialness;
Reduce intra- and intergroup politics; and
Pose new requirements for conceptual thinking.

To predict the behavior of managers in organizations when and if MIS mature fully, Argyris studied a group charged with implementing such changes. His assumption was that this group and the manner in which it worked were prototypes for the future rational organization they were trying to achieve. The group under study was a team of about 20 management-science/operations research professionals, headed by a trained mathematical statistician in the context of a multibillion dollar corporation. The researcher observed and tape recorded work meetings of this group.

The tape-recorded meetings were analyzed and statements made in them were categorized on a six-point scale from facilitating to inhibiting interpersonal relationships and problem solving. Analysis of the scores presented profiles of the meetings.

Two basic patterns were found. Both patterns were characterized by a high degree of "owning" ideas, and contributed in pattern A to the group's norms of concern (first) and conformity (second) and in pattern B to conformity (first) and concern (second). Based on these findings and on an earlier study of line managers, Argyris's conclusion was that MIS professionals and line managers have a comparable degree of interpersonal competence and that both groups react to stress and tension in ways that tend to inhibit effective problem solving. He also concluded that the MIS group, dedicated to implementing rational designs for management, dealt with their own professional problems in an emotional way, although "intellectually" disguised.

Argyris's in-depth study of the work behavior of an MIS group is illuminating. It strengthens the long-held suspicion that groups emphasizing systematic and rational decision making behave and react emotionally even when applying knowledge and intellect. Yet, the authors think it is somewhat daring to predict, using as a base observations of each of the groups separately, relationships between implementors and users in an environment of mature MIS that does not yet exist.

Boland (1978)

In contrast to Argyris's study, Boland actually observed the performance of mixed teams and their effects on problem definition, design quality, and types of organizational control strategies. The mixed teams in this study each consisted of one nurse and one system designer. The teams were assigned the task of finding and solving problems in a hypothetical hospital similar to the one in which the nurses were employed.

All the nurses had similar jobs and experience in one large hospital. Pairs of systems designers evaluated as equally competent and with no prior hospital design experience were assigned by firms with large and active groups of information system implementors. Nurse/designer teams were formed randomly and assigned to one of two groups of teams, one designer from each firm in each group. The groups were subjected to different treatments termed "protocols of traditional rationality" (traditional) and "protocols of alternative rationality" (alternative). These protocols are exhibited in Figure 8.1.

Each group of teams was also divided into two subgroups: problem finders (to identify the problems and solutions) and problem solvers (to solve a specific problem). A pilot test involved 4 teams; the full test, 18 teams. After a two-hour interview, team reports were evaluated by a panel of seven graduate students and a panel of three expert nurses (for a detailed discussion of the evaluation method, see Boland (1978), p. 890).

The main findings were as follows:

There was no significant difference in the number and quality of problems identified by the designers in the problem-finding groups under both treatments.

Nurses under the alternative treatment identified more problems than did nurses under the traditional treatment. Since some of these problems were not identified by the designers, these teams performed better.

Teams under the alternative treatment had significantly higher idea-quality scores.

The traditional teams emphasized control through efficiency, accuracy, and proceduration. The alternative teams emphasized coordination among departments.

The traditional teams focused on data needs of the nurses; the alternative teams concentrated on the system and the process.

The traditional problem-solving teams saw the computer as the center of the system, whereas the alternative teams viewed the nurse as the center.

FIGURE 8.1

## Protocols of Traditional and Alternative Rationality

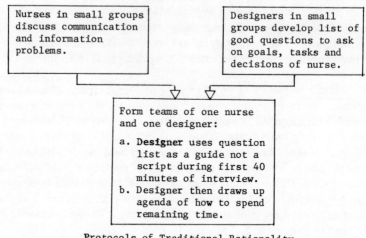

| | |
|---|---|
| Nurses in small groups discuss communication and information problems. | Designers in small groups develop list of good questions to ask on goals, tasks and decisions of nurse. |

Form teams of one nurse and one designer:

a. **Designer** uses question list as a guide not a script during first 40 minutes of interview.
b. Designer then draws up agenda of how to spend remaining time.

Protocols of Traditional Rationality

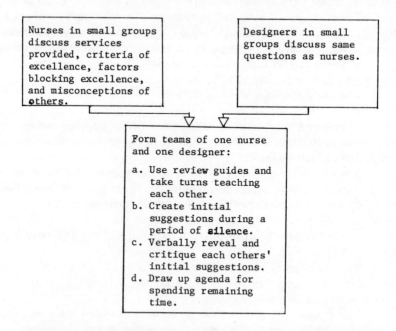

| | |
|---|---|
| Nurses in small groups discuss services provided, criteria of excellence, factors blocking excellence, and misconceptions of others. | Designers in small groups discuss same questions as nurses. |

Form teams of one nurse and one designer:

a. Use review guides and take turns teaching each other.
b. Create initial suggestions during a period of silence.
c. Verbally reveal and critique each others' initial suggestions.
d. Draw up agenda for spending remaining time.

The traditional teams reduced and limited nurse responsibility, whereas the alternative teams expanded it.

Nurses in the alternative teams understood the problems identified by the designers and the solutions to them, understood the system better, and learned more from the experience.

It is important to recognize both the lack of structure of this experiment and the subjectivity of the evaluations. Although Boland controlled for many potential intervening variables such as experience, skills, sex, and capabilities, these may still have influenced the evaluation interview because of its unstructured nature. The author recognized that different panels may have produced different evaluations. There is also some doubt whether the behavior of nurses in designer/nurse teams can be generalized to designer/manager teams in managerial contexts.

Having made these points, however, the originality of Boland's approach should be commended as should the careful design of the "unstructured" experiment and his significant findings in a field that needs much more research. It is a pity that this study did not also collect data on the relationships between nurses and designers in addition to evaluating the performance of teams operating in different modes. However, the findings listed, especially the last four, lead the authors to hypothesize that the alternative approach would create more positive relationships than would the traditional.

TURNOVER OF MIS STAFF

Proposition 8.6: Above a given level, turnover of MIS personnel adversely affects the success of system development and operation.

It has been suggested that concern regarding turnover rates of MIS implementors has been overstated. One survey found no difference between successful and unsuccessful companies with respect to systems personnel turnover. But even these authors note the importance of reducing turnover to acceptable levels (Garrity 1963; Willoughby 1972).

This optimistic view is, however, by no means universal, nor are all survey findings consistent. Very high rates of turnover are sometimes reported for MIS implementors and it has been claimed that the development of systems has suffered as a result. Some data are provided by Lehman's (1979) survey and are exhibited in Table 8.5. These data suggest turnover rates considerably higher for project managers and functional analysts than for technical staff, but even among the latter the rates are by no means negligible. Perhaps even more significant is that turnover rates on late projects are consistently higher than the mean; although it is unclear which is the cause and which the effect, this problem clearly warrants attention. As an aside, it may be mentioned that one case in Lehman's study, excluded from the data in the table, exhibited a uniform turnover rate of 200 percent in all categories!

TABLE 8.5

Personnel Turnover

| Position | Average (percent) | Late Projects (percent) |
|---|---|---|
| Project manager | 68 | 90 |
| Functional analyst | 60 | 97 |
| DP analyst | 20 | 28 |
| Programmer | 38 | 53 |
| Support librarian | 32 | 37 |
| Secretary | 63 | 79 |
| Administration | 33 | 40 |
| User representative | 32 | 39 |
| Other | 9 | 0 |

Source: John H. Lehman, "How Software Projects Are Really Managed," Datamation 25 (January 1979), p. 121. Reprinted with permission of DATAMATION® magazine, © Copyright by TECHNICAL PUBLISHING COMPANY, A DUN & BRADSTREET COMPANY, 1979—all rights reserved.

It has been noted that role dissatisfaction is common for information services staff; this, presumably, is one cause of high turnover. Such dissatisfaction has been attributed to the creation of specialized EDP departments that do not provide career paths into general management. In one survey of 100 computer programming department managers, 73 percent of the respondents indicated that they would eventually like to be promoted to higher managerial positions in which they would no longer be directly involved in software development; 96 percent of these same respondents believed that programmers cannot reasonably expect promotion to top positions in the organization. These data clearly indicate considerable grounds for frustration and probably apply to systems analysts as well as to programmers. Implementors at the technical level seem, therefore, to turn to other organizations for higher rank and salary. Several authors suggest that alienation may be reduced by developing career paths that permit easy interchange of personnel between information system and other departments (Brill 1974; Delaney 1977; Lucas 1973).

Pathak and Burton (1976) have conducted an empirical study aimed at identifying an efficient mix of incentives for data processing managers. A questionnaire was administered to 105 members of two North Carolina chapters of the Data Processing Management Association (DPMA). Seventy-six completed questionnaires were returned and analyzed.

In the questionnaire, the managers were asked to evaluate the financial incentives they receive, nonfinancial incentives, and the fulfillment of their needs. For nonfinancial needs, Pathak and Burton used Dubin's nonfinancial incentives (status pay, privilege pay, and power pay) and for needs they used a modified version of Maslow's hierarchy of needs. On each of these topics, the DP managers were asked to evaluate on a seven-point scale "How much is there now?" "How much should there be?" and "How important is this to me?" The first question measured the need fulfillment level; the difference between "should be" and "is now" measured the need deficiency level; the third question measured need importance.

In addition to incentive levels, overall job satisfaction was measured using Tausky's global index of job satisfaction. Tables 8.6 and 8.7 present Pearson product-moment correlation coefficients between job satisfaction and each work incentive and means of responses for work incentive evaluations.

Of the nine incentives studied, only three, security needs, self-actualization, and privilege pay, are effective in the sense that their fulfillment is positively and significantly correlated with satisfaction and their deficiency is negatively and significantly correlated with satisfaction. The other six incentives do not meet these criteria. To be relevant as motivators, incentives must, furthermore, be relatively important and relatively ungratified. Of the three effective incentives, two—security and self-actualization—are high both in importance and fulfillment, and therefore "gratified." Privilege pay was found to be low in both fulfillment and importance and therefore classifies as a "latent" motivator.

Pathak and Burton's study implies a high level of job satisfaction for data processing managers and, when compared with the turnover rates displayed above, raises some difficult questions. If DP managers are so satisfied, why is their turnover rate so high? The processes at work here clearly warrant further study.

TABLE 8.6

Correlations between Work Incentives and Job Satisfaction

(n = 76)

| Work Incentives | Need Fulfillment | Need Deficiency | Need Importance |
|---|---|---|---|
| Financial incentives | 0.0658 | -0.0119 | 0.2540[a] |
| | | | |
| Maslow's needs | | | |
| Security | 0.4256[b] | -0.3965[b] | -0.0330 |
| Social | 0.27592 | -0.1552 | 0.0712 |
| Esteem | 0.0153 | -0.1837[c] | -0.0880 |
| Autonomy | 0.0817 | -0.1836[c] | -0.2178[c] |
| Self-actualization | 0.5311[b] | -0.5045[b] | -0.2549[a] |
| | | | |
| Dubin's nonfinancial incentives | | | |
| Status pay | 0.673 | -0.0643 | 0.1049 |
| Privilege pay | 0.2047[d] | -0.2446[c] | 0.0196 |
| Power pay | 0.2339[c] | -0.0677 | 0.3823[b] |

[a]p < 0.01.
[b]p < 0.001.
[c]p < 0.05.
[d]p < 0.005.

Source: D. S. Pathak and G. E. Burton, "Shifting to the Human Side," Data Management 14 (December 1976): 23. Copyright DATA MANAGEMENT magazine. Data Processing Management Association. ALL RIGHTS RESERVED.

TABLE 8.7

Response Means for Need Fulfillment, Need Deficiency, and Need Importance

(n = 76)

| Work Incentives | Need Fulfillment | Need Deficiency | Need Importance |
|---|---|---|---|
| Financial incentives | 3.737 | 1.974 | 5.947 |
| Maslow's needs | | | |
| Security | 5.500 | 0.842 | 6.342 |
| Social | 5.224 | 0.487 | 5.342 |
| Esteem | 4.868 | 0.842 | 5.289 |
| Autonomy | 4.803 | 0.921 | 5.487 |
| Self-actualization | 4.891 | 1.234 | 6.111 |
| Dubin's nonfinancial incentives | | | |
| Status pay | 3.341 | 1.465 | 4.650 |
| Privilege pay | 4.316 | 0.868 | 4.868 |
| Power pay | 4.558 | 0.853 | 5.368 |

Source: D. S. Pathak and G. E. Burton, "Shifting to the Human Side," Data Management 14 (December 1976): 23. Copyright DATA MANAGEMENT magazine. Data Processing Management Association. ALL RIGHTS RESERVED.

## CAPABILITIES OF SYSTEM IMPLEMENTORS

The capabilities required of system implementors stem, of course, from the definitions of their jobs. There are a number of job categories, each with its particular demands, discussed below. A number of authors, however, have suggested some traits beneficial in all information system personnel; these tend, naturally, to be rather nonspecific and smack of motherhood and apple pie but are worth noting, nevertheless. Those capabilities considered generally useful include:

Training and talent, including design and programming talent (Dearden 1972; Emery 1969; Murdick and Ross 1972; Nolan and Knutsen 1974; Shults and Bruun 1974);

High competence and computer orientation (Gibson and Nolan 1974; Rubenstein et al. 1967; Singer 1969;

Experience in both the systems field and in the organization's operations (Emery 1969; Gibson and Nolan 1974; Townsend 1970); and

Knowledge of the process of management (Hayes and Nolan 1974; Murdick and Ross 1972).

Two surveys both found that the breadth and depth of technical skills in the systems staff, broad organizational perspective, and ability to communicate with nontechnical personnel all differentiated successful from unsuccessful MIS efforts.

Proposition 8.7: The better the fit between MIS executives' styles and the state of MIS, the greater the likelihood of success.

Proposition 8.8: The higher the level of managerial and interpersonal skills of MIS executives, the greater the likelihood of MIS project success.

In addition to the general capabilities listed in the previous section, some traits desirable specifically in information system supervisors have also been identified. These include:

Leadership and the ability to command respect and confidence in the organization (Cochran 1978; McKinsey 1968);

Political ability, experience, and judgment (Cochran 1978; Grayson 1973; Morgan and Soden 1973);

Personnel development skills—the ability to act as motivator, educator, and change agent (Cochran 1978; Diebold 1968; Gupta 1974; Heany 1972);

Management skills (<u>Financial Executive</u> 1974; Gupta 1974)
(failures to complete MIS development projects on time and within
budget are rampant and epitomize MIS executives' lack of management skills in planning, organization, and control) (Morgan and
Soden 1973); and

Appropriate philosophy (MIS developers have been categorized
by Morgan and Soden [1973] into five types: flamboyant conceptual-
izer, benign underachiever, tyrant, efficiency expert, and fast
tracker. In their view, each of these types is strong in some management activities and weak in others. Consequently, each of these
types fits a different stage of MIS maturity. Their experience is
that the type of architect employed by a company will directly affect
its ability to move from stage to stage as well as the time it spends
in any one state of development).

The view has been expressed, and fairly widely accepted, that
no person can possess all the special skills required in implementing MIS. The question that then arises is whether the chief implementor should possess primarily managerial skills or technical
skills. A number of pieces of evidence point to a consensus on the
primacy of managerial skills. First, this view is implicit in the
preceding lists of skills required of information system managers.
Second, Garrity's (1963) survey found that the computer manager
can function effectively with limited technical knowledge; however,
the systems managers in successful companies tend to have both
systems and operations experience. Third, the survey by Spaniol
and Smith (1976) indicates that practicing data processing managers
are aware of the need for additional management skills and are actively engaged in their acquisition (Dearden 1972; Diebold 1969;
<u>Financial Executive</u> 1974; Garrity 1963; Hammond 1974a; Hanold
1972; Heany 1972; Ransdell 1975; Spaniol and Smith 1976).

Spaniol and Smith mailed questionnaires to the members of
the Data Processing Management Association (DPMA) to survey the
need for continuing education among data processing managers.
Over 4,000 completed questionnaires were returned, a response
rate of 19.1 percent. Analysis of the responses indicated an eager-
ness for continuing education, primarily in the areas listed in Table
8.8. Of the ten areas of interest in that table, seven are general
management, personal development, or data processing management skills. At the time of the survey, 52 percent of respondents
were actively engaged in training to improve their managerial
skills.

TABLE 8.8

Perceived Need for Additional Training: Top Ten Subject
Areas Selected by DPMA Respondents

| Subject Area | Percent Selecting |
|---|---|
| Data communications | 55.6 |
| Data base concepts | 54.9 |
| Written communication | 48.8 |
| Verbal communication | 47.9 |
| DP management assessment | 47.9 |
| Speed reading | 47.2 |
| Telecommunications concepts | 44.7 |
| Cost-benefit analysis | 44.4 |
| Memory training | 43.2 |
| Development of DP standards | 40.6 |

Source: Roland Spaniol and Eugene Smith, "The DP Professional and Education: Preliminary Survey Results," Data Management 14 (August 1976): 30. Copyright DATA MANAGEMENT magazine, Data Processing Management Association. ALL RIGHTS
RESERVED.

Proposition 8.9: The better the ability to define
traits required of systems analysts and programmers and the better the controls established on their
performance, the greater the likelihood of MIS project success.

Very little work seems to have been done on formally establishing links between systems analyst capabilities and system success. Wofsey (1968) lists 25 traits posited as desirable by various
authors and organizations; these are exhibited in Table 8.9, in which
the authors have added two additional sources to the original seven.
Surprisingly, technical knowledge is not included in these lists. In
addition, complaints about the unresponsiveness of many systems
to users' real needs would seem to indicate that a knowledge of management processes is also necessary at this level; it appears only
once in the table.

Programmer performance is noted for extreme variability,
which has been attributed, among other things, to whim, the assump-

tion of implicit objectives, incompetence, and differences of programming style. A list of traits desired in programmers by a number of corporations has been compiled by the Bureau of Labor Statistics (Table 8.10). Although many people have expressed views on desired personality traits for MIS personnel and long lists of such traits are available, there is little evidence to support any of these conjectures and very little is known of the personality sets conducive to good performance of MIS jobs (Fisher 1969; Kernighan and Plauger 1974; Naur and Randell 1969; Schulman and Weinberg 1973; Willoughby 1972).

Some interesting, although not necessarily representative, data on desired educations for information systems staff were provided by a survey at Ford Motor Company. Table 8.11 exhibits the educational qualifications desired of MIS implementors by 21 systems managers questioned. For the positions listed, none of the respondents was interested in hiring anyone with less than a baccalaureate. Systems analysts and OR analysts are largely sought outside the population of computer science graduates. The respondents also had clear ideas about the kinds of additional educational backgrounds desired of candidates. These are exhibited in Table 8.12 and reflect the organizational needs of each manager. Managers in production organizations preferred engineering or science backgrounds; those in marketing organizations tended to prefer additional education in business. Comments by several managers that "past experience with Computer Sciences people had been unfavorable because the individuals had lacked any understanding about organizational disciplines such as Management and Accounting" underscores the emphasis on management traits (Roark 1976).

ORGANIZATION OF MIS IMPLEMENTORS

> Proposition 8.10: Matrix organization of MIS imple-
> mentors enhances the likelihood of MIS project
> success.

Traditionally, there have been two major forms of organization for information system implementors. The first is functional, with each individual assigned a clearly defined function such as programming or systems analysis. The second is project team or application, in which a team is responsible for all aspects of development and implementation or operation and with much less emphasis on clear-cut functional assignments. Sudden changes have been reported from one of these forms of organization to the other, usually when a project is in trouble, and both types of organization have been

## TABLE 8.9

### Desirable Characteristics for Systems Analysts

| Characteristic | Reference | | | | | | | | |
|---|---|---|---|---|---|---|---|---|---|
| | 1 | 2 | 3 | 4 | 5 | 6 | 7 | 8 | 9 |
| Logical ability | X | X | X | X | X | X | | | |
| Thoroughness | X | X | X | X | X | X | | | |
| Ability to work with others | X | X | | X | | X | X | | X |
| Resourcefulness | X | X | | X | | X | X | | |
| Imagination | X | X | | X | | X | | | |
| Oral ability | X | X | X | X | | | X | | |
| Abstract reasoning | | | X | | | | X | | |
| Emotional balance | X | | | X | | | X | | |
| Interest in analysis | X | | | X | | X | | | |
| Writing ability | X | X | | X | | X | | | |
| Curiosity | X | X | | | | | | | |
| Decisiveness | X | | | | | X | X | | |
| Empathy | X | | | | | X | | | |
| Mature judgment | | X | | X | | | | | |
| Practicality | X | X | | | | | | | |
| Ability to observe | | X | | | | | | | |
| Dislike of inefficiency | | X | | | | | | | |
| Initiative | | | X | | | | | | |
| Integrity | X | | | | | | | | |
| Intelligence | | X | | | | | | | |
| Interest in science and technology | | | | | | | X | | |

| | | |
|---|---|---|
| Numerical ability | | |
| Open-mindedness | X | |
| Selling ability | X | |
| Understanding of organizational functions | | X |
| Creativity | | X |
| Perception | | X |
| Ability to motivate people | | X |

1. "Army civilian career program for comptroller functional area." Department of the Army, Washington, D.C., Sept. 30, 1959, p. 60.

2. Administrative planning for business data automation. n.c., Sperry Rand Corp., 1958, pp. 12–13.

3. Ned Chapin, "An introduction to automatic computers," 2nd edition. (Princeton, N.J., Van Nostrand, 1963): 400.

4. Conversion planning manual. (n.c., Remington Rand UNIVAC, n.d.): 8.

5. Managing the ADP program. Management Science Training Institute, a Division of Diebold, New York, 1958, p.11.04.

6. Gordon L. Murray, Systems and methods appraisal, selected papers 1957. (n.c., Haskins and Sells, n.d.): 207.

7. Occupations in electronic data processing systems (Washington, D.C., U.S. Department of Labor, January 1959): 27.

8. William L. Ramsgard, "The Systems Analyst: Doctor of Business," Journal of Systems Management 25 (July 1974): 8–13.

9. John M. Nicholas, "Transactional Analysis for System Professionals," Journal of Systems Management 29 (October 1978): 6–11.

Source: Marvin M. Wofsey, Management of Automatic Data Processing (Washington, D.C.: Thompson, 1968). Adapted from Theodore C. Willoughby, "Staffing the MIS Function," Computing Surveys 4 (December 1972): 246.

# TABLE 8.10

## Desired Programmer Traits

| Trait | Number of Corporations Listing Trait |
|---|:---:|
| Understanding of underlying principles | 16 |
| Report-writing ability | 15 |
| Responsibility for planning | 15 |
| Adaptability to a variety of duties | 14 |
| Judgment based on quantity | 13 |
| Adaptability to precise standards | 13 |
| Judgment based on quality | 12 |
| Adaptability to deadlines, pressure | 12 |
| Observation | 12 |
| Rapid arithmetic | 11 |
| Knowledge of accounting | 11 |
| Knowledge of decimals, fractions | 11 |
| Adaptability for repetitive operations | 5 |
| Knowledge of calculus | 5 |
| Knowledge of theoretical mathematics | 4 |
| Rapid coordination | 0 |
| Rapid manipulation of small objects | 0 |

Source: U.S., Bureau of Labor Statistics, Bulletin 1276. Reprinted from Theodore C. Willoughby, "Staffing the MIS Function," Computing Surveys 4 (December 1972): 247.

TABLE 8.11

Desired Education for Ford Systems Recruits

| Category | Percentage of 1976 Recruits | | | |
| --- | --- | --- | --- | --- |
| | Bachelor | Masters, Computer Sciences | Masters, Other | Total |
| Programmers | 66 | 17 | 17 | 100 |
| Analyst-programmers | 44 | 28 | 28 | 100 |
| Systems analysts | 36 | 0 | 64 | 100 |
| OR analysts | 0 | 33 | 67 | 100 |
| Technical specialists | 0 | 50 | 50 | 100 |
| Total | 49 | 22 | 29 | 100 |

Source: Mayford L. Roark, "Information System Education: What Industry Thinks," Data Management 14 (June 1976): 26. Copyright DATA MANAGEMENT magazine. Data Processing Management Association. ALL RIGHTS RESERVED.

TABLE 8.12

Desired Additional Education for Ford Systems Recruits

| Category | Business Administration | Percentage of 1976 Projected Recruits | | | | |
| --- | --- | --- | --- | --- | --- | --- |
| | | Engineering | Sciences | Liberal Arts | No Preference | Total |
| Programmers | 40 | 13 | 21 | 5 | 21 | 100 |
| Analyst-programmers | 38 | 10 | 3 | | 49 | 100 |
| Systems analysts | 33 | 42 | 17 | | 21 | 100 |
| OR analysts | 100 | | | | | 100 |
| Technical specialists | 17 | 49 | 17 | | 17 | 100 |
| Total | 41 | 17 | 13 | 3 | 17 | 100 |

Source: Mayford L. Roark, "Information System Education: What Industry Thinks," Data Management 14 (June 1976): 26. Copyright DATA MANAGEMENT magazine. Data Processing Management Association. ALL RIGHTS RESERVED.

found in companies with successful computer programs (Ahituv and Hadass 1978; Gibson and Nolan 1974; McKinsey 1968; Scamell and Baugh 1975; Stuart 1968).

As yet, there has been very little empirical research, other than case studies, on the optimal form of organization for implementors. Lehman (1979) found that some form of project-related organization was overwhelmingly preferred, with only 2 of the 38 organizations choosing functional organization. The predominant approach, accounting for three of every five cases, was a matrix organization, in which implementors were assigned to project managers for the duration of the project. This study found an average of five teams per project, each team under a technical leader who reported to the project manager. The percentage of projects using each type of team is reproduced in Table 8.13. It has been suggested elsewhere that the best team size for effective communication between members is three (Lehman 1979; Scamell and Baugh 1975).

TABLE 8.13

Project Teams

| Type | Used (percent) |
| --- | --- |
| Programmer/analyst teams | 75 |
| Analyst teams | 20 |
| Programmer teams | 18 |
| Test/acceptance teams | 40 |
| Integration teams | 36 |
| Interface teams | 13 |

Source: John H. Lehman, "How Software Projects Are Really Managed," Datamation 25 (January 1979): 121. Reprinted with permission of DATAMATION® magazine, © Copyright by TECHNICAL PUBLISHING COMPANY, A DUN & BRADSTREET COMPANY, 1979—all rights reserved.

In his study of software projects, Lehman (1979) also investigated the locus of the development effort and related interfunctional assignments. He found that in about half the cases software development was carried out in the data processing organization with potential users or functional analysts seconded to the development team. In one-third of the projects, the user department employed functional analysts who presented system specifications to the development team. In the remaining 14 percent of the cases, implementors were assigned to a development team within the user organization. The cross-functional assignments necessitated by mixed user-implementor teams clearly contain potential for both cooperation and conflict that have been discussed above and are taken up again in Chapter 9.

## TOP MANAGEMENT-IMPLEMENTOR RELATIONS

Problems in the relationships between top managers and MIS executives seem to center around issues of control and communications.

> Proposition 8.11: The more rigorous the controls established by top management over MIS staff, the greater the likelihood of success of MIS projects.

Problems between top management and implementors seem to originate mainly in the difficulty management encounters in attempting to control the information system function. It has been indicated earlier in this chapter that the selection process for MIS executives is particularly ineffective. Once an MIS chief is selected, it is only with great difficulty that top management can extract performance commitments from that person. Finally, there is a lack of standards against which corporate management and MIS executives can evaluate their control procedures. Thus, it is very hard to manage computer professionals and this must lead to conflict (Lucas 1973; Morgan and Soden 1973).

> Proposition 8.12: The better the communications between top management and MIS staff, the greater the likelihood of MIS project success.

In addition to control problems, there are communications problems between implementors and top executives. On the one hand, an MIS director may have difficulty influencing top management and convincing them of the importance of MIS. On the other hand, MIS executives may have trouble understanding management goals. The relative importance placed by information staff on efficient use of machine time versus efficient use of management time is one trade-off that seems to cause particular difficulty (Carlson 1967; Diebold 1969; Emery 1973).

Communications problems between top management and information staff may be critical because the relationship of the MIS manager with top management must be strong enough to permit the manager to weather inevitable conflicts with users and to permit adoption of policies that will permit efficient use of the information system. It has been suggested that outside consultants may be effective not so much because of their capabilities but because of their ease of access to top management; perhaps internal information management must have such access if it is to be effective (Argyris 1971; Gibson and Nolan 1974; Sass 1975).

CONCLUSION

Given the centrality of MIS implementors to the process of information system development, it is surprising that so little research has been devoted to them. Some of the areas in which the need is most pressing are:

Devising effective selection criteria for MIS staff and executives;

Identifying reasons for high turnover of MIS personnel and suggesting solutions, whether they be appropriate career paths or other incentives;

Determining the educational and personal qualifications that make for the best implementors and devising appropriate training programs;

Analysis of the interaction of organizational modes for implementors with success and suggestion and examination of additional alternatives; and

Study of the relationships between implementors and top executives and their effects on the success and failure of MIS and MIS projects.

# 9

## USERS OF MIS

> I said it in Hebrew—I said it in Dutch—
> I said it in German and Greek;
> But I wholly forgot (and it vexes me much)
> That English is what you speak!
> Lewis Carroll, The Hunting of the Snark

The users of MIS are the last element in the behavioral subsystem; executives and implementors having already been discussed. Since the authors define the success of an informational system in terms of its use, the users clearly become a critical element. In fact, the raison d'etre of all other elements of MIS is to elicit a positive response from users. It is therefore important to understand the way users interface with the other elements, especially since these interfaces are by no means straightforward.

The users of MIS are those members of the organization to whom outputs of systems are addressed for decision-making purposes. By this definition, not all members of the organization who come into contact with MIS are necessarily users. Clerical or other operating personnel who receive output for operational purposes do not fall within this definition, nor do personnel who prepare data or put them into the systems but do not use output for decision making.

The variables describing the user community are divided for the purposes of this discussion into two main groups. The first group consists of variables that can be considered in relative isolation from one another; namely, user requirements, the ranks of users, user motivation, and user personality. The remaining variables form a complex subsystem that interrelates users with MIS. Included in this group are user attitudes, user involvement, conflict, user education, role definition, and the degree of project formalization. This subsystem must be dealt with as a whole.

USER REQUIREMENTS

Proposition 9.1: The lower the level of management, the more easily information needs can be identified.

Proposition 9.2: The more easily management needs for information can be accurately defined in advance, the greater the likelihood of success.

Many authorities suggest that managers' real needs for information are either ad hoc or so complex as to defy definition by even the most skillful managers. Cases are cited in which, when attempts were made to identify management needs, few top managers could tell what kind of information or models they wanted or what they would do with them if they had them. This state of affairs is further complicated by hesitancy on the part of some managers to formally identify the criteria they wish to be used in decision making; an extreme position even holds that managers do not really know what decisions they should be making or how to make them (Aron 1969; Brady 1967; Hayes and Nolan 1974; Head 1970, Kennedy and Mahapatra 1975). A list of problems observed during case studies of a number of implementations is presented by Carlson et al. (1977).

At first reading, there is something of a paradox in the literature on this topic. Despite the contentions mentioned in the preceding paragraph, it is also widely assumed that users' information needs should be defined in advance; in fact, it is difficult to imagine systems being built without some such prior definition. These seemingly inconsistent viewpoints can be at least partly reconciled by recourse to the differentiation of decisions by degrees of structure and routine. At the structured decision end of the continuum, which generally coincides with lower levels of management, information needs should be amenable to prior definition, and the normative injunction to do so is quite valid. At the unstructured end, which frequently characterizes top management decision making, such prior definition is much more difficult and may not be feasible (Kennedy and Mahapatra 1975; Simon 1977). Since the number of systems at the unstructured end of the scale is growing, this problem has become increasingly evident and has even given birth to that subspecialization of MIS known as Decision Support Systems (DSS).

To the extent that uncertainties relate to the form in which information is to be presented, rather than to its content, the solutions proposed generally suggest maximal flexibility for users to adapt systems to their own needs and user involvement in iterative experiments in which the requirements are successively refined by empirical observation and feedback from users until a consensus is achieved (Carlson 1974; Kennedy and Mahapatra 1975; King and Cleland 1975; Shio 1977; Smith 1977). The paper by Boland (1978) discussed in Chapter 8 explores empirically how such interactions are best structured.

Two basic methods are suggested for information analysis (defining information requirements); these have been identified as asking users what information they need and telling them (Miller 1964). This distinction seems to parallel that made between data analysis and decision analysis (Munro 1978; Munro and Davis 1977). Asking users about information requirements presumes that managers know what decisions they are to make and how they will make them; all that remains to be done is to obtain from them their information needs. This method proceeds by analyzing the data available and tracing its current and potential uses in decision making. Telling users what information they need entails examining the decision process, validating or improving it, then providing the information needed to apply the decision rules adopted. Data analysis is equivalent, at the tactical level, to the strategic bottom-up approach to system development; decision analysis is the tactical equivalent to a top-down strategy.

Empirical research in this area has been performed by Munro and Davis (1977). Their study was designed to compare the effectiveness of data analysis and decision analysis in determining management information needs. The criterion of effectiveness was the perceptions of users of the value of information obtained by each of the methods. An identical set of four different decision situations was analyzed in each of four colleges. In each college, two of the situations were analyzed by data analysis and the other two by decision analysis. The decision types, functional areas, and specific problems are exhibited in Table 9.1. Following the analyses, managers evaluated the information statement requirements for their own areas of responsibility; each manager evaluated the statements obtained from all four participating colleges for that manager's decision problem. The evaluation was by means of semantic differentials.

The hypotheses, expectations, and findings of Munro and Davis are summarized in Table 9.2. The authors believe that this study is a good example of the type of work that needs to be done. Of particular interest in this study is that the researchers state their prior expectations on some of the hypotheses, which turned out to be different from the results actually obtained. This is significant because their expectations reflected the conventional wisdom in the field, as do so many of the writings on MIS. Even in those cases where the hypotheses are intuitively obvious, as in this case, intuition may frequently vary from the findings of empirical research. That the results refute some of the "common sense" expectations emphasises the need for research in the entire discipline, criticism of the seeming triviality of some of the hypotheses notwithstanding.

Munro and Davis' study also relates to the areas in which MIS are applied. A proposition concerning the effects of the decision areas to which MIS are applied is specified in the chapter on MIS structure.

TABLE 9.1

Decision Situations Analyzed for
Information Requirements

| Decision Type | Functional Area One (Academic Area) | Functional Area Two (Administrative Area) |
|---|---|---|
| Programmed | Determining the academic standing of students with low performance. | Investing short-term surplus funds. |
| Nonprogrammed | Advising faculty as to the appropriate action to be taken with regard to a proposed new innovative academic program. | Projecting enrollment for the coming year. (Time of the decision is early spring.) |

Source: Reprinted by special permission from the MIS Quarterly, from "Determining Management Information Needs: A Comparison of Methods," by M. C. Munro and G. B. Davis, in Volume 1, Number 2, published in 1977. Copyright 1977 by the Society for Management Information Systems and the Management Information Systems Research Center.

TABLE 9.2

Munro and Davis's Study of Information Requirement Analysis:
Hypotheses, Expectations, and Findings

| Hypotheses | Expectations | Findings |
|---|---|---|
| **Methods hypothesis**<br>The perceived value of the information generated by the decision analysis method is not significantly different from that generated by the data analysis method. | | Not rejected.<br>Neither method perceived as generating significantly more valuable information than the other. |
| **Functional areas hypothesis**<br>The perceived value of information generated within one functional area is not significantly different from that generated within another functional area. | | Rejected at 0.86 level.<br>The value of information produced is perceived as being significantly different in different functional areas. |
| **Functional areas/methods interaction**<br>There is no significant interaction, in terms of the perceived value of information between the information analysis methods used and the functional areas in which they are used. | | Not rejected.<br>The perceived value of information produced by a method does not depend on the functional area in which the method is applied. |

| Hypothesis | Predicted | Result |
|---|---|---|
| **Decision types hypothesis** The perceived value of information generated from analysis of a programmed decision is not significantly different from that generated from analysis of a nonprogrammed decision. | Decision analysis and data analysis would both perform better on programmed decisions than on nonprogrammed ones. | Rejected at 0.91 level. Both techniques produce higher value information on nonprogrammed than on programmed decisions. |
| **Decision types/methods interaction hypothesis** There is no significant interaction, in terms of the perceived value of information between the information analysis methods used and the decision types in which they are used. | For highly structured decisions, since the requirements are obvious, neither approach would generate information that would be perceived as more valuable than that generated by the other method. | Rejected at 0.83 level. The performance results of data analysis on programmed decisions was quite low relative to the performance results of either decision analysis or data analysis on nonprogrammed decisions. There is an interaction between the decision type and method used. |

Source: Adapted by special permission from the MIS Quarterly, from "Determining Management Information Needs: A Comparison of Methods," by M. C. Munro and G. B. Davis, in Volume 1, Number 2, published in 1977. Copyright 1977 by the Society for Management Information Systems and the Management Information Systems Research Center.

USER RANK

> Proposition 9.3: The higher the level of management
> interfacing with it directly, the more successful a
> system.

At least four different surveys, altogether covering hundreds
of corporations, have examined the levels of management using computer information systems (Brady 1967; Ference and Uretsky 1976;
Grindlay and Cummer 1973; Whisler 1970). Not one of these surveys
found any instance of chief executive officers using MIS in person.
One additional survey of 55 companies found two cases of presidents
personally interacting with a computer system (Boulden 1971). In
fact, top management rarely receives output of any kind directly
from a computer. But cases have been identified of vice-presidents
dealing directly with MIS. The major effect of computers on top
management seems to be indirect, affecting the ways in which middle management contributes to top management decision making
(Head 1970; Higgins and Finn 1976; Mintzberg 1976; Shio 1977).

The reason for so little direct use of MIS by top management
is implicit in the preceding discussion of information requirements.
Since top management decision making is seldom routine and is
highly unstructured, systems to serve this level of management are
the most difficult to define and construct. It is natural, therefore,
that MIS to serve top management directly should often be the last to
be implemented. Thus, the level of management using MIS directly
may be a good additional criterion of success and a refinement of
the criterion of general level of use in the organization as a whole.

USER PERSONALITY

Following the discussion of two fairly clear issues affecting the
use of MIS, the authors now enter what is probably one of the most
complex and also one of the most significant areas—the effect of
user personality on the use of MIS. One highly regarded psycholo-
gist, H. J. Eysenck, has defined personality as follows:

> Personality is the more or less stable and enduring
> organization of a person's character, temperament,
> intellect, and physique, which determines his unique
> adjustment to the environment. Character denotes a
> person's . . . system of conative behavior ("will");
> Temperament, his . . . system of affective behavior
> ("emotion"); Intellect, his . . . system of cognitive

behavior ("intelligence"); Physique, his . . . system
of bodily configuration and neuroendocrine endowment.*

Not all the dimensions of personality are significantly relevant to a
study of MIS; those that are, and have been studied, are intellect
and some aspects of temperament. The authors shall refer to these
as the cognitive and noncognitive aspects, respectively, of user
personality interaction with MIS.

The topic of user personality variables of MIS is close to that
of MIS structure. Thus, many studies have implications for both
these areas. Several of the studies described here are of this nature. In those cases, only the material relating directly to this
chapter is included; more complete description of these studies are
to be found in the chapter on structure of MIS.

> Proposition 9.4: Certain noncognitive personality sets
> induce more effective use of MIS and increase the like-
> lihood of success.

There is probably a large number of noncognitive personality
traits that affect MIS use by managers. As only the first tentative
steps have been taken in studying this area, it is yet too early even
to attempt to list the relevant characteristics. Those that have so
far received attention are evaluative defensiveness, anxiety, and
motivation (achievement motivation [need achievement] and reward
motivation).

Informal definitions of these terms are as follows:

Evaluative defensiveness is the employment of distorted self-
evaluation as a mechanism of ego defense;

Anxiety is a feeling of unease that may motivate behavior.
Anxiety may have one of two effects: facilitating, when it promotes
greater efforts to achieve a goal, uncertainty about whose attainment generated the anxiety; and debilitating, when the level of
anxiety is such that efforts to achieve the goal are reduced or aban-
doned;

Motivation is a characteristic that induces individuals to pur-
sue goals in the face of difficulty or resistance;

Need achievement is motivation arising from a felt need to
complete, once undertaken, a task; and

---

*H. J. Eysenck, The Structure of Human Personality, 2d ed.
(London: Methuen, 1960), p. 2.

Reward motivation is motivation arising from an anticipation of rewards associated with task completion.

Of the two studies related directly to this hypothesis, the more ambitious is that of Wynne and Dickson (1975), who examined the effects of experienced managers in an experimental human-machine decision-system simulation. This study proposed five hypotheses. Three naive hypotheses stated that people with low evaluative defensiveness, high need-achievement, and high facilitating anxiety, each considered separately, would exhibit better performance; these were naive hypotheses in the sense that they ignored expected interactions between the independent variables. These hypotheses we re rejected.

Two additional hypotheses, which recognized variable interactions, were as follows:

4. Higher indicated levels of need-achievement were perhaps excessive [given the absolutely high need-achievement to be expected in this group of subjects] and if so would serve, especially when coexistent with high anxiety, to lower criterion performance.

5. The previously hypothesized relationship between low evaluative defensiveness and better performance would be mediated, as indicated above by the two measures of anxiety.* [P. 33]

The findings concerning these last two hypotheses are exhibited in Tables 9.3 and 9.4 and indicate strong relationships between personality, defined by a number of variables, and performance. The data are interpreted by the authors of the study as follows:

1. Better criterion performance was associated with:
   a. need-achievement levels which were modest relative to the group's mean level.
   b. lower evaluative defensiveness, even at higher levels of need-achievement, especially when coupled with acknowledged high levels of debilitating anxiety.

---

*Bayard E. Wynne and Gary W. Dickson. "Experienced Managers' Performance in Experimental Man-Machine Decision System Simulation." Academy of Management Journal 18 (March 1975), p. 33. Reprinted by permission.

TABLE 9.3

Analysis of Variance Test: Need-Achievement versus Total Anxiety, Noting Evaluative Defensiveness

| Joint Levels of | | Sample Size | Mean Performance | F-test Conclusions[1] | Evaluative Defensiveness Mean Value[2] |
| Need Achievement | Total Anxiety | | | | |
| --- | --- | --- | --- | --- | --- |
| Low | Low | 6 | 7.480 | | 11.17 |
| Low | High | 6 | 7.260 | $F_{(1,21)} = 6.52$ | 15.83 |
| High | Low | 6 | 6.450 | | 17.67 |
| High | High | 6 | 5.977 | $\hat{\alpha}_c \simeq 0.007$ | 20.83 |

[1]Significance noted is primarily because of the need achievement dichotomy, but the performance loss with high anxiety is repeated.

[2]These values correlate with mean performance at $-0.988$ ($\hat{\alpha}_c \simeq 0.01+$).

Source: Bayard E. Wynne and Gary W. Dickson, "Experienced Managers' Performance in Experimental Man-Machine Decision System Simulation," Academy of Management Journal 18 (March 1975): 35. Reprinted by permission.

## TABLE 9.4

Analysis of Variance Test: Debilitating versus Facilitating Anxiety, Noting Evaluative Defensiveness

| Expected Level of Deception | Joint Levels of Achievement Anxiety | | Sample Size | Mean Performance | F-test Conclusions | Evaluative Defensiveness Mean Value[1] |
| --- | --- | --- | --- | --- | --- | --- |
| | Debilitating | Facilitating | | | | |
| Lowest | High | Low | 6 | 7.867 | $F_{(3, 20)} = 3.995$ | 12.67 |
| Low | Medium | Medium | 6 | 6.890 | | 13.67 |
| High | Low | High | 6 | 6.570 | | 18.83 |
| Mixed | (High) or (Low) | (High) (Low) | 6 | 5.843 | $\hat{\alpha}_c \simeq 0.023$ | 20.33 |

[1]These values correlate with mean performance at $-0.899$ ($\hat{\alpha}_c \simeq 0.05+$).

Source: Bayard E. Wynne and Gary W. Dickson, "Experienced Managers' Performance in Experimental Man-Machine Decision System Simulation," Academy of Management Journal 18 (March 1975): 35. Reprinted by permission.

2. Poorer criterion performance was associated with:
   a. relatively high need-achievement levels.
   b. claimed higher ratios of facilitating and debilitating anxiety in conjunction with greater evaluative defensiveness.* [P. 36]

In a different study, by Chervany and Dickson (1974), subjects using summary data in a laboratory achieved better results than did those using detailed raw data. Therefore, it can be inferred that the summary data were "better," but these same subjects took longer to reach their decisions and had less confidence in the results. One might speculate, therefore, that the anxiety generated by use of the summary data had a positive effect on performance.

A prevalent opinion implies that a good system, in itself, will provide motivation for use; users will be working with better data in more useful forms and this will increase their confidence. But, since using better systems seems to require more effort of users and also seems to raise their anxiety levels, it is not at all clear that there will be greater use. This may explain a number of surveys that found low motivation on the part of managers to use information systems (Grindlay and Cummer 1973; Guthrie 1974). Perhaps the payoffs to use need to be more direct than those provided by better performance; in one experiment, paid subjects realized significantly greater profits and used more decision time than did unpaid subjects (Mock 1973).

An additional subjective personality factor that has not yet been studied systematically, but has received considerable comment in the literature, is status perception. High-level management seems to have some reservations about interfacing directly with computer systems, especially in the presence of their peers, since this may be interpreted as a loss of intuitive skills with consequent loss of status. Some managers perceive MIS as a threat to their control over the work environment (Alexander 1969; Argyris 1971; Hayes and Nolan 1974).

Although much more research is needed in this field before any prescriptive statements can be responsibly made, what does seem to be clear is that noncognitive personality factors have a considerable effect on the use of MIS. It is possible that the practical payoffs to research in this area are much higher than in the more technical areas of MIS construction.

---

*Wynn and Dickson, "Experienced Managers' Performance," p. 36.

Proposition 9.5: Users with different cognitive styles will react differently to a given MIS, thus affecting the likelihood of success.

The proposition on noncognitive personality attributes of managers implies that these attributes affect use in general, irrespective of the particular MIS involved. The proposition on cognitive styles has to do with the interaction between cognitive styles of users and particular systems.

There is a definition of cognitive styles commonly accepted in the lteratures on management in general and on information systems in particular, derived from the Jungian typology of personality. This typology is based on four human cognitive functions: sensation, thinking, feeling, and intuition (Jung 1971):

Under sensation I include all perceptions by means of the sense organs: by thinking I mean the function of intellectual cognition and the forming of logical conclusions; feeling is a function of subjective valuation; intitution I take as perception by way of the unconscious, or perception of unconscious contents.* [P. 518]

Each individual exhibits all of these characteristics to some degree and is typified by which of them habitually predominate. But these characteristics are not really all independent. As Jung (1971) noted:

When we think, it is in order to judge or reach a conclusion, and when we feel it is in order to attach a proper value to something. Sensation and intuition, on the other hand, are perceptive functions—they make us aware of what is happening but do not interpret or evaluate it.† [P. 539]

Thus, thinking and feeling both have to do with evaluation, and if one mode is employed at a given time, the other is ruled out. The degree to which each is employed determines a point on the continuum between thinking only and feeling only. Similarly, sensation

---

*The Collected Works of C. G. Jung, trans. R.F.C. Hull, Bollingen Series XX, Vol. 6: Psychological Types, copyright © 1971 by Princeton University Press, p. 518.
†The Collected Works of C. G. Jung, p. 539.

and intuition refer to modes of perception, with a continuum of combinations between the extremes. Thus, one can be thought of as typified by one's attributes in a two-dimensional perception/ evaluation space.

A number of studies have adopted this theory of cognitive style; in fact, it is one of the few areas of MIS research in which some degree of consistency has been achieved. Mason and Mitroff (1973) employed this typology to explicate their definition of an information system. They posited that the various cognitive styles would require different types of information systems. McKenney and Keen (1974) showed empirically that some tasks are more appropriate to given cognitive styles than are others, thus supporting Mason and Mitroff's thesis. They also cite a study by Botkin that showed that managers with different cognitive styles use information systems in different ways. Benbasat and Schroeder found that the number of reports requested by subjects in an experiment varied with their cognitive styles (Benbasat and Schroeder 1977).

An additional significant study in this area is that of Bariff and Lusk (1977). Their study replicated previous findings of the identifiability of cognitive styles and drew some normative conclusions that refer to one of the present authors' previous variables— user requirement definition. They used psychological tests that measured facets of users' cognitive styles in the design of user reports. Frequency of the reports and their level of aggregation were the main design variables. This field study was performed in a community nursing service in a large eastern city, and involved 17 individuals identified as the organization's decision network.

In Bariff and Lusk's study, two behavioral variables were measured: cognitive style and implementation apprehension. The operationalization of these variables and the tests used are exhibited in Table 9.5.*

Based upon hierarchical level in the organization, the 17 users involved were divided into two groups: supervisors and administrators. Bariff and Lusk hypothesized that supervisors have different

---

*The psychological tests used in the Bariff and Lusk study are as follows: for Cognitive Style, Watkin Embedded Figures Test, Bieri Cognitive Complexity Test and Category Width*; for Resistance to Change, F-Scale*, Dogmatism* and Flexibility*; for Defense Mechanisms, Defense Mechanism Inventory (DMI); for Stress Level, Taylor's Manifest Anxiety Scale* and Tolerance of Ambiguity*. An Extroversion Test* was also administered. Tests marked with asterisks were later selected as discriminant variables.

cognitive style and implementation apprehension than do administrators. This was tested by screening the test variables, stepwise. Seven of the variables were selected as discriminant variables.

TABLE 9.5

Behavioral Variables, Factors, and Measures Used
in the Bariff and Lusk Study

| Behavioral Variable | Factor | Measure |
|---|---|---|
| Cognitive style | Cognitive complexity | Differentiation/ integration |
| | Field independence-dependence | |
| | Thinking mode | |
| | Cognitive controls | |
| Implementation-apprehension | Resistance to change | Dogmatism scale |
| | Defense mechanisms | Ego defense |
| | Stress level | Manifest anxiety |
| | | Tolerance of ambiguity |

Source: Adapted by permission from M. L. Bariff and E. J. Lusk, "Cognitive and Personality Tests for the Design of Management Information Systems," Management Science Volume 23, Number 8, pp. 822-823 (April 1977), Copyright (1977) The Institute of Management Sciences.

The study showed that the two groups were low-analytic in comparison with national norms, and that the scores on the implementation apprehension measures (flexibility, anxiety, and tolerance of ambiguity) were more "benevolent" than the norms. From these findings, Bariff and Lusk concluded that reports should be designed with minimal complexity (that is, raw and disaggregated data and high frequency) and that anxiety and resistance to change would not interfere with the implementation stage.

Two subsequent tests over a period of three months validated these findings. The users were asked to evaluate three sets of reports (different each time) varying in data content, format, and length. The user evaluations of readability, completeness of data, ability to locate and extract data, and amount of detail all supported Bariff and Lusk's hypothesis. Based on this experience, Bariff and Lusk also suggested that psychological tests are more useful (and sometimes more economical) in designing MIS reports than are interviews, and are an indicator of user acceptance of the reports.

This is clearly a research area of great potential value. Bariff and Lusk's second independent variable—implementation apprehension—is closely connected with user attitudes, and so leads into the next subsystem of variables to be discussed.

## ATTITUDES, INVOLVEMENT, AND RELATIONSHIPS

There is a long and rather complicated chain of interactions between users, implementors, and their behaviors, which culminates in the establishment of user attitudes toward MIS. These attitudes play a significant role in determining the success and failure of MIS. The establishment of attitudes is treated here as a process that parallels the process of MIS development. Potential users enter the process with prior attitudes toward MIS. These attitudes undergo change as a result of experiences or involvement in the development and use of a system. Thus, posterior attitudes are derived from the effects of the experience on prior attitudes. These effects of experience are modulated by a number of factors that can contribute to the quality of the experience. The following discussion examines the variables affecting this evolution of users' attitudes.

### Prior Attitudes

Proposition 9.6: The greater the perceived need for MIS and the lower the level of apprehension about them, the greater the likelihood of success.

Prior attitudes toward MIS are molded by the felt need for such systems and by anticipations of their effects. The organizational environment has also been considered as a determinant of user attitudes. One study concludes that this environment, rather than the backgrounds of individual managers, is the key factor in attitude formation (Guthrie 1974). Another study found no consistent relationship between situational factors and use (Lucas 1975b). Thus, this is still an unresolved issue.

Surveys of both top and middle management indicate that the felt need for MIS development is rather low (Adams and Schroeder 1973; Guthrie 1974). This could be either because managers are satisfied with the systems they have or because they do not believe that formal systems can help them with their unstructured tasks or perhaps because their appreciation of such systems is too low.

The evidence on anticipated effects of MIS is not at all conclusive. Guthrie (1974) found no support for the idea that managers are apprehensive about MIS. In the particular situation studied by Bariff and Lusk (1977) no evidence was found that anxiety or change resistance would impair implementation. Grindlay and Cummer (1973), however, found a pervasive concern among managers for the effects of MIS on the people in the organization, attaining in some cases the proportions of a fear among managers of loss of direct person-to-person contact with fellow managers and employees. It has even been reported that middle managers at the staff level have recurring nightmares about being displaced by a computer. Such a situation may create an atmosphere conducive to rumor or false information that fosters negative attitudes and resistance to change and innovation.

Prior attitudes are affected by a number of personal and situational factors. These were the subject of a report by Gibson (1975). Gibson's study shows that prior attitudes are determined not only by situational factors but that these are mediated by personal variables. The case history of Gibson's research project, in addition to providing some insight into the personal determinants of attitudes, also further illuminates the problem of information requirement definition. The purpose of this study was originally to assist implementing a decision-support computer model for a medium-sized bank in New England and to observe, record, and analyze events and behavior during this process. The specific problem was to select sites for branch banks.

In the early phases of the project, Gibson and his associates discovered that the decision-making process in the bank was much less structured and clear cut than some employees claimed; the researchers therefore instructed the model developers to design a simulation of branch operations, rather than a straightforward modeling of the formal decision process.

A delay in development of the model forced Gibson to abandon testing of the original hypotheses on implementation of a model in an organization. Instead, he turned to investigating the social and political interactions within the bank. To this end, a questionnaire was administered to a stratified random sample of 52 officers (out of 130); it dealt with personal and work history and attitudes toward banking and the use of computers. The results of this survey generally confirmed that there were two informal but distinct "coalitions" among the employees, which he dubbed "bankers" and "marketers." The former were more conservative, cautious, and resistant to computer operations. Age, years in the bank, education, and participation in an in-house orientation program were found to be the best predictors of attitudes. Some illustrative data are exhibited in Table 9.6.

Conclusions drawn from this work were that the personal interactions within the bank (or any organization) are extremely pertinent to successful implementation of a computer system; that decision making is often "political and even idiosyncratic" in nature; that mutual involvement is important for success; and, most important for the current discussion, that the way employees perceive the organization and their role (that is, their attitudes) affect their behavior.

In the conception of the authors of this book, the attitudes of users prior to a system development cycle are modified by their experiences during development and subsequent use of the system. The elements of this experience are collected under the heading "involvement." Before presenting propositions on the aspects of posterior attitude formation, it may be useful to present the findings of two studies by Lucas that touch on all the elements of this topic.

The first study reported by Lucas is of a field investigation of the factors related to favorable user attitudes toward computer operations (Lucas 1974a). He hypothesized that perceived high quality of computer service, perceived management support, involvement in computer system design, and contact with the computer department would be associated with favorable perceived computer potential and attitudes toward MIS staff.

Data were gathered from six companies by a Likert-type attitude questionnaire administered to 683 users in positions ranging from clerk to vice-president. Table 9.7 summarizes the findings relating to this hypothesis. Clearly, users' attitudes toward information systems are affected by the quality of their experience with them. This study by Lucas also examined the effects of employing external consultants (a topic included in Chapter 8, where Lucas's findings on that subject are also mentioned).

Lucas's second field study focused on three questions: What variables are associated with high performance? What variables are associated with the use of an information system? and How is the use of an information system related to performance? (Lucas 1975b). He postulated that use of an information system, U, is given by:

$$U = f(P, S, I, D, A)$$

TABLE 9.6

Illustrative Items Related to Attitudes of Coalitions

| Item | Predicted | Mean Scores of Groups | | |
|---|---|---|---|---|
| | | "Bankers" (n = 10) | Middle (n – 31) | "Marketers" (n = 11) |
| When it comes to using computers in this bank, a little knowledge is a dangerous thing. | B>Mid>Mkt | 5.0 | 4.5 | 3.0 |
| Computers are at their best when used for routine operations. | B>Mid>Mkt | 4.1 | 3.5 | 2.6 |
| In the face of competition from other banks, we should expect considerable loyalty from our commercial customers. | B>Mid>Mkt | 4.8 | 3.0 | 2.6 |
| This organization is not a good place to work. | Mkt>Mid>B | 1.5 | 2.0 | 2.4 |

Note: Each item was rated on a scale from 1, "strongly disagree," to 7, "strongly agree."

Source: Reprinted by permission of the publisher from Chapter 4. "A Methodology for Implementation Research," by Cyrus F. Gibson in Implementing Operations Research/Management Science, Randall L. Schultz and Dennis P. Slevin (eds.), p. 62. Copyright 1975 by Elsevier North Holland, Inc.

where   P = performance
        S = situational factors
        I = personal factors
        D = decision style
        A = attitudes and perceptions,
and that performance, P, is given by:

$$P = f(S, I, D, U).$$

TABLE 9.7

Correlations between Key Variables

| Variable | Computer Potential[a] | Attitudes toward EDP Staff[a] |
|---|---|---|
| Perceived quality of EDP service | 0.50 | 0.40 |
| Perceived management support | 0.29 | 0.34 |
| Involvement in designing systems | 0.22 | NS[b] |
| Week's contact with EDP | NS[b] | NS[b] |

[a]Pearson Correlation significant at the 0.01 level.
[b]Not significant.
Source: Reprinted from "Measuring Employee Reactions to Computer Operations" by Henry C. Lucas, Jr. SLOAN MANAGE-MENT REVIEW, Vol. 15, No. 3, pp. 59-67, by permission of the publisher. Copyright © 1974 by the Sloan Management Review Association. All rights reserved.

The study was conducted in the sales force of three divisions of a major manufacturer of ready-to-wear clothing and related to the information system that served the sales force—primarily a monthly report. Operationalizations of the variables and sources of data are exhibited in Table 9.8. Conclusions were based on analysis of the data from computer files, personnel records, and questionnaires completed by 316 salesmen and 82 account executives—about 90 percent of the 439-member sales force. Stepwise, multiple regression was used to predict performance and use.

The analysis showed that all use variables were included in the regression as possible predictors of performance of account executives but not of salesmen. Situational factors proved to be good

## TABLE 9.8

### Variables in the Study

| Variable Class | | Variables | Source |
|---|---|---|---|
| Performance | P1 | Total dollar bookings, 1973 season | Computer files |
| Situational | S1 | Number of accounts | Computer files |
| | S2 | Number of buying entities (approximate) | Computer files |
| | S3 | Length of time in present territory (months) | Questionnaire |
| | S4 | Length of time in present position (months) | Questionnaire |
| Personal | I1 | Age | Personnel records |
| | I2 | Education | Personnel records |
| Use of system | U1 | Working with customer in store | Questionnaire |
| | U2 | Detailed analysis of buying entity/account | Questionnaire |
| | U3 | Overall progress | Questionnaire |
| | U4 | Summary this year versus last | Questionnaire |
| | U5 | Planning | Questionnaire |
| | U6 | Cancellations | Questionnaire |
| Decision style | D1 | Records orientation— keep own item records | Questionnaire |
| | D2 | Calculations performed with sales report data | Questionnaire |
| Attitudes and perceptions | A1 | Quality of output | Questionnaire |
| | A2 | Computer potential | Questionnaire |
| | A3 | Management computer support | Questionnaire |

Source: Reprinted by permission from Henry C. Lucas, Jr., "Performance and the Use of an Information System," Management Science, Volume 21, Number 8 (April 1975), p. 912. Copyright (1975) The Institute of Management Sciences.

indicators of performance, especially $S_1$ and $S_2$, both indicating the number of customers. Low performance was also found to predict use of the system, as Lucas anticipated, although the relationship was a weak one. Finally, positive attitudes predict high levels of information system use; since this was an existing system, the attitudes are those established as a result of experience with the system.

In conclusion, it is worthy of note that Lucas also measured decision style. However, since the characteristics he employed for ascertaining this variable were different from those of studies previously cited, it is impossible to synthesize or compare the results. It is also noteworthy, and a commentary on the state of research in MIS, that although both Gibson and Lucas attempted to measure attitudes, their characteristics of definition are so different that comparison of the results is infeasible.

As mentioned earlier, the posterior attitudes of users are influenced by their involvement in system development. It is generally believed that such involvement has a positive effect on attitudes and it is widely prescribed as a panacea for change resistance. Some studies have found that involvement in development and use of a system increases appreciation and fosters favorable attitudes, but many psychological problems have been identified in cases where users participated actively in the development process. Two studies (Luthans and Koester 1976; Koester and Luthans 1979) even suggest that familiarity with computer systems may breed contempt, rather than use.

In their two experiments, Koester and Luthans showed that people with previous computer experience tend to disparage information systems, whereas people with no experience are influenced by them. Their experiments called for answers to a 20-item multiple-choice test, the questions being very difficult and the possible answers being either all correct or all incorrect. Then the subjects were advised that because of the difficulty of the test they might revise their answers. A control group was supplied with no additional data or with irrelevant data for making revisions. The others were divided into two groups; one group received suggested answers on a mimeograph list, the second group received the same list on a computer printout. All three groups were composed of some people with and some people without previous computer experience.

The subjects in the first experiment were undergraduate students of business administration at the University of Nebraska; those in the second experiment were finance and accounting staff of the production division of a large oil company, some of whom actually used computerized MIS. After the subjects revised their answers, the number of changes was counted for each subject. The results of the two experiments are reproduced as Table 9.9. In both cases, the mean number of changes introduced by the control group was significantly lower, whereas computer-experienced subjects were affected more by mimeograph data and the inexperienced by computer output. Thus, the bias in computer information is dependent on the user's previous experience, which does affect the choice activity of decision makers.

These experiments have been described in detail not so much for their results but because they are a good example of what the authors called "orderly progression of scientific enquiry by moving from the laboratory to the field setting in the search for generalizability."* This is precisely the kind of orderly progression that is the rationale for the paradigm presented in this book.

Change Resistance

> Proposition 9.7: The lower the level of stress engendered by system development, the lower the level of resistance and the greater the likelihood of success.

Virtually all studies of experience with MIS development indicate that it is a stressful problem for participants, with heavy emotional and psychological costs involved. These problems have been reported at all levels of management and in many different types of organizations. The problems raised include changes in success criteria, fear of job downgrading and reduction of freedom of action, breakup of work relationships, perceived threats to decision-making functions and prerogatives of exercising managerial judgment, decreased feelings of being essential, perceived threats to self-esteem, and psychological failure. These perceived effects can complicate the design process when they generate resistance. Resistance can take many forms, from apathy and quitting through quiet destructiveness and open opposition.

Totally negative views of imposed changes tend to create genuine resistance. The results are unresponsive and uncreative work behavior, uncertainty, anxiety, and even a surprising amount

---

*Robert Koester and Fred Luthans. "The Impact of the Computer on the Choice Activity of Decision Makers: A Replication with Actual Users of Computerized MIS." Academy of Management Journal 22 (June 1979): 416-422.

TABLE 9.9

Number of Changes in Answers for Computer-Experienced
and Inexperienced Subjects

| Group | Students | | | Finance and Accounting Staff | | |
|---|---|---|---|---|---|---|
| | N | Mean Number of Changes | Standard Deviation | N | Mean Number of Changes | Standard Deviation |
| Experienced | | | | | | |
| Control | 80 | 2.66 | 2.57 | 31 | 0.419 | 0.84 |
| Printout | 61 | 4.45 | 3.12 | 29 | 1.483 | 2.16 |
| Mimeograph | 59 | 5.82 | 4.08 | 28 | 2.679 | 4.53 |
| Inexperienced | | | | | | |
| Control | 24 | 2.62 | 1.75 | 30 | 0.333 | 0.83 |
| Printout | 26 | 6.28 | 3.16 | 46 | 1.783 | 2.88 |
| Mimeograph | 20 | 4.10 | 2.21 | 39 | 1.487 | 2.16 |

Source: For students, Fred Luthans and Robert Koester, "The Impact of Computer Generated Information on the Choice Activity of Decision Makers," Academy of Management Journal 19 (June 1976): 328–332; for accounting staff, Robert Koester and Fred Luthans, "The Impact of the Computer on the Choice Activity of Decision Makers: A Replication with Actual Users of Computerized MIS," Academy of Management Journal 22 (June 1979): 416–22.

of sabotage. Thus, the introduction of computer systems can cause significant attitude changes that adversely affect performance and retard development (Alexander 1969; Argyris 1971; Colton 1972-73; Daniel 1976; Gibson and Nolan 1974; Grindlay and Cummer 1973; Grossman 1972; Ramsgard 1974; Schwartz 1969; Singer 1969; Srinivasan and Dascher 1977).

Sorensen and Zand (1975) have applied a theory of organizational change to predicting the success of system implementations. In analyzing the lack of success so common to implementation of computer models, the authors examined the changes that occur within the organization. As noted, there is a tendency to resist change. This tendency can be beneficial in terms of stability but can be detrimental to attempts to overcome problems by use of a new system.

As their analytical framework, Sorenson and Zand (1975) adopted the Lewin-Schein theory of change, which they describe as a three-step process:*

> . . . unfreezing, changing, and refreezing. Unfreezing refers to overcoming resistance to change by introducing disequilibrium into the present, stable equilibrium. Changing refers to exposure to new information, attitudes, and theories in order to achieve new perception and to learn new behavioral patterns. Refreezing refers to reinforcement, confirmation, and support of new behavior.† [P. 217]

The researchers hypothesized that high levels of unfreezing, changing, and refreezing would be found in high-success model implementations, and that low levels of unfreezing, changing, and refreezing would be found in low-success cases.

A pilot test was used to develop scales to measure the independent variables (unfreezing, changing, and refreezing) and the

---

*For detailed discussions of this theory see Lewin (1947) and Schein (1964).

†Reprinted by permission of the publisher from Richard E. Sorensen and Dale E. Zand. "Improving the Implementation of OR/MS Models by Applying the Lewin-Schein Theory of Change," Chapter 10. In Implementing Operations Research/Management Science, Randall L. Schultz and Dennis P. Slevin (eds). New York: American Elsevier, 1975. Copyright 1975 by Elsevier North Holland Inc.

dependent variable (success). Success was considered to consist of development of a solution, profitability, client's satisfaction, and consultant's satisfaction.

The questionnaire consisted of 60 questions to be answered on a five-point scale and dealt with the subject's perceptions about one successful and one unsuccessful project. The instrument was sent to 391 members of the Metropolitan New York Chapter of the Institute of Management Sciences. The 193 responses provided data on 280 OR/MS projects.

The hypotheses were tested at the 0.05 level of significance, using Pearson product-moment correlation coefficients, Spearman rank-order correlation coefficients, and Kendall rank-order correlation coefficients. The results, exhibited in Table 9.10, supported the hypotheses. A retest indicated a high level of reliability for the questionnaire.

Sorensen and Zand believed it is the responsibility of the management scientist, to improve the chances of successful implementation, by becoming resistant to change within an organization. They concluded from their study that application of Lewin-Schein change theory can be of significant help in achieving this result.


Involvement

> Proposition 9.8: The higher the level of user partici-
> pation in system design and implementation, the higher
> the level of use and the greater the likelihood of success.

Involvement of users is recommended not just to reduce resistance; participation or involvement of users in stages prior to use is widely considered an important prerequisite to the proper design of an MIS. Areas in which involvement has been considered desirable include:

Project selection;
Project definition;
Establishing design criteria;
Project planning and design;
Responsibility for functional specifications;
Project staffing;
Responsibility for implementation progress and results; and
Establishing operating criteria.

Participation by users is considered especially important in the project selection and planning stages.

TABLE 9.10

Sorensen and Zand: Experimental Results

| Variable | Pearson Product Moment | | Spearman Rank Order | | Kendall Rank Order | | |
|---|---|---|---|---|---|---|---|
| | $\rho_{x,s}$ | $t^a$ | $\rho_s$ | $t^a$ | $\tau$ | SD | $Z^a$ |
| U+ | 0.45 | 8.44 | 0.46 | 8.75 | 0.31 | 0.04 | 7.86 |
| U– | -0.46 | -8.76 | -0.46 | -8.87 | -0.31 | 0.04 | -7.83 |
| C+ | 0.40 | 7.30 | 0.39 | 7.12 | 0.28 | 0.04 | 7.30 |
| C– | -0.58 | -11.87 | -0.57 | -11.78 | -0.41 | 0.04 | -10.42 |
| R+ | 0.85 | 27.12 | 0.84 | 26.30 | 0.61 | 0.04 | 15.70 |
| R– | -0.62 | -13.20 | -0.61 | -13.15 | -0.43 | 0.04 | -11.00 |

[a] 278 d.f.; all t and Z values significant at the 0.0005 level.

U+ signifies the index of items favorable toward unfreezing.
U– signifies the index of items unfavorable toward unfreezing.
C+ signifies the index of items favorable toward changing.
C– signifies the index of items unfavorable toward changing.
R+ signifies the index of items favorable toward refreezing.
R– signifies the index of items unfavorable toward refreezing.

Source: Reprinted by permission of the publisher from Chapter 10, "Improving the Implementation of OR/MS Models by Applying the Lewin–Schein Theory of Change," by Richard E. Sorensen and Dale E. Zand in Implementing Operations Research/Management Science, Randall L. Schultz and Dennis P. Slevin (eds.) p. 227. Copyright 1975 by Elsevier North Holland Inc.

Although it has not been established that user involvement is
absolutely necessary, it has been found by field studies to contribute to successful implementation and that its absence contributes
to failure.  There are two reasons for this:  First, appropriately
qualified operating managers are likely to be a better source of
ideas for profitable changes than are computer professionals, thus
leading to better systems; and second, acceptance of a system by
users is largely conditioned on the users' belief that they contributed
to its development.  As suggested above, however, the results of
participation are not necessarily all positive, especially when the
experience is a negative one.

A major problem with obtaining user involvement is the
amount of time required.  Considerable time needs to be expended
if involvement is to be meaningful, but the perceived need for information system development is low and is coupled with the natural tendency to resist change; thus, managers are unwilling to
devote the study, time, and effort to make participation meaningful.
The result is a widespread abdication by users of their responsibilities in system design and the transfer, by default, of those responsibilities to the computer professionals (Alter 1976; Atkins
1976; DeBrabender and Edström 1977; Carlson et al. 1977; Carlson
1967; Colton 1972-73; Diebold 1969; Ference and Uretsky 1976;
Fisher 1969; Garrity 1963; Guthrie 1974; Hammond 1974a; Higgins
and Finn 1976; Holland et al. 1974; Jenkins 1969; King and Cleland
1975; Lucas 1973, 1974a; McKenney and Keen 1974; McKinsey
1968; Murdick and Ross 1972; Schwartz 1969, 1970; Shaw 1976;
Shio 1977; Singer 1969; Srinivasan and Dascher 1977; Swanson 1974).

Conflict Caused by User-Implementor Interactions

> Propositions 9.9:  The lower the level of conflict be-
> tween users and implementors, the greater the like-
> lihood of success.

The relationships between manager-users and MIS implementors are so fraught with difficulties that they often lead not only
to resistance but even to open conflict.  Such conflict may inhibit
the successful implementation of MIS projects.  User interaction
with implementors is most noticeable at the systems analysis and
programming stages, which involve the transfer of system plans
and policies into an operating environment.  The unfavorable user
attitudes generated by conflict in these and other stages can lead to
a mutual unwillingness to cooperate, a refusal on the part of potential users to participate in design and operation of the information

system, and rejection by technicians of good ideas that may be generated by the line managers (DeBrabender and Edström 1977; Gibson and Nolan 1974; Keen 1975; Lucas 1973; Render and Villere 1977; Schwartz 1969; Wynne and Dickson 1975).

## Communications

> Proposition 9.10: The better the communications between users and implementors, the lower the level of conflict.

When users do become involved, communication problems are rampant, evidenced by numerous reports of an unbridged culture gap between implementors and users. Computer technicians are accused of being complicators, not simplifiers, using jargon that confuses, intimidates, or angers users. Thus, management is often confused by technological arguments put forward by systems people.

This communications gap has been attributed to different styles of thinking and problem solving in the two groups, an approach consistent with the authors' distinction between the various cognitive styles of users. Argyris (1971) reports that MIS specialists are not equipped to cope with the emotional problems caused by their systems and have difficulty in coping with executives' feelings and behavior. Line managers and MIS professionals have comparable degrees of interpersonal competence. Under stress, people with this degree of interpersonal competence tend to react in ways that inhibit effective problem solving (Alexander 1969; Argyris 1971; Brill 1974; DeBrabender and Edström 1977; Diebold 1969; Doktor 1976; Grayson 1973; Head 1967; Jenkins 1969; Lewis 1976; McKenney and Keen 1974; McKinsey 1968; Render and Villere 1977; Srinivasan and Dascher 1977; Townsend 1970).

DeBrabender and Edström (1977) have studied user involvement as a two-party communication relationship between user and implementor. They believe that user involvement is the factor most consistently and significantly related to successful implementation of computer systems. They see user involvement as a dyadic relationship between user and specialist. Using the model of Thompson (1962), they postulate that this interaction can develop in one of three ways: exchange of information, use of rewards or bribes, or use of punishment or coercion. Either of the last two indicate conceptual discordance between the parties, with the likelihood of reduced voluntary compliance on the part of the party coerced or bribed.

The mandatory-optional dimension is seen as a continuum, not a dichotomy.  Another such continuum pertinent to this theory is the programmed-heuristic dimension.  A party's positions on each of these continua reflect individual, interpersonal, and organizational factors.  Figure 9.1 illustrates effective communication in all possible combinations of these dimensions.  A direct arrow indicates straightforward exchange of information; a curved arrow indicates greater freedom in seeking solutions because of heuristic orientation toward the problem; an adjoint arrow indicates extra effort that must be made to motivate the party for whom the transaction is optional.

To help insure the establishment of the effective communications patterns, DeBrabender and Edström offer three guidelines for management during the design phase: a less formal approach should be taken, asymmetry in the relationship between the parties should be reduced, and a semantic bridge should be established.  Often, this will require mediation of a third party, and DeBrabender and Edström discuss the status and orientation the third party should have in the various circumstances.  Although acknowledging that effective communication will not guarantee successful MIS implementation, they believe that, all other things being equal, there will be a greater chance of success under these conditions than there would be otherwise.

DeBrabender and Edström's article is highly theoretical in nature, often to the point of obscurity.  As they state, experimental substantiation is needed.  Given the critical nature of the communication problem, even theoretically derived concepts are better than none, and empirical results would be even more welcome.

Relocation of Power

> Proposition 9.11: The weaker the perception of power
> loss by users, the lower the level of conflict.

MIS imply an organizational design in which competence and cooperation become more important than power and competition, and the change tends to create fears and resistance on the part of individuals and groups.

Whisler (1970) suggested that during the development of new systems, top management entrusts middle management with decisions in their area of expertise, providing them with a highly active and powerful role during the transition, especially if they choose to become actively involved.  When the transition is completed, some of middle management's responsibilities have become incorporated

FIGURE 9.1

Effective Exchange of Information in Different Situations

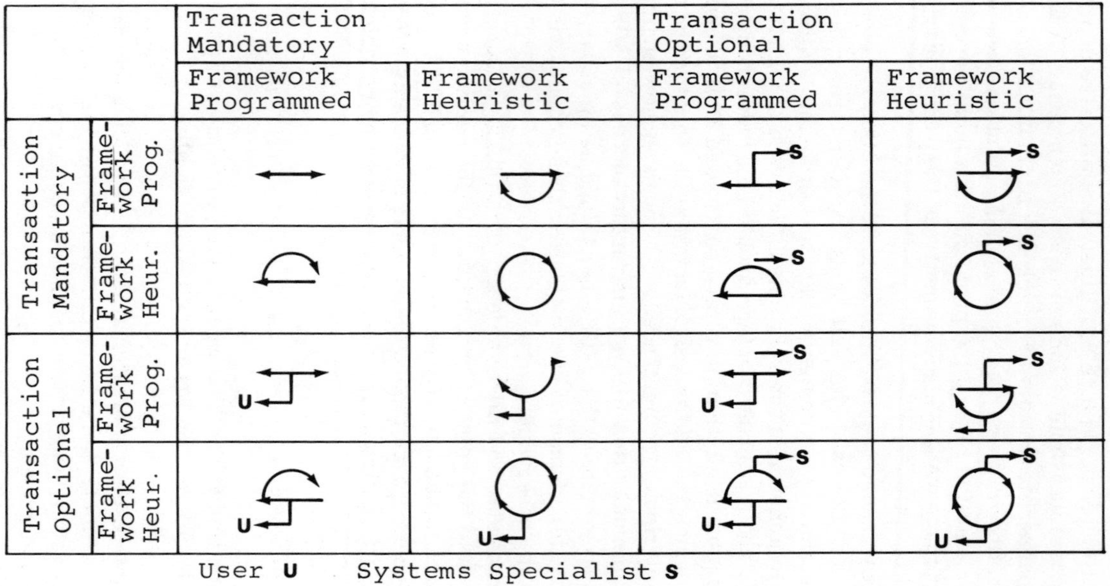

User **U**     Systems Specialist **s**

Source: Reprinted by permission from DeBrabender, Bert and Edstrom, Anders N., "Successful Information System Development Projects," Management Science, Volume 24, Number 2 (October 1977) p. 194, Copyright © (1977) The Institute of Management Sciences.

into programmed decisions and many middle management people have reduced responsibilities for decision making. There is also a specialization effect, the more creative aspects of decision making tending to move from line to staff people. Those with line responsibilities may lose, or feel they have lost, the authority to deal with exceptions and problems of change.

As a gradual transfer of power has taken place to the information services department, users become less powerful and more frustrated, the frustration being reflected in unfavorable attitudes toward the information system and its staff (Argyris 1971; Emery 1973; Garrity 1963; Lucas 1973; Nolan 1977; Render and Villere 1977; Whisler 1970).

Implementation Practices

> Proposition 9.12: The more sensitive implementors
> are to users' personal needs and the better adapted
> their implementation practices to those needs, the
> lower the level of conflict.

How the information system staff go about their tasks also affects their relationships with users. For example, frequent changes to systems without consulting users can adversely affect their attitudes. In general, the system design and operating policies of the information services staff and the technical quality of their systems influence user attitudes and perceptions of that staff.

Many writers place the onus for cooperation on the implementors. They argue that it is the implementor who should take the first step in bridging the communication gap. To help the user, implementors must develop an understanding of the user's work and information needs. Information analysis has been advocated not only as a basis for system design but also to facilitate communication between users and analysts.

Successful systems personnel learn to take managers' attitudes and preferences into account and to accommodate and support users' more intuitive cognitive styles. Sensitivity to users is reflected in, among other things, associating the importance of information with the importance of the manager responsible for that information (Alexander 1969; Alter 1976; Aron 1969; Balderston 1975; DeBrabender and Edstrom 1977; Carlson et al. 1977; Gibson and Nolan 1974; Keen 1975; King and Cleland 1975; Kneitel 1975b; Lucas 1973; McKenney and Keen 1974; Mintzberg 1971, 1976; Nolan 1977; Sihler 1971; Srinivasan and Dascher 1977).

Proposition 9.13: The higher the degree of user involvement, the greater the likelihood of success.

Cooperation between users and implementors is important because neither, alone, can design and implement an MIS—dialogue and teamwork are essential. Involvement of qualified managers has been recommended as an additional means of bridging the communication gap. Argyris (1971) reports a case in which the solution chosen was to place members of line management on MIS teams to act as a liaison; these line managers made significant suggestions during development of the system, but reported great role strain. Thus, stimulating effective user involvement creates great challenges and can cause friction between the groups involved; if involvement is achieved, however, it can result in more favorable user attitudes and perceptions of the information system and its staff. The theory of DeBrabander and Edström, discussed above, suggests a framework for establishing positive relations between users and implementors (Argyris 1971; Carlson 1967; Diebold 1969; Grossman 1972; Jenkins 1969; King and Cleland 1971, 1975; Lucas 1973; McKinsey 1968; Murdick and Ross 1972; Nolan and Knutsen 1974; Schwartz 1970).

Swanson (1974) tested the relationship between user involvement and MIS appreciation in an engineering department of a large international manufacturer of complex electronic equipment. He viewed users' involvement as composed of two types: a priori involvement of a manager (consisting of cooperative involvement with MIS design, implementation, and operation processes) and inquiry involvement of a manager (consisting of cooperative involvement with the MIS inquiry process). He also defined MIS appreciation by a manager as being the manager's manifold of beliefs about the relative value of the MIS as a means of inquiry.

Swanson made three conjectures:

(5) An increase in the a priori involvement of an individual with an MIS will increase his MIS appreciation;
(6) An increase in the MIS appreciation of an individual will increase his inquiry involvement, and vice versa; and hence, indirectly (7) An increase in the a priori involvement of an individual with an MIS will increase his inquiry involvement. *

---

*Reprinted by permission from E. Burton Swanson, "Management Information Systems: Appreciation and Involvement," Management Science, Volume 21, Number 2 (October 1974), p. 180. Copyright (1974) The Institute of Management Sciences.

The study focused on an inquiry-type MIS, the use of which Swanson monitored for 30 consecutive working days. A questionnaire was then administered to all 46 users who had access to the system. The analysis is based on recorded use of the system and on 37 completed questionnaires. Table 9.11 describes the operationalizations of the three relevant variables.

TABLE 9.11

Operationalization of Variables in Swanson's Study

| Variable | Indicators | Measure |
|----------|-----------|---------|
| Inquiry involvement | Submission of a report-producing query. | Relative frequency (number of days one or more queries were made per 30 days sampled). |
| A priori involvement | Initiation of ten different kinds of change in the design or operation of the system. | Users were asked to rank the frequency (from "once a week" to "never") in which they initiated each of the ten kinds of potential change. The scores of the ten questions were averaged to an index. |
| MIS appreciation | 16 verbal evaluations of the system (data, reports, interface documentation, personal). | Simple average of the 16 evaluations. |

Source: Adapted by permission from E. Burton Swanson, "Management Information Systems: Appreciation and Involvement," Management Science, Volume 21, Number 2 (October 1974), pp. 177-88. Copyright (1974) The Institute of Management Sciences.

Rather than evaluation on a continuum, the measures were used to dichotomize the users into two groups for each variable: "involved" and "uninvolved," "appreciative" and "unappreciative." Contingency tables were used to test the three conjectures. The results strengthen Swanson's propositions about the existence of relationships between the kinds of MIS involvement and MIS appreciation. There was no attempt to test the direction of the relationships or causality. Swanson concludes that MIS appreciation coproduces, and is coproduced by, MIS involvement.

It is important to note Swanson's awareness that:

> Although the scaling technique applied to MIS apprecia-
> tion was successful in discriminating effectively among
> questionnaire respondents, the technique applied to
> a priori involvement (the initiation of change in the
> design or operational state of the system) still seems
> to me a good choice, the method for effectively opera-
> tionalizing its measure remains a problem. More
> sophisticated measures of inquiry involvement are also
> called for.*

### Conflict Reduction

A number of means have been suggested for lowering the level
of conflict between users and implementors and for encouraging
user participation in system development. These include increasing sensitivity of implementors to users' reactions, education of
users, role definition, and project formality. The first of these
has been discussed in this book under "Implementation Practices."
The three remaining means are briefly discussed below.

### Education

> Proposition 9.14: Appropriate education promotes
> favorable user attitudes, facilitates user involvement,
> and increases the likelihood of success.

A number of authors suggest education as a means of bridging the gap between users and implementors and facilitating cooperation. Indeed, several case reports attribute success in part to
appropriate training of users, and training has been widely employed in conjunction with computer system introduction. Argyris
(1971), however, is rather skeptical and states that it remains to
be demonstrated that such learning transfers to real-world situations in which individuals are in conflict. He notes that MIS people,
who presumably possess the requisite technical qualifications, have
the same problems dealing with each other as they have with line

---

*Reprinted by permission, ibid., p. 187. Copyright (1974)
The Institute of Management Sciences.

managers. The strategy suggested by Argyris is to raise the interpersonal competence of both managers and MIS personnel in dealing
with emotionality and strain. As interpersonal skills are improved,
he believes, people will turn naturally to education.

Interestingly, it has been found that recent training of any
kind in management, not only in information systems, clearly induces perceptions of need for, and positive effects of, information
system change (Guthrie 1974). This is clearly an area in which
additional research might yield great practical benefits (Argyris
1971; Aron 1969; Bonini 1978; Carlson et al. 1977; DeBrabender and
Edström 1977; Dickson et al. 1977; Financial Executive 1974;
Grindlay and Cummer 1973; Guthrie 1974; Hammond 1974a; Heany
1972; Higgins and Finn 1976; King and Cleland 1975, Montijo 1967;
Murdick and Ross 1972; Nolan and Knutsen 1974; Nolan 1977;
Srinivasan and Dascher 1977; Young 1978; Whisler 1970).

## Role Definition

> Proposition 9.15: The clearer the allocation of func-
> tions between users and implementors, the lower the
> level of conflict and the greater the likelihood of
> success.

It has been recommended that status incongruence between
users and implementors be avoided. Users and implementors
should share status and background, but their roles should be
clearly defined. One such definition has planners making recommendations, line managers making decisions, and implementors
building systems (Hammond 1974a; Sihler 1971).

## Formality

> Proposition 9.16: The more formal the lines of com-
> munication between users and implementors, the lower
> the level of conflict and the greater the likelihood of
> success.

Without project management guidelines, implementors and
users have to develop their own procedures for dealing with each
other, and conflict may ensue. Thus, it is suggested that care
should be taken to improve the administrative and organizational
processes that facilitate clear communications between system
development groups and users. Performance measures and

short-term control devices should be formal for the more routine tasks, and MIS technical personnel should be removed from frequent interaction with users (DeBrabender and Edstrom 1977; Dickson et al. 1977; Gibson and Nolan 1974; Knutsen and Nolan 1974; Nolan 1977).

## CONCLUSION

Since the authors regard an MIS as successful when it is widely used, the user becomes an important element of the system. This observation should lead to a change in the frequently current approach to system design and development strategies. The emphasis in such strategies should be on solving the behavioral problems raised by MIS, rather than being the almost exclusive preoccupation with technical issues that is now prevalent. This is proposed not because technical issues are unimportant but because the most elegant technical solution must be considered a failure if potential users do not use it.

An element of prime importance in the development strategy is the involvement of users in the development process. This very involvement, however, tends to generate conflict between users and implementors. The indifference of passive uninvolvement may be transformed by unsatisfactory involvement into open hostility. The cure may prove worse than the malady.

Thus, there is urgent need for research on how to make user involvement a positive experience, motivating use of the finished system. Research is also needed on how to prevent outbreaks of conflict, which can make development a negative experience, leading to an aversion to using the system, with failure as a consequence.

It is clear that the success of a system, as measured by its use, is dependent on the integration of users into the system development process in such a way that they will be motivated to use the end product.

# 10
# THE CONCEPT OF FIT:
# A SUMMARY AND CONCLUSIONS

> The Butcher would gladly have talked till next day.
> But he felt that the Lesson must end.
> Lewis Carroll, The Hunting of the Snark

The preceding chapters of this book have discussed the relationships between single variables or small groups of variables, and the success or failure of management information systems. In attempting to summarize this material, the authors are impressed by the large number of variables involved and the difficulty in reducing discussion of them, as a whole, to simple terms. In this context, the concept of the fit of an information system is particularly useful. Given a vector of values of variables that define the structure of an MIS, as detailed in Chapter 6, the success of an MIS depends on the extent that the particular values fit the situation—specifically, the organizational and extraorganizational environments (Chapter 2) and the behavioral variables (Chapters 7, 8, and 9). This, then, explains why a system that is successful in one situation may be unacceptable in another.

In a sense, the discussion of fit inverts the nature of the conceptual and empirical experiments described. Until now, the authors have concentrated on elucidating the values of variables that promote success or lack of it in given circumstances. In discussing fit, the information system is taken as given, and the effects on success or failure of placing it in different circumstances are evaluated. A study by Robey and Zeller (1978) provides an excellent example of this concept.

That study focused on the implementation of the same system in two similar departments of a very large corporation. The system was adopted and used extensively by one of the departments (success) and was discontinued by the second department after six months (failure).

In their efforts to trace the reasons for the different outcomes, the researchers administered questionnaires to four users in the "success" department and seven users in the "failure" department. The questionnaires were designed to measure the attitudes in the groups toward the system. Robey and Zeller also conducted interviews with the personnel and studied organizational records. Two significant differences were found between the attitudes of the adopting and rejecting users: The adopting group viewed more favorably the effect of the system on their performance and the urgency and importance of the system to the organization. These differences were found after success or failure were determined, so they cannot be claimed as their cause. Table 10.1 exhibits these findings and also the areas in which no significant differences in attitudes were found. The data were analyzed using the Mann-Whitney U test.

TABLE 10.1

Differences in Attitudes between the Adopting Group
and the Rejecting Group

| Area of Concern | Level of Statistical Significance |
| --- | --- |
| Performance | 0.055 |
| Interpersonal relations | — |
| Organizational changes | — |
| Goals | — |
| Support from others | — |
| User-developer relationships | — |
| Urgency and importance | 0.036 |

Dash signifies no significant difference between groups, according to Mann-Whitney U Test results.

Conclusion: The differences on Performance and Urgency and Importance indicate that the adopting group's attitudes were more favorable toward QIS than were the rejecting group's.

Source: Reprinted by permission from Daniel Robey and Richard L. Zeller, "Factors Affecting the Success and Failure of an Information System for Product Quality," Interfaces 8 (February 1978) 2: 74. Copyright (1978) The Institute of Management Sciences.

Based on the interviews and their study of the company records, Robey and Zeller identified some organizational and procedural differences between the two departments in the way the system was introduced and supported. These differences are summarized in Table 10.2. These differences may help to explain why the system was a good fit in the one situation but not in the other.

TABLE 10.2

Organizational and Procedural Differences between Adopting and Rejecting Departments

| Department Characteristics | Adopting | Rejecting |
|---|---|---|
| Size | Relatively smaller | Bigger |
| Specialization | Relatively less | More |
| Formality | Relatively more formal | Less formal |
| Centralization | Relatively more centralized | Less centralized |
| System's support | Supported by management | No support |

Source: Daniel Robey and Richard L. Zeller, "Factors Affecting the Success and Failure of an Information System for Product Quality," Interfaces 8 (February 1978) 2: 70-75.

The implications of this study are clearly limited by its methodology as well as by the specific nature of the two departments involved. Some insight is provided, however, into the effect of the fit of a system on success and failure. Furthermore, the two significant differences that they found relate to individuals and their performance and to organizational importance. It is helpful to consider each of these aspects of fit—individual fit and organizational fit—separately.

INDIVIDUAL FIT

Individual fit refers to the extent to which different people need different information and the ability of a given system to meet those varying needs. In Chapter 9 the authors presented at length the differences in cognitive style between individuals and the available empirical evidence on the effects of those differences on the success and failure of information systems. Since different people look at problems in different ways and require different kinds of information in different formats, the question has been raised of whether the concept of a general system that can be used by a number of people over a long period of time is valid. The problem of fit is exacerbated by the observation that it is more important that a model match a manager's understanding of the real world than that it contain a complete or correct representation of reality (Hayes and Nolan 1974; Mitroff, Nelson, and Mason 1974).

> Proposition 10.1: The better the fit of a system to a manager's cognitive style, the greater the likelihood that the manager will use it.

> Proposition 10.2: The more adaptable a system to different managers and different needs, the better the fit.

The behavioral dependence of information systems suggests the validity of tailoring them to users' needs. A tailoring capacity would be reflected in the adaptability and coverage of a system. It is widely agreed that systems should be responsive and flexible to support the changing needs of different users. Adaption to managers' needs implies either batch processing systems designed so all management needs are anticipated and the right reports delivered at the right time or providing each manager with the ability to query the system whenever desired, presumably by means of a terminal in on-line mode. Since adaption to managers' needs requires the ability to change systems readily, this implies an interactive capability; thus, the on-line real-time solution is usually preferred (Adams and Schroeder 1973; Aron 1969; Kriebel 1972; Mock 1973; Sprague and Watson 1975).

Coverage of an information system refers to the subset of the information made available to a user. On the one hand, simple data processing systems fail to provide management with a complete picture; on the other hand, large, all-inclusive models overwhelm many managers' abilities to understand the underlying assumptions and to integrate the output into their decision processes. Furthermore, such complex systems have difficult design and data management problems. In a case report on MIS at Xerox (Canada), it was found that simulation models were most readily understood by managers; this system provided managers with a variety of models with differing degrees of scope and complexity so managers did not have to struggle with a detailed model if they were interested only in general solutions. It has also been suggested that information availability should be tailored to managers' areas of responsibility. In this context, the concept of "information threshold" has been introduced— the depth to which a given manager may wish to delve into a data base for information (Aron 1969; Hayes and Nolan 1974; Head 1967; Kronenberg 1967; Seaberg and Seaberg 1973).

There are also problems associated with fitting information structures to users, however. Holland et al. (1974) report that users have very strong possessive feelings about "their" data and are reluctant to share them. In their survey of 20 systems, 17 were originally designed for only one or two specific users (even when later expansion was intended); these systems expanded little after original implementation, in spite of resource availability. Often, the original users of models are the only ones with sufficient understanding and confidence in them to make use of them and the models fall into disuse with their departure (Hammond 1974a).

A study implicitly incorporating the concept of individual fit is that of Maish (1979), who, to determine the factors associated with favorable values for these variables, focused on the behavior and feelings of information system users. In the authors' present context, favorable behavior and feeling may be viewed as prima facie evidence of good individual fit, and factors that promote them may be considered to promote such fit.

Maish's study was conducted in four federal government agencies in Washington, D.C., that implemented or redesigned systems in the year of the study. A self-administered questionnaire was distributed among users by top management of each agency. The questionnaires consisted mainly of Likert-type questions, some previously used by Lucas. Sixty-two questionnaires (42 percent) were completed and analyzed.

Maish found positive correlations between the two focal variables, feelings and behavior, which the authors regard as surrogates for fit, and a series of other variables. Feelings were registered in degrees of positivity. Behavior was measured as the average score of nonroutine activity—"requesting optional features of the system, making extra use of terminals, requesting system changes, and assisting the system designers." The findings are exhibited in Tables 10.3 and 10.4. Maish also compared his findings with those of Lucas (1973) and other researchers in the field.

Although he examined numerous factors, Maish unfortunately reported only those items that produced positive associations. One is curious about those variables not reported and their association (even if negative, small, or insignificant) with user behavior and feelings. In any event, those factors that are significantly associated with positive user behavior contribute to our understanding of the elements of good individual fit.

TABLE 10.3

Findings about User Behavior

| Association | Kendall's tau | Pearson |
|---|---|---|
| Feelings about staff | | |
| Positive behavior is associated with | 0.327 | 0.309 |
| positive feelings about the information | (58) | (58) |
| system staff. | 0.003 | 0.018 |
| Management support | | |
| Positive behavior is associated with | 0.257 | 0.193 |
| a feeling of good management support. | (58) | (59) |
| | 0.035 | 0.143(NS) |
| Prepared to use system | | |
| Positive behavior is associated with | 0.320 | 0.356 |
| the feeling of being prepared to | (50) | (50) |
| use a new system. | 0.006 | 0.011 |
| Grade GS-12 or better | | |
| Positive behavior is associated with | 0.259 | 0.178 |
| a middle to upper civil service | (57) | (57) |
| grade GS-12 or better. | 0.037 | 0.184(NS) |
| Access | | |
| Positive behavior is associated with | 0.428 | 0.541 |
| good access to the information | (58) | (58) |
| system. | 0.0005 | 0.001 |
| Gives information wanted | | |
| Positive behavior is associated with | 0.285 | 0.266 |
| a feeling that the system produces | (47) | (47) |
| the information wanted. | 0.015 | 0.070 |
| Ease of correction | | |
| Positive behavior is associated with | 0.389 | 0.103 |
| ease of correcting data or instructions | (35) | (35) |
| on an on-line system | 0.018 | 0.555(NS) |
| Flexible formats | | |
| Positive behavior is associated with | 0.323 | 0.286 |
| the flexibility of on-line formats. | (32) | (32) |
| | 0.022 | 0.112(NS) |

Note: The upper number is the coefficient; the second, shown in parentheses, is the number of respondents; and the third is the level of significance. NS signifies not significant.

Source: Reprinted by special permission from the MIS Quarterly, from "A User's Behavior Toward His MIS," by A. M. Maish, in Volume 3, Number 1, published in 1979. Copyright 1979 by the Society for Management Information Systems and the Management Information Systems Research Center.

## TABLE 10.4

### User Feelings about the System

| Association | Kendall's tau | Pearson |
|---|---|---|
| **Feelings about staff** | | |
| Positive feelings about the system are associated with positive feelings about the system staff. | 0.475 (58) 0.000 | 0.568 (58) 0.001 |
| **Batch quality** | | |
| Positive feelings about the system are associated with positive feelings about batch output quality. | 0.411 (48) 0.001 | 0.533 (48) 0.001 |
| **On-line quality** | | |
| Positive feelings about the system are associated with positive feelings about on-line system quality. | 0.566 (35) 0.000 | 0.624 (35) 0.001 |
| **Involved in design or change** | | |
| Positive feelings about the system are associated with the impression that users are involved in the design of changes or of new systems. | 0.279 (56) 0.010 | 0.197 (56) 0.147 |
| **Problems listened to** | | |
| Positive feelings about the system are associated with the impression that user problems are well provided for. | 0.250 (55) 0.033 | 0.291 (55) 0.031 |
| **Newer employee** | | |
| Positive feelings about the system are associated with less than five years of service with the agency. | 0.314 (56) 0.016 | 0.310 (56) 0.020 |

Note: The upper number is the coefficient; the second, shown in parentheses, is the number of respondents; and the third is the level of significance.

Source: Reprinted by special permission from the MIS Quarterly, from "A User's Behavior Toward His MIS," by A. M. Maish, in Volume 3, Number 1, published in 1979. Copyright 1979 by the Society for Management Informations Systems and the Management Information Systems Research Center.

ORGANIZATIONAL FIT

Organizational fit deals with the extent that an information
system is adapted to the particular organization in which it is used.
Very little work seems to have been done on this topic directly, but
there are some more or less oblique references in terms of system
feasibility, integration, the organizational interface, and organizational weltansicht.

Proposition 10.3: Technical, economic, and organizational feasibility are prerequisites for good organizational fit.

The feasibility of an information system is regarded as consisting of technical, economic, and operational or organizational
aspects. The technical aspect is the ability of a system to cope
with problems relevant to the organizationa. The economic aspect
is the economic value of information and the cost of producing it.
It has been argued that it is impossible to determine the value side
of the equation; as a result, decisions tend to be based on cost comparisons, rather than cost-benefit analyses. The organizational
aspect is the degree to which an organization is ready to accept and
use a particular information system (this is the topic of Chapter 2).
The economic and technical components of information system feasibility have been discussed in greater detail in Chapters 3 through 5
(Emery 1973; Hammond 1974a; McKinsey 1968).

Proposition 10.4: The greater the degree of integration, the better the organizational fit.

Integration, in the context of organizational fit, is the integration of information systems and organizational activities. This
is expressed in a variety of ways in recommendations relating to
the system design phase. Some examples of such recommendations
are: the integration of MIS objectives and plans in general corporate
objectives; the study of information flows in the organization to build
systems that assemble the basic data and make it available to all
functional groups; and the planning of business transaction systems,
management information systems, and planning and control systems
on a coordinated and unified corporation-wide basis (Aron 1969;
Emery 1973; McFarlan 1971; Schwartz 1970).

Proposition 10.5: The more closely an information
system interfaces with the organization, the better
the organizational fit.

Information systems exist within an organizational context and their introduction requires solutions to problems of organizational behavior in planning, design, implementation, and operation. Lucas posited two organizational models—the power model and the conflict model—that can be applied to relationships between information systems and organizations. He found that information services have a high score on all variables in the power model and potential for high scores on all variables in the conflict model. This may help to explain the propensity of organizations to reject information systems (Lucas 1973; Schwartz 1970).

> Proposition 10.6: The more closely an information system reflects the organization's view of the world, the better the organizational fit.

It has been noted that information structures are a function of organizations' needs and consequently should reflect overall corporate design and character. Thus, an information system fits an organization to the extent that it reflects its weltansicht or view of the world. This has been stated by a number of authors in various ways, such as that it is less important that models contain complete or correct representations of reality than that they should reflect the organization's own understanding of the reality, or that information is meaningful only if it is tied to an appropriate story that has meaning to the users and to their organization (Coe 1974; Hayes and Nolan 1974; Mitroff, Nelson, and Mason 1974; Sihler 1971).

In concluding the discussion of individual and organizational fit, a study is presented in which these concepts were used to develop a methodology for system design. The authors, Souder et al. (1975), believed that the use of project selection models has lagged far behind their potential application; these are computer models designed to evaluate proposed projects and portfolios. They believed that a main cause is that models are not tailored to organizations, are not perceived as useful by potential users, and are therefore not received with enthusiasm.

A central thesis of the study was that a model must fit an organization's decision-making climate and a person's willingness to adopt it (WTA). The authors developed a questionnaire-based method to select a model appropriate for a given organization (the "design method").

The design method used a Likert-type questionnaire to gather opinions of the extent to which a computerized model would be compatible with the employees' work. Analysis identifies statistically significant specific variables. Examples of such variables are upward compatibility, downward compatibility, communicability, appropriateness of outputs, and appropriateness of mathematics. The variables are grouped into Personal Decision Variables (individual fit) and Organizational Factors (organizational fit). For a diagrammatic representation of the variable system see Figure 10.1.

Subjects for the design method participate in formal and informal lectures and are given an opportunity to try various models. The values given to the variables for a specific model ("model characteristics") are then obtained by administering questionnaires to the people familiar with it. Weights are assigned to the variables, reflecting the importance of each as indicated in the questionnaire responses. The weighted variables are combined in a predictive equation for the organization. The final result of the predictive equation is a value for the organization's WTA for that model. An example of the application of the predictive equation is exhibited in Table 10.5.

Souder et al. admit there is a sizable error factor in the predictive equation and that averaging the variables has a smoothing effect, so the WTA value is inaccurate. They believe, however, that the level of accuracy is reasonable and that a relatively high or low score for a particular model gives an indication of its acceptability. Three examples are cited of successful use of the design method. In one case, willingness to adopt was changed from negative to positive. The other two cases exhibited long-term adoption of computer models, a stated goal of the design method. In this book, the authors are less interested in the design-specific aspects of this study than in its demonstration of the operationalization and application of the concept of fit.

A discussion of organizational fit would be incomplete without some reference to its other side: the adaptions required of organizations. Two studies, one by Whisler and the other by Vertinsky et al., indicate the inevitability of MIS acting as an agent for such organizational change.

Whisler (1970)

Whisler conducted a field study among 23 life insurance companies. They were not a random sample, but were chosen because they had become computer users, they differed in size, and they were willing to participate in the study. An officer in each company was provided with an interview guide, to reduce interviewer bias, that was used to make information-gathering interviews (questions dealt with experiences, organizational structure, jobs, and individual reactions). Certain specified documents were also obtained and the results were used to make "systematic comparisons." Whisler

FIGURE 10.1

Example of a Specific Variables System

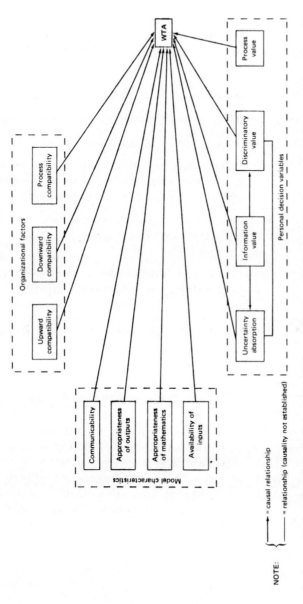

Source: Reprinted by permission of the publisher from W. E. Souder et al., "An Organizational Intervention Approach to the Design and Implementation of R & D Project Selection Models," in Implementing Operations Research/Management Science, Randall L. Schultz and Dennis P. Slevin, eds. (New York: American Elsevier, 1975), pp. 133–52. Copyright 1975 by Elsevier North Holland, Inc.

TABLE 10.5

Example of Predictive Equation

---

$$WTA = -0.51 + (0.61 \times MC) + (0.42 \times PDV) + (0.14 \times OF) \pm \epsilon$$

where:
| | | |
|---|---|---|
| MC | = | average score, model characteristics |
| PDV | = | average score, personal decision variables |
| OF | = | average score, organizational factors |
| MC | = | communicability score + appropriateness of outputs score + availability of inputs score + appropriateness of mathematics score ÷ 4 |
| PDV | = | uncertainty absorption + discriminatory value score + process value score + information value score ÷ 4 |
| OF | = | upward compatibility score + downward compatibility score + process compatibility score ÷ 3 |
| $\pm \epsilon$ | = | error term (range is from −0.51 to 0.35) |

---

Source: Reprinted by permission of the publisher from W. E. Souder et al., "An Organizational Intervention Approach to the Design and Implementation of R & D Project Selection Models," in Implementing Operations Research/Management Science, Randall L. Schultz and Dennis P. Slevin, eds. (New York: American Elsevier, 1975), p. 142. Copyright 1975 by Elsevier North Holland, Inc.

believed this approach would provide "interpretive richness" not otherwise available. One weakness of the study was caused by several ambiguously phrased questions that produced unusable data.

## Effects on Structure and Control

The findings indicated that with the advent of computers all the companies experienced employment displacement at the clerical level. At the supervisory level, there were mixed results (slight increases or decreases in personnel, or, in most cases, no change); none experienced a decrease at the managerial level, and most had no change. Whisler believed that after some time the decreases at the lower level would be reflected in employment displacement throughout the organization.

It was found that the computer tended to reduce the span of control within the organizations, with the largest declines occurring in the companies that had used computers the longest. However, corporate growth was seen to offset this effect. There was weak evidence of a decline in the number of organizational levels in the computer-affected areas.

There were many changes in organization structure, such as creation of new departments and transfer of activities, with a tendency to move from parallel to functional departmentation. Again, corporate growth acted as a restraint on this trend.

In assessing the computer's effect on organizational control, Whisler found that there had been a definite increase in central control. Further, the computer had taken over some phases of control, such as quality checks, resulting in tightening control of a person's behavior within the organization. There were mixed results concerning whether computer use resulted in clearer perceived lines of authority, and Whisler concluded that change (such as the adoption of the computer) caused blurring in the patterns of authority and control.

## Effects on Decision Making

Whisler's study indicated that computer applications in all cases caused a consolidation of decision-making areas, usually paralleled by organizational consolidation as well. Also found was a tendency to push decision making to a higher level, perhaps because the computer system so structured the lower-level operations that any decision to be made had an increased potential effect. Another change observed was an increase in dependence on computer personnel for help in decision making.

All the companies perceived the computer as having increased the quantifying and rationality of decision making, with a decreasing reliance on "rule of thumb." Middle management seemed to be the level most affected by the computer, but the nature of the effect is not clear. Top management's decision making was little affected by the computer, but Whisler concluded that it would become more so over time.

The new technology tended to create an inflexibility in decision making, because of the high cost of changing an established computer system. Thus, the computer creates a stimulus for change by providing current, in-depth information, but makes that change harder to effect.

### Effects on Job Content

Whisler's study found that with the computer, clerical jobs tended to become more routine. Most supervisory jobs had not changed, but those that did tended to be enlarged. Changes in managerial jobs were not clear cut. In terms of interpersonal communications on the job, evidence seemed to indicate that in the transition phase, communications increased, especially at the managerial level and somewhat at the supervisory level; but the more established the computer system, the less communication there was, chiefly at the clerical and supervisory levels.

The effect on job skills is most notable at the clerical level, where 90 percent of the jobs showed changes, with 70 percent of those changes being an upgrading of skill level. Whisler explained that although the jobs had become routine, greater precision was demanded, which was interpreted as an increase in skill. Skill changes caused by use of the computer diminished at successively higher levels in the organization.

### Vertinsky, Barth, and Mitchell (1975)

Vertinsky, Barth, and Mitchell attempted to investigate the dynamics of direct and indirect social change caused within organizations by OR/MS implementation. The authors believed that operations research and management science express the weltanschauung of an organizations management and that successful implementation is more likely if the management has a holistic, teleological, scientific perspective of the organization. They stated that individual attitudes, organizational patterns, and environmental interactions should be in line with this goal-oriented approach. They believed an evolutionary or planned change is more effective than a random one, but that, in any case, motivation of key individuals is important.

A pilot study was carried out in several organizations in western Canada in an attempt to test the researchers' notions of OR/MS as a change agent. OR/MS practitioners and client managers were administered questionnaires and semistructured interviews; data gathered concerned management style in terms of weltanschauung, skills associated with the computer system, modes of interaction, and personal characteristics of personnel involved with the system.

Results led the researchers to derive an expectancy theory model, derived from Lawler's (1971) theory, to explain the process of social change resulting from OR/MS implementation. The variables that affect the motivation to establish and use the system were seen as:

The manager's expectancy that implementation would lead to task accomplishment;

The manager's expectancy that such task accomplishment would lead to desired payoffs; and

The manager's degree of preference (valence) for different payoffs.

The authors summarized the major findings of the study as follows:

1. OR/MS solutions leading to significant social change tend to mobilize counter forces aimed at reversing or at least containing these changes.
2. Forced implementation of OR/MS solutions does not necessarily lead to changes in management approaches and may often result in counter-productive long-term consequences.
3. Changes in management approaches depend on the intensity of dissonance stemming from a manager's perceptions of conflict between his management style and OR/MS. The choice of strategy for reducing dissonance is determined by the level of motivation to use OR/MS that exists in the organization.
4. Use of OR/MS when solutions do not significantly affect the function or structure of the organizational unit may lead to long-run social change if the following conditions are met: (a) dissonance is experienced in using OR/MS; (b) use is continuous; (c) modes of interaction with OR/MS are informed and trusting.
5. The establishment of trusting, informed relationships with OR/MS practitioners depends on both the level of motivation for use of OR/MS in the organization and the interpersonal competence of the OR/MS practitioners.

6. The manager's quantitative aptitude increases
   the likelihood of successful and informed use of
   OR/MS.*

Although they acknowledge that their limited sample precludes gen-
eralizing the results, the researchers believed that their study provides a basis for further research.

In concluding this discussion, it is clear that the achievement
of fit is the result of a lengthy process of adaption in which systems
are designed to be appropriate for the specific natures of individual
organizations. Concurrently, the organizations undergo changes imposed by the exigencies of information systems and by their desires
to use such systems better. The success of organizations in building and operating information systems depends in part on their capacity for change and their ability to adapt so they provide an environment an MIS can fit with relative ease. Research that would provide
insight of how to implement this process of adaption most efficacious-
ly would clearly be of great interest both scientifically and practi-
cally.

## CONCLUSION: RESEARCH INTO MIS

It is now time to bring together a number of threads that have
been spun in the course of this study and to weave them into a single
fabric. This book began with an analogy between information systems and biological nervous systems. This analogy was based on
the functions of information in both kinds of systems and on their
complexity. The large number of variables discussed in the preceding chapters, the complexity of the interactions between them,
the evident interdependence of these variables with decision making
in organizations, and the use of information for evaluation and control do nothing to weaken the analogy; on the contrary, they tend to
strengthen it.

After beginning with the broad analogy of MIS as organizational
nervous systems and then decomposing them into their numerous
components, an attempt was made to render this detail applicable

---

*Reprinted by permission of the publishers from Ilan Vertin-
sky, Richard J. Barth, and Vance F. Mitchell. "A Study of OR/MS
Implementation as a Social Change Process," Chapter 12 in Randall
L. Schultz and Dennis P. Slevin (eds.), Implementing Operations
Research/Management Science, pp. 253-272. Copyright 1975 by
Elsevier North Holland, Inc.

with the help of the concept of fit. Given a description of an information system as a vector of variable values, one can evaluate its efficacy in terms of its individual fit to users in the organization and organizational fit to the character of the organization as an entity.

This concept of fit emphasizes the contingent nature of MIS success. Information systems that are highly successful in one organization may be very ineffective in another because a structure that fits one situation may be a bad fit in another. One may think of the individual and organizational environments of MIS as a pattern. The structure of MIS is another pattern. If the two patterns interlock, success will result. Incompatible patterns, however attractive each may be alone, will achieve no results. It would appear that the prime practical motivation for research in MIS is the need to understand how these two patterns may be mutually adapted.

The paradigm developed in this book is intended to provide a common framework for this essential research into MIS. The need for such a framework is amply demonstrated by the research efforts described in these chapters. Any attempt to synthesize the results of a number of studies in the same area is plagued by lack of consistency in definitions of variables and by the lack of a common theoretical framework to provide consistent underlying assumptions. It is the lack of such a framework that prevents the orderly and cumulative acquisition of knowledge in the area. This is especially important because of the multiple forms that research in MIS can adopt.

Four principal modes of research are employed in the study of MIS and it may be useful to briefly describe and assess each of them. The four modes are laboratory experiments, field experiments, surveys, and case studies (Van Horn 1973).

The major advantage of laboratory experiments is that they permit isolation and control of a small number of variables that may then be studied intensively. Thus, they may provide insight into the precise relationships between the variables studied. The major disadvantage of this form of research is that the extent that the relationships found in the laboratory carry over into the greater complexity of real-world situations is never clear, because of the necessary simplicity of the situations used as test vehicles and the isolation of those situations from most of the variables of real situations.

Field experiments consist of experiments performed on organizations. Potentially, this is one of the most powerful methods of research since it is essentially an extension of the laboratory approach to real situations. The major problems are finding organizations that are prepared to act as subjects for such experiments and achieving sufficient control over the subject organization so situations may be replicated with only the variables under study being altered. It is almost inconceivable that it would be possible to replicate any situation with sufficient accuracy so the effects of two different sets of variables could be validly compared.

Surveys are a useful means of obtaining snapshots of practices and situations at any time. However, they usually provide little insight of the causes of phenomena observed in such a study, nor do they usually provide information concerning the processes behind the observed phenomena. There is also the problem that respondents are generally self-selected, leading to suspicions of bias in the results.

Case studies have the advantage of capturing reality in greater detail than do any other mode of research. Case studies typically provide information on a greater number of variables and more information on the processes behind them than do the other methods. Usually, however, they are restricted to one event in a single organization. Thus, it is difficult to acquire data from a sufficiently large sample of organizations to provide statistically meaningful results. This is especially true when the case reports are not prepared under the guidance of a common model.

In light of the advantages and disadvantages of each of the research methodologies mentioned, it is clear that a comprehensive program of research in MIS must use all of them for various aspects of the program. This need to integrate the results of different research methodologies strengthens even further the need for a common framework into which the results may be incorporated. The reader, it is hoped, will find the paradigm presented in this book to be such a framework—this is its stated purpose.

Not only are various research methods necessary in the study of MIS, but there is a need to draw on several disciplines. MIS development and use are social and political process joined with a highly technical process. Thus, a complete picture of the processes requires the application of concepts and methodologies from areas as diverse as general systems theory, organizational development, project management, and organizational behavior. Again, the synthesis of results from so many different fields demands the existence of a general and comprehensive framework such as that given in this book.

The framework developed in this book, and in which the authors have incorporated much of the knowledge available in the field of MIS research, is clearly not a final product. New variables may be unearthed, different partitions into subsystems may also prove useful, additional disciplines may be found applicable, and emphases may change. However, given the state of the art, the authors are confident that widespread adoption of this paradigm can only advance the ability to understand the results of existing research in MIS and motivate and facilitate new research until there is a better paradigm.

# APPENDIX: OPERATIONALIZATION
# OF THE VARIABLES:
# SUGGESTIONS AND EXAMPLES

To demonstrate the feasibility of using in empirical studies the variables discussed in this book, and as a supplement to the definitions and discussion in the text, operational measures are presented in this appendix. It should be noted that these operationalizations are offered as suggestions; the precise measure adopted would need to be fitted in each case to the specific research design. Thus, the operationalization of a variable might be different for a laboratory experiment from that of a field survey, especially where behavioral variables are concerned. For convenience of use and cross-reference, a separate table corresponds to each chapter of this book. The variables are listed in the order of their presentation in the chapters. These tables have been compiled by the authors.

Suggestions for Operational Measures for the
Environment Variables of MIS
(Chapter 2)

| Variable | Operational Measures |
|---|---|
| Extraorganizational environment | Availability of trained manpower<br>Availability of hardware<br>Availability of software<br>Availability of decision techniques |
| Organizational structure | Number of product-market units<br>Number of profit centers<br>Number of divisions<br>Number of groups |
| Organizational time frame | Planning horizon<br>Average length of strategic decision process<br>Rate of technological change in industry |
| Organizational maturity | Degree of system formalization<br>Level of quantification<br>Availability of decision-relevant data |
| Resource allocation | Size of budget<br>Liquidity |
| The psychological climate | Attitudes toward information systems<br>Perceptions of information systems<br>Expectations from information systems |
| Size of the organization | Annual sales<br>Work force<br>Assets<br>Market share |

Suggestions for Operational Measures for Strategic Planning Variables of MIS
(Chapter 3)

| Variable | Dimension | Operational Measures |
|---|---|---|
| Development strategy | Degree of comprehensiveness | Top-down/Inside-out/Parallel/Bottom-up/ Evolutionary |
| | Integration of systems[1] | Proportion of data in shared data bases<br>Number of applications using common files<br>Number of functions served by application |
| | Pioneering | Number of similar applications in existence<br>Number of firms with similar problems<br>Number of firms in industry<br>Number of firms of same size |
| Purpose | Formality | Overall purpose defined in writing<br>Purpose included in terms of reference of responsible executive |
| Priorities | | Comprehensive list of projects prepared<br>All projects priority-ordered<br>Priorities consistent with purpose |
| Functions | Profitability | Direct contribution to profitability<br>Indirect contribution to profitability |
| | Institutional | Consistent with purpose<br>Relative degree of progress in MIS in different areas of the organization<br>Availability of requisite human resources |
| | Major problems | Proportion of resources involved<br>Contribution to total revenue<br>Amount of management time devoted<br>Implicit in statement of purpose |
| | Sophistication | Applications perceived as trivial or commensurate with organizational standards of management |
| Goals | Operationalization | Information content<br>Reliability<br>Service levels<br>Economy or efficiency<br>Intangible benefits<br>Improved operations |

(continued)

| Variable | Dimension | Operational Measures |
|---|---|---|
| | Consistency | Service levels consistent with cost goals<br>Service levels consistent with reliability<br>Reliability consistent with cost goals<br>Goals consistent with organizational<br>  sophistication |
| Requirements | Information content | Accuracy<br>Integrity<br>Timeliness<br>I/O characteristics |
| | Operating<br>characteristics | Mode of operation<br>Priority scheduling<br>User interface |
| | Capacity | Transactions per hour<br>Input rate<br>Response times |
| | Sophistication | Use of modern information processing<br>  and management science techniques |
| Documentation | | Formality<br>Completeness<br>Up to date<br>Clarity<br>Planned and existing systems included |

[1]This is the same variable that appears under this name in Table A. 9, and the operationalization is identical. Here, the reference is to planning variable values, whereas under MIS fit, the reference is to existing values.

TABLE A.3

Suggestions for Operational Measures for MIS Strategy Variables
(Chapter 4)

| Variable | Dimension | Operational Measures |
|---|---|---|
| Hardware strategy | Computer capabilities | Storage size<br>Speed<br>Reliability<br>Accessibility<br>Operating system characteristics |
| | Selection process | Selection criteria<br>System evaluation procedures |
| | Form of acquisition | Purchase/rent/lease/service bureaus |
| | Equipment deployment | Degree of centralization<br>Existence of central unit<br>Number of peripheral units |
| Software strategy | Project complexity | Programming man-hours<br>Program complexity<br>Number of organizational functions involved<br>Degree of technological sophistication |
| | Programming languages | Level of languages<br>Types of languages<br>Degree of standardization in language usage |
| | Acquisition | Internal/external<br>Type of program |
| | Estimates | Types of estimates undertaken<br>Degree of standardization of estimating procedures<br>Accuracy of estimates |
| | Standardization | Degree of standardization of software development practices<br>Types of standard practices employed<br>Areas of standardization |

(continued)

| Variable | Dimension | Operational Measures |
|---|---|---|
| Organizational strategy | Location | Identification with specific functional area |
| | Degree of centralization | Parallelism to corporate structure<br>Number of units<br>Proportion of organizational units served by individual MIS unit |
| | Organization of implementors | Team/functional/matrix |
| | User interface | Number of implementors in non-MIS units<br>Number of user representatives in MIS units |
| | Steering committee | Existence<br>Organizational level<br>Functional composition |
| | Study group | Existence<br>Composition<br>Skill level<br>Proportion of technical members |
| | Data base administrator | Existence<br>Rank<br>Degree of independence |
| | Corporate computer staff | Existence<br>Level of education<br>Experience level |
| | External assistance | Use<br>Budget for<br>Length of time used<br>Functions assigned |

TABLE A.4

Suggestions for Operational Measures for
Project Implementation Variables
(Chapter 5)

| Variable | Dimension | Operational Measures |
|----------|-----------|---------------------|
| MIS project stages | Execution-control cycles | Phases implemented<br>Sequence of phases<br>Average time allocated for each stage |
| | Level of control | Control phases implemented<br>Relative rank of controlling body<br>Average time between control phases |

TABLE A.5

Suggestions for Operational Measures for MIS Structure Variables
(Chapter 6)

| Variable | Dimension | Operational Measures |
|---|---|---|
| Data characteristics | | Managers' perceptions of accuracy, content, recency, frequency, and feedback time<br>Expert evaluations<br>Level of aggregation |
| Processing capabilities | | Flexibility<br>Packages available<br>Input/output ratio |
| Data base | Data base characteristics | Existence<br>Structure<br>Degree of integrity<br>Percent of time used<br>Percent of applications using<br>Number of data bases |
| | Data base capabilities | Need for auxiliary systems<br>Ease of use<br>Versatility<br>Number of options |
| | Data base development | Parallel/transformed<br>Ad-hoc/planned<br>Flexible/rigid |
| | Data base content | Relevance<br>Accessibility<br>Redundancy<br>Coverage of data required |
| User interface characteristics | I/O characteristics | Length of training needed<br>Symbols used<br>Adaptability of output formats<br>Length of output<br>Contextual richness of outputs |
| | Mode of operation | OLRT-hybrid-batch<br>Existence of direct access<br>Response time<br>Ease of use<br>Degree of "human" behavior<br>Time-sharing ability<br>Modes of communication |
| | Integration of systems | Proportion of data in shared data bases<br>Number of applications using common files<br>Number of organizational functions served by each application |

## TABLE A.6

Suggestions for Operational Measures for
Executive Responsibility Variables
(Chapter 7)

| Variable | Dimension | Operational Measures |
| --- | --- | --- |
| Association | | Formal commitment<br>Degree of perceived association<br>Degree of involvement<br>Prior involvement |
| Rank of responsible executive | | Number of levels below chief officer |
| Functions | Amount of time | Proportion of executive time devoted<br>Frequency of meetings<br>Length of meetings<br>Proportion of activities |
| | Devotion | Rank order in priorities<br>Congruence with personal goals |
| Capabilities | | Formal computer education<br>Formal management education<br>Prior managerial success |

Suggestions for Operational Measures for System Implementor Variables
(Chapter 8)

| Variable | Dimension | Operational Measures |
|---|---|---|
| Functions | Goals | Existence<br>Degree of comprehensiveness<br>Clarity<br>Level of specification |
| | Breadth | Procedural constraints<br>Degree of discretion (budget) |
| Recruitment | Origin | Proportion recruited inside organization<br>Average number of years with the organization |
| | Method | Use of testing<br>Tests used<br>Selection criteria |
| | Type | Proportion with management science background<br>Proportion with operating management experience |
| Turnover | Rate | Annual turnover<br>Number of years in the unit<br>Function of exiters |
| | Level | Relative rates in various levels |
| Capabilities | Management | Formal management education<br>Past managerial experience<br>Employees' evaluation of interpersonal skills |
| | Analysts and programmers | Formal computer education<br>Average years of experience |
| Organization | Structure | Functional/project team<br>Unit size<br>Unit discretion |
| Relationships with top management | | Degree of control of top management<br>Ease of communications<br>Accessibility of top management |

Suggestions for Operational Measures for MIS User Variables
(Chapter 9)

| Variable | Dimension | Operational Measures |
|---|---|---|
| Requirements | | Complexity of decisions (number of decision variables)<br>Number of decisions<br>Frequency of decisions<br>Degree of structure in decisions |
| Rank | | Distance from top<br>Line/staff<br>Salary |
| Personality | Noncognitive | Motivation<br>Anxiety<br>Defensiveness |
| | Cognitive | Intuitive/analytic<br>Detail/"broad brush" |
| Attitudes | | Attitudes toward MIS<br>Felt need<br>Perceived effect<br>MIS appreciation |
| Change resistance | | Intensity of resistance to change<br>Type of resistance |
| Involvement | | Prior involvement<br>Development involvement<br>Use involvement<br>Number of tasks<br>Time invested in MIS |
| Conflict | Communications | Time spent together<br>Degree of convergence of technical vocabularies<br>Degree of similarity in educational and professional backgrounds |
| | Relocation of power | Number of decisions relocated<br>Importance of decisions relocated |
| | Implementation practices | Degree of sensitivity to users |
| Conflict reduction | Education | Time passed since management education<br>Users' cooperation in training design<br>Time invested in studying proposed system |
| | Role definition | Degree of formality of terms of reference<br>Degree of formality of task assignments |
| | Formalization | Level of documentation<br>Degree of prior scheduling of meetings |

# TABLE A.9

Suggestions for Operational Measures
for MIS Fit Variables
(Chapter 10)

| Variable | Dimension | Operational Measures |
|---|---|---|
| Individual fit | System adaptability | Number of decision models<br>Rigidity of use<br>Tailoring capabilities |
| Organizational fit | Feasibility | Availability of resources<br>Availability of technical knowledge<br>Consistent with organizational strategy |
| | Integration of information systems with the organization[1] | Consistency of MIS goals with organizational goals |
| | Organizational interface | Power of the information function<br>Level of conflict of information systems with other organizational functions |
| | Information view | Degree of qualitative information<br>Relates to quantitative organizational goals<br>Congruent with users' weltansicht |

[1]This variable appears in Table A.2, referring to planning variables. Here, the reference is to existing values.

# REFERENCES

Ackoff, Rusell L. 1967. "Management Misinformation Systems." Management Science 14 (December): 147-56.

Adams, Carl R., and Schroeder, Roger G. 1973. "Managers and MIS: 'They Get What They Want.'" Business Horizons 16 (December): 63-68.

Adcock, William J.; Letzler, Walter A.; Terrey, John V.; and Terry, Mack W. 1968. "A Framework for Evaluation of Management Information Systems." A Research Study for D.P. Group, Information Systems Planning, International Business Machines Corp. Sloan School of Management, Massachusetts Institute of Technology.

Ahituv, Niv, and Hadass, Michael. 1978. "Organizational Structure of a Complex Data Processing Department." Information & Management 1: 53-57.

Alexander, Tom. 1969. "Computers Can't Solve Everything." Fortune 80 (October): 126.

Alter, Steven. 1977. "A Taxonomy of Decision Support Systems." Sloan Management Review 19 (Fall): 39-56.

_____. 1976. "How Effective Managers Use Information Systems." Harvard Business Review 54 (November-December): 97-104.

Alter, Steven, and Ginzberg, Michael. 1978. "Managing Uncertainty in MIS Implementation." Sloan Management Review 20 (Fall): 23-31.

Ansoff, H. Igor. 1967. "Making Effective Use of Computers in Managerial Decision Making." Automation (October): 68-73.

Anthony, Robert N. 1965. Planning and Control Systems: A Framework for Analysis. Boston: Harvard University Graduate School of Business Administration.

Argyris, Chris. 1971. "Management Information Systems: The Challenge to Rationality and Emotionality." Management Science 17 (February): B275-91.

241

Aron, J. D. 1969. "Information Systems in Perspective." Computing Surveys 1 (December): 213-36.

_____. 1967. "Real-Time Systems in Perspective." IBM Systems Journal 6: 49-67.

Atkins, William. 1976. "Why Do Systems Fail—Part II." In Proceedings of the Eighth Annual Conference, pp. 51-52. Chicago: Society for Management Information Systems.

Balderston, Jack L. 1975. "The Tiger in the Management Jungle." Journal of Systems Management 26 (May): 7-9.

Bariff, M. L., and Lusk, E. J. 1977. "Cognitive and Personality Tests for the Design of Management Information Systems." Management Science 23 (April): 820-29.

Bean, Alden S.; Neal, Rodney D.; Radnor, Michael; and Tansik, David A. 1975. "Structural and Behavioral Correlates of Implementation in U.S. Business Organizations." In Implementing Operations Research/Management Science, edited by Randall L. Schultz and Dennis P. Slevin, pp. 77-132. New York: American Elsevier.

Beckhard, Richard. 1969. Organization Development: Strategies and Models. Reading, Mass.: Addison-Wesley.

Beehler, Paul J. 1976. "Integrated MIS: A Data Base Reality." Journal of Systems Management 27 (February): 34-39.

Benbasat, Izak, and Schroeder, Roger G. 1977. "An Experimental Investigation of Some MIS Design Variables." MIS Quarterly 1 (March): 37-49.

Berkowitz, Nathan, and Munro, Robertson. 1969. Automatic Data Processing and Management. Belmont, Ca.: Dickenson.

Birkhahn, Paul D. 1976. "Planning to Meet Management's Needs." In Proceedings of The Eighth Annual Conference, pp. 97-104. Chicago: Society for Management Information Systems.

Blumenthal, Sherman. 1969. Management Information Systems: A Framework for Planning and Development. Englewood Cliffs, N.J.: Prentice-Hall.

Boland, Richard J., Jr. 1978. "The Process and Product of System Design." Management Science 24 (May): 887-98.

Bonini, Charles P. 1978. "Computers, Modeling, and Management Education." California Management Review 21 (Winter): 47-55.

Borovits, Israel, and Ein-Dor, Phillip. 1976. "Computer Selection in Israel." Israel Review of Business Economics 1 (May): 45-55. (Hebrew).

Botkin, J. W. 1974. "An Intuitive Computer System: A Cognitive Approach to the Management Learning Process." Ph.D. dissertation, Harvard University.

Boulden, J. B. 1971. "Computerized Corporate Planning." Long Range Planning 3 (June): 2-9.

Boulding, Kenneth E. 1956. "General Systems Theory: The Skeleton of Science." Management Science 2 (April): 197-208.

Brady, Rodney H. 1967. "Computers in Top-Level Decision Making." Harvard Business Review 45 (July-August): 67-76.

Brandon, Dick H. 1970. Management Planning for Data Processing. Princeton, N.J.: Brandon Systems Press.

Brehmer, Berndt. 1976. "Social Judgment Theory and the Analysis of Interpersonal Conflict." Psychological Bulletin 83: 985-1003.

Brennan, John M. 1975. "Small Business Gets Big DP Help." Journal of Systems Management 26 (June): 26-27.

Brill, Alan E. 1974. "The Alienation of the Systems Analyst." Journal of Systems Management 25 (January): 26-29.

Brooks, F. P., Jr. 1975. The Mythical Man-Month. Reading, Mass.: Addison-Wesley.

Brown, Foster, 1977. "The Systems Development Process." Journal of Systems Management 28 (December): 34-39.

Burdeau, H. B. 1974. "Environmental Approach to MIS." Journal of Systems Management 25 (April): 11-13.

Burnett, Gerald J., and Nolan, Richard L. 1975. "At Last, Major Roles for Minicomputers." Harvard Business Review 53 (May-June): 148-56.

Caldwell, John. 1975. "The Effective Reports Crisis." Journal of Systems Management 26 (June): 7-12.

Carlson, Eric D. 1979. "An Approach for Designing Decision Support Systems." Data Base 10 (Winter): 3-23.

_____, ed. 1977. "Proceedings of a Conference on Decision Support Systems." Data Base 8 (Winter).

_____. 1974. "Evaluating the Impact of Information Systems." Management Informatics 3 (April): 57-67.

Carlson, Eric D.; Grace, Barbara F.; and Sutton, Jimmy A. 1977. "Case Studies of End User Requirements for Interactive Problem-Solving." MIS Quarterly 1 (March): 51-63.

Carlson, Walter M. 1967. "A Management Information System Designed by Managers." Datamation 13 (May): 37-43.

Cave, William C., and Salisbury, Alan B. 1978. "Controlling the Software Life Cycle—The Project Management Task." IEEE Transactions on Software Engineering SE-4 (July): 326-34.

Chapanis, Alphonse. 1975. "Interactive Human Communication." Scientific American 232 (March): 36-42.

Chapin, Ned. 1963. An Introduction to Automatic Computers. 2nd ed. Princeton, N.J.: Van Nostrand.

Chervany, Norman L., and Dickson, Gary W. 1974. "An Experimental Evaluation of Information Overload in a Production Environment." Management Science 20 (June): 1335-44.

Chrysler, Earl. 1978. "Some Basic Determinants of Computer Programming Productivity." Communications of the ACM 21 (June): 472-83.

Churchman, C. West. 1971. The Design of Inquiring Systems. New York: Basic Books.

Cochran, Terry L. 1978. "Development and Compensation of Systems Supervisors." Journal of Systems Management 29 (January): 14-17.

Coe, Ted L. 1974. "Allocating the Corporate Information Processing Resource." Journal of Systems Management 25 (August): 18-22.

Cohen, I. K., and Van Horn, Richard L. 1972. "A Laboratory Research Approach to Organizational Design." Brussels: European Institute for Advanced Studies in Management, Working Paper 72-16.

Colton, Kent W. 1972-3. "Computers and Police: Patterns of Success and Failure." Sloan Management Review 14 (Winter): 75-97.

Cooke, Lawrence H., Jr. 1976. "The Chief Programmer Team Administrator." Datamation 22 (June): 85-86.

Cooper, John D. 1978. "Corporate Level Software Management." IEEE Transactions on Software Engineering SE-4 (July): 319-26.

Cosier, Richard A.; Ruble, Thomas L.; and Aplin, John C. 1978. "An Evaluation of the Effectiveness of Dialectical Inquiry Systems." Management Science 24 (October): 1483-90.

Daly, Edmund B. 1977. "Management of Software Development." IEEE Transactions on Software Engineering SE-3 (May): 229-42.

Daniel, Leland M. 1976. "Planning MIS Acceptance." Journal of Systems Management 27 (January): 20-21.

David, E. E. 1969. Remarks in Software Engineering, Report edited by Peter Naur and Brian Randell. NATO: Scienfific Affairs Division.

Davis, Gordon B. 1974. Management Information Systems: Conceptual Foundations, Structure and Development. New York: McGraw-Hill.

Dean, Neal J. 1968. "The Computer Comes of Age." Harvard Business Review 46 (January-February): 83-91.

Dearden, John. 1972. "MIS is a Mirage." Harvard Business Review 50 (January-February): 90-99.

Dearden, John, and Nolan, Richard L. 1973. "How to Control the Computer Resource." Harvard Business Review 51 (November-December): 68-78.

DeBrabender, Bert, and Edström, Anders N. 1977. "Successful Information System Development Projects." Management Science 24 (October): 191-99.

Delaney, William A. 1977. "Software Managers Speak Out." Datamation 23 (October): 77-78.

Department of the Army. 1959. Army Civilian Career Program for Comptroller Functional Area. Washington, D. C.

Dickson, Gary W.; Senn, James A.; and Chervany, Norman L. 1977. "Research in Management Information Systems: The Minnesota Experiments." Management Science 23 (May): 913-23.

Dickson, Gary A., and Simmons, John K. 1970. "The Behavioral Side of MIS." Business Horizons 13 (August): 59-71.

Diebold, John. 1969. "Bad Decisions on Computer Use." Harvard Business Review 47 (January-February): 14-28, 176.

Dinter, Heinz. 1971. "Criteria for the Organizational Effectiveness of Data Processing." Data Management 9 (August): 33-34.

Doktor, Robert. 1976. "Cognitive Style and the Use of Computers and Management Information Systems." Management Datamatics 5 (April): 83-88.

Edwards, James B. 1974. "Wanted: Someone to Manage Information." Data Management 12 (July): 22-25.

Ein-Dor, Phillip. 1975. "Parallel Strategy for MIS." Journal of Systems Management 26 (March): 30-35.

Ein-Dor, Phillip, and Segev, Eli. 1980. "Organizational Arrangements for MIS Units." Information and Management 3: 19-26.

_____. 1978a. Managing Management Information Systems. Lexington, Mass.: D. C. Heath.

_____. 1978b. "Organizational Context and the Success of Management Information Systems." Management Science 24 (June): 1064-77.

_____. 1978c. "Strategic Planning for Management Information Systems." Management Science 24 (November): 1631-41.

_____. 1977. "Information System Responsibility." MSU Business Topics 25 (Autumn): 33-40.

Emery, James C. 1973. "An Overview of Management Information Systems." Data Base 5 (Winter): 1-15.

_____. 1969. "Management Information System." In Progress in Operations Research vol. 3, edited by Julius S. Aronofsky, pp. 489-524. New York: John Wiley & Sons.

Erikson, W. J. 1966. "A Pilot Study of Interactive Versus Non-Interactive Debugging." Santa Monica: System Development Corporation, TM-3296 (December).

Eysenck, H. J. 1960. The Structure of Human Personality. 2nd ed. London: Methuen.

Farley, John U.; Howard, John A.; and Hulbert, James. 1971. "An Organizational Approach to an Industrial Marketing Information System." Sloan Management Review 13 (Fall): 35-54.

Farrington, Norman. 1977. "High Level Business Software." Journal of Systems Management 28 (October): 24-31.

Ference, Thomas P., and Uretsky, Myron. 1976. "Computers in Management: Some Insights into the State of the Revolution." Management Datamatics 5 (April): 55-63.

Financial Executive. 1974. "Managing MIS—Special Section." 42 (June): 23.

Fisher, D. L. 1969. "Management Controlled Information Systems." Datamation 15 (June): 53-57.

Fronk, William C. 1978. "Solving Five Systems Development Problems." Journal of Systems Management 29 (July): 34-37.

Garrity, John T. 1963. "Top Management and Computer Profits." Harvard Business Review 41 (July-August): 6-12, 172-74.

Gehring, Philip F., and Pooch, Udo W. 1977. "Software Development Management." Data Management 15 (February): 14.

Geisler, Robert. 1970. "The THOMIS Medical Information System." Datamation 16 (June): 133-36.

Geller, Dennis P. 1976. "How Many Directions is Top-Down?" Datamation 22 (June): 109-12.

Geoffrion, Arthur M. 1976. "Better Distribution Planning with Computer Models." Harvard Business Review 54 (July-August): 49-58.

Gershefski, George W. 1969. "Building a Corporate Financial Model." Harvard Business Review 47 (July-August): 61-72.

Gibson, Cyrus F. 1975. "A Methodology for Implementation Research." In Implementing Operations Research/Management Science, edited by Randall L. Schultz and Dennis P. Slevin, pp. 53-76. New York: American Elsevier.

Gibson, Cyrus F., and Nolan, Richard L. 1974. "Managing the Four Stages of EDP Growth." Harvard Business Review 52 (January-February): 76-88.

Gibson, James L.; Ivancevich, John M.; and Donnelly, James H., Jr. 1973. Organizations: Structure, Processes, Behavior. Dallas: Business Publications.

Gibson, Lawrence D.; Mayer, Charles S.; Nugent, Christopher E.; and Vollman, Thomas E. 1973. "An Evolutionary Approach to Marketing Information Systems." Journal of Marketing 37 (April): 2-6.

Gold, M. 1967. "Methodology for Evaluating Time-Shared Computer Usage." Ph.D. dissertation, Sloan School of Management, Massachusetts Institute of Technology.

Grant, E. E., and Sackman, H. 1967. "An Exploratory Investigation of Programmer Performance Under On-Line and Off-Line Conditions." IEEE Transactions on Human Factors in Electronics HFE-8 (March): 33-48.

Grayson, C. Jackson, Jr. 1973. "Management Science and Business Practice." Harvard Business Review 51 (July-August): 41-48.

Grindlay, Andrew A., and Cummer, Gordon. 1973. "Comment: Computer-Based Decision Systems and Canadian Management." Management Science 20 (December): 562-74.

Grossman, Jerome H. 1972. "Management Information Systems in Medicine." Sloan Management Review 13 (Winter): 1-7.

Gupta, Roger. 1974. "Information Manager: His Role in Corporate Management." Data Management 12 (July): 26-29.

Guthrie, Art. 1974. "Attitudes of the User-Manager Towards Management Information Systems." Management Informatics 3: 221-32.

Hamilton, William J., and Moses, Michael A. 1974. "A Computer-Based Corporate Planning System." Management Science 21 (October): 148-59.

Hammond, John S., III. 1974a. "Do's and Don'ts of Computer Models for Planning." Harvard Business Review 52 (March-April): 110-23.

_____. 1974b. "The Roles of the Manager and Management Scientist in Successful Implementation." Sloan Management Review 15 (Winter): 1-24.

Hanold, Terrance. 1972. "An Executive View of MIS." Datamation 18 (November): 65-71.

Hansen, James V. 1975. "Progress in Healthcare Systems." Journal of Systems Management 26 (April): 14-21.

Hax, Arnoldo. 1973. "Planning a Management Information System for a Distributing and Manufacturing Company." Sloan Management Review 14 (Spring): 85-98.

Hayes, Robert H., and Nolan, Richard L. 1974. "What Kind of Corporate Modeling Functions Best." Harvard Business Review 52 (May-June): 102-12.

Head, Robert V. 1974. "Real Time Applications." Journal of Systems Management 25 (September): 7-13.

_____. 1970. "The Elusive MIS." Datamation 16 (September): 22-27.

_____. 1967. "Management Information Systems: A critical Appraisal." Datamation 13 (May): 22-26.

Heany, Donald F. 1972. "Education: The Critical Link in Getting Managers to Use Management Systems." Interfaces 2 (May): 1-7.

_____. 1965. "Is TIMS Talking to Itself." Management Science 12 (December): B146-55.

Hedberg, Bo. 1975. "Computer Systems to Support Industrial Democracy." In Human Choice and Computers, edited by E. Mumford and H. Sackman. New York: American Elsevier.

Henry, David. 1977. "Systems Project Management—A Snap!" Journal of Systems Management 28 (February): 35-38.

Herzlinger, Regina. 1977. "Why Data Systems in Nonprofit Organizations Fail." Harvard Business Review 55 (January-February): 81-86.

Higgins, J. C., and Finn, R. 1976. "Managerial Attitudes Towards Computer Models for Planning and Control." Long Range Planning 9 (December): 107-12.

Hodge, Bartow. 1974. "The Computer in Management Information and Control Systems." Data Management 12 (December): 26-30.

Holland, W. E.; Kretlow, William J.; and Ligon, Jerry C. 1974. "Socio-Technical Aspects of MIS." Journal of Systems Management 25 (February): 14-16.

Holt, H. O., and Stevenson, F. L. 1978. "Human Performance Considerations In Complex Systems." Journal of Systems Management 29 (October): 14-20.

Huse, Edgar F. 1975. Organization Development and Change. St. Paul: West.

Jenkins, William E. 1969. "Airline Reservation Systems." Datamation 15 (March): 29-32.

Jones, T. C. 1978. "Measuring Programming Quality and Productivity." IBM Systems Journal 17: 39-63.

Juergens, Hugh F. 1977. "Attributes of Information System Development." MIS Quarterly 1 (June): 31-41.

Jung, C. G. 1971. Collected Works, translated by R. F. C. Hall. Psychological Types, vol. 6. Princeton: Princeton Univ. Press.

Kalogeras, C. M. 1977. "Centralized vs. Local DP Organization." Journal of Systems Management 28 (March): 28-31.

Keen, Peter G. W. 1976. "'Interactive' Computer Systems for Managers: A Modest Proposal." Sloan Management Review 18 (Fall): 1-17.

_____. 1975. "Computer-Based Decision Aids: The Evaluation Problem." Sloan Management Review 16 (Spring): 17-29.

Kelsch, August L. 1978. "Dispersed and Distributed Data Processing." Journal of Systems Management 29 (March): 32-37.

Kennedy, Miles H. 1974. "Real Time vs. Exception Reports." Journal of Systems Management 25 (April): 22-26.

Kennedy, Miles H., and Hoffer, Jeffrey A. 1978. "Real-Time Data Processing and Real-Time Decision Making." Journal of Systems Management 29 (October): 21-25.

Kennedy, Miles H., and Mahapatra, Sitikantha. 1975. "Information Analysis for Effective Planning and Control." Sloan Management Review 16 (Winter): 71-83.

Kenneron, Walter. 1970. "MIS Universe." Data Management 8 (September): 62-64.

Kernighan, Brian P., and Plauger, P. J. 1974. "Programming Style: Examples and Counterexamples." Computing Surveys 6 (December): 303-19.

King, William R. 1973. "The Intelligent MIS—A Management Helper." Business Horizons 16 (October): 5-12.

King, William, and Cleland, David I. 1975. "The Design of Management Information Systems: An Information Analysis Approach." Management Science 22 (November): 286-97.

_____. 1974. "Environmental Information Systems for Strategic Marketing Planning." Journal of Marketing 38 (October): 35-40.

_____. 1973. "Decision and Information Systems for Strategic Planning." Business Horizons 16 (April): 29-36.

_____. 1971. "Manager-Analyst Teamwork in MIS." Business Horizons 14 (April): 59-68.

Kneitel, Arnold M. 1975a. "Will the Real User Please Stand Up." Management Datamatics 4 (June): 83-93.

_____. 1975b. "Current Myths about Information Processing." Journal of Systems Management 26 (May): 36-41.

Knutsen, K. Eric, and Nolan, Richard L. 1974. "Assessing Computer Costs and Benefits." Journal of Systems Management 25 (February): 28-34.

Knutsen, Joan, and Scotto, Marie. 1978. "Developing a Project Plan." Journal of Systems Management 29 (October): 37-41.

Koester, Robert, and Luthans, Fred. 1979. "The Impact of the Computer on the Choice Activity of Decision-Makers: A Replication with Actual Users of Computerized MIS." Academy of Management Journal 22 (June): 416-22.

Kriebel, C. H. 1973. Discussion comments on a paper by Emery. Data Base 5 (Winter): 11-13.

_____. 1972. "The Future MIS." Business Automation 19 (June): 18.

_____. 1968. "The Strategic Dimension of Computer Systems Planning." Long Range Planning 1 (September): 7-12.

Kroeber, Donald W., and Watson, Hugh J. 1979. "Is There a Best MIS Department Location?" Information & Management 2: 165-73.

Kronenberg, R. A. 1967. "Weyerhaueser's Management Information System." Datamation 13 (May): 28-30.

Kuhn, Thomas H. 1972. "The Structure of Scientific Revolutions." In International Encyclopaedia of Unified Science, vol. 2, no. 2. Chicago: University of Chicago Press.

Lanahan, John R. 1976. "Planning." In Proceedings of the Eighth Annual Conference, pp. 67-71. Chicago: Society for Management Information Systems.

_____. 1973. "Data Base Applications at Inland Steel." Data Base 5 (Winter): 87-94.

Laverdiere, Raymond G., and Smith, Ephraim P. 1975. "Information Systems and Management." Managerial Planning 23 (May-June): 20-23.

Lawler, E. E. 1971. Pay and Organizational Effectiveness. New York: McGraw-Hill.

Lawrie, John W.; Ryan, John M.; and Carlyle, Alistair. 1974. "Terminals and Their Impact on Employee Motivation." Datamation 20 (August): 59-62.

Lehman, John H. 1979. "How Software Projects Are Really Managed." Datamation 25 (January): 119-29.

Lewin, Kurt. 1947. "Group Decision and Social Change." In Readings in Social Psychology, edited by Eleanor E. Maccoby, Theodore M. Newcomb, and Eugene L. Hartley, pp. 197-211. New York: Holt, Rinehart and Winston.

Lewis, L. J. 1976. "Service Levels: A concept for the User and the Computer Center." IBM Systems Journal 15: 328-57.

Lieberman, Arthur Z., and Whinston, Andrew B. 1975. "A Structuring of an Events-Accounting Information System." The Accounting Review 50 (April): 246-58.

Lucas, Henry C., Jr. 1975a. Why Information Systems Fail. New York: Columbia University Press.

_____. 1975b. "Performance and the Use of an Information System." Management Science 21 (April): 908-19.

_____. 1974a. "Systems Quality, User Reactions and the Use of Information Systems." Management Informatics 3 (August): 207-12.

_____. 1974b. "Measuring Employee Reactions to Computer Operations." Sloan Management Review 15 (Spring): 59-67.

_____. 1973. "A Descriptive Model of Information Systems in the Context of the Organization." Data Base 5 (Winter): 27-39.

Lucas, Henry C., Jr., and Sutton, Jimmy A. 1977. "The Stage Hypothesis and the S-Curve: Some Contradictory Evidence." Communications of the ACM 20 (April): 254-59.

Luthans, Fred., and Koester, Robert. 1976. "The Impact of Computer Generated Information on the Choice Activity of Decision Makers." Academy of Management Journal 19 (June): 328-32.

McFadden, Fred R., and Suver, James D. 1978. "Costs and Benefits of a Data Base System." Harvard Business Review 56 (January-February): 131-39.

McFarlan, F. Warren. 1976. "Planning the Information Function." In Proceedings of the Eighth Annual Conference, pp. 63-64. Chicago: Society for Management Information Systems.

_____. 1971. "Problems in Planning the Information System." Harvard Business Review 49 (March-April): 74-89.

McKenney, James L., and Keen, Peter G. W. 1974. "How Managers' Minds Work." Harvard Business Review 52 (May-June): 79-90.

The McKinsey Quarterly. 1968. "Unlocking the Computer's Profit Potential: A Research Report to Management." (Fall).

McLaughlin, R. A., and Knottek, Nancy. 1978. "DP Salary Survey." Datamation 24 (November): 87-95.

McLean, Ephraim R., and Soden, John V., eds. 1977. Strategic Planning for MIS. New York: Wiley-Interscience.

MacCrimmon, Kenneth R. 1974. "Descriptive Aspects of Team Theory: Observation, Communication and Decision Heuristics in Information Systems." Management Science 20 (June): 1323-34.

Maish, Alexander M. 1979. "A User's Behavior Toward His MIS." MIS Quarterly 3 (March): 39-52.

Management Science Training Institute. 1958. "Managing the ADP Program." New York.

Mandell, Steven L. 1975. "The Management Information System is Going to Pieces." California Management Review 17 (Summer): 50-56.

Manley, John H. 1975. "Implementation Attitudes: A Model and a Measurement Methodology." In Implementing Operations Research/Management Science, edited by Randall L. Schultz and Dennis P. Slevin, pp. 183-202. New York: American Elsevier.

March, James G., and Simon, Herbert A. 1958. Organizations. John Wiley & Sons.

Martin, Merle P. 1975. "Judicial Information Systems." Journal of Systems Management 26 (December): 31-38.

Mason, Richard O. 1969. "A Dialectical Approach to Strategic Planning." Management Science 15 (April): B403-14.

Mason, Richard O., and Mitroff, Ian I. 1973. "A Program for Research on Management Information Systems." Management Science 19 (January): 475-87.

Meldman, Jeffrey A. 1977. "A New Technique for Modeling the Behavior of Man-Machine Information Systems." Sloan Management Review 18 (Spring): 29-46.

Merwin, Richard E. 1978. "Software Management: We Must Find A Way." IEEE Transactions on Software Engineering SE-4 (July): 307-8.

Miller, Floyd. 1977. "Selection of Software." Journal of Systems Management 28 (July): 12-15.

Miller, J. C. 1964. "Conceptual Models for Determining Information Requirements." In AFIPS Conference Proceedings vol. 25: Spring Joint Computer Conference, pp. 609-20. Baltimore: Spartan Books.

Miller, William B. 1978. "Fundamentals of Project Management." Journal of Systems Management 29 (November): 22-29.

Milutinovich, J., and Kanter, H. A. 1975. "Organizing the MIS Department." Journal of Systems Management 26 (April): 36-41.

Mintzberg, Henry. 1976. "Planning on the Left Side and Managing on the Right." Harvard Business Review 54 (July-August): 49-58.

_____. 1975a. "Making Management Information Useful." Management Review 64 (May): 34-38.

_____. 1975b. Impediments to the Use of Management Information. New York: National Association of Accountants.

_____. 1972. "The Myths of MIS." California Management Review 15 (Fall): 92-97.

_____. 1971. "Managerial Work: Analysis from Observations." Management Science 18 (October): B97-110.

Mitroff, Ian I.; Barabba, Vincent P.; and Kilman, Ralph H. 1977. "The Application of Behavioral and Philosophical Technologies to Strategic Planning: A Case Study of a Large Federal Agency." Management Science 24 (September): 44-58.

Mitroff, Ian I.; Nelson, John; and Mason, Richard O. 1974. "On Management Myth-Information Systems." Management Science 21 (December): 371-82.

Mock, Theodore F. 1973. "A Longitudinal Study of Some Information Structure Alternatives." Data Base 5 (Winter): 40-49.

Montijo, R. E. 1967. "California DMV Goes On-Line." Datamation 13 (May): 31-36.

Moore, Jeffrey H. 1979. "A Framework for MIS Software Development Projects." MIS Quarterly 3 (March): 29-38.

Morgan, Howard L., and Soden, John V. 1973. "Understanding MIS Failures." Data Base 5 (Winter): 151-71.

Munro, Malcolm C. 1978. "Determining the Manager's Information Needs." Journal of Systems Management 29 (June): 34-39.

Munro, Malcolm C., and Davis, Gordon B. 1977. "Determining Management Information Needs: A Comparison of Methods." MIS Quarterly 1 (June): 55-67.

Murdick, Robert G. 1977. "MIS for MBO." Journal of Systems Management 28 (March): 34-40.

Murdick, Robert G., and Ross, Joel E. 1975. Information Systems for Modern Management. Englewood Cliffs, N.J.: Prentice-Hall.

_____. 1972. "Future Management Information Systems." Journal of Systems Management 23 (April): 22-25 and (May): 32-35.

Murray, Gordon L., ed. (n.d.) Systems and Methods Appraisal, Selected Papers 1957. (n.c.): Haskins and Sells.

Myers, M. Scott. 1975. "Awareness Improves Communication." Journal of Systems Management 26 (March): 26-28.

Naur, Peter, and Randell, Brian, eds. 1969. Software Engineering. NATO: Scientific Affairs Division.

Neumann, Seev, and Segev, Eli. 1979. "A Case Study of User Evaluation of Information Characteristics for Systems Improvement." Information & Management 2 (December): 271-78.

Nicholas, John M. 1978. "Transactional Analysis for System Professionals." Journal of Systems Management 29 (October): 6-11.

Nolan, Richard L. 1979. "Managing the Crises in Data Processing." Harvard Business Review 57 (March-April): 115-26.

_____. 1977. "Effects of Chargeout on User/Manager Attitudes." Communications of the ACM 20 (March): 177-84.

_____. 1973a. "Managing the Computer Resource: A Stage Hypothesis." Communications of the ACM 16 (July): 399-405.

_____. 1973b. "Computer Data Base: The Future is Now." Harvard Business Review 51 (September-October): 98-114.

Nolan, Richard L., and Knutsen, K. Eric. 1974. "The Computerization of the ABC Widget Co." Datamation 20 (April): 71-76.

Ochsman, Robert B., and Chapanis, Alphonse. 1974. "The Effects of 10 Communication Modes on the Behavior of Teams During Co-operative Problem-Solving." International Journal of Man-Machine Studies 6: 579-619.

Oliver, Paul. 1978. "Examining Programming Costs." Computer Decisions 10 (April): 50-52.

O'Toole, Raymond J. W., and O'Toole, Edward F. 1966. "Top Executive Involvement in the EDP Function." Management Controls 13 (June): 125.

Pathak, D. S., and Burton, G. E. 1976. "Shifting to the Human Side." Data Management 14 (December): 20-24.

Phillips, J. Donald, and Boockholdt, J. L. 1977. "Mini Systems for Mini Businesses." Journal of Systems Management 28 (May): 28-31.

PoKempner, Stanley J. 1973. "Management Information Systems—A Pragmatic Survey." The Conference Board Record 10 (May): 49-54.

Powers, Richard F., and Dickson, Gary W. 1973. "MIS Project Management: Myths, Opinions and Reality." California Management Review 15 (Spring): 147-56.

Price, James L. 1968. Organizational Effectiveness: An Inventory of Propositions. Homewood, Ill.: R. D. Irwin.

Putnam, Lawrence H. 1978. "A General Empirical Solution to the Macro Software Sizing and Estimating Problem." IEEE Transactions on Software Engineering SE-4 (July): 345-61.

Ramsgard, William L. 1974. "The Systems Analyst: Doctor of Business." Journal of Systems Management 25 (July): 8-13.

Ransdell, William H. 1975. "Managing the People Who Manage the Computer." Journal of Systems Management 26 (September): 18-21.

Remington Rand Univac. (n.d.) "Conversion Planning Manual."

Render, Barry, and Stair, Ralph M. 1977. "Management Science and the Small Business." Journal of Systems Management 28 (March): 20-22.

Render, Barry, and Villere, Maurice F. 1977. "Games Systems People Play." Journal of Systems Management 28 (May): 18-21.

Roark, Mayford L. 1976. "Information System Education: What Industry Thinks." Data Management 14 (June): 24-28.

_____. 1970. In Proceedings of the Second Annual Conference. Chicago: Society for Management Information Systems.

Robey, Daniel, and Zeller, Richard L. 1978. "Factors Affecting the Success and Failure of an Information System for Product Quality." Interfaces 8 (February): 70-75.

Rolefson, Jerome F. 1978. "Project Management—Six Critical Steps." Journal of Systems Management 29 (April): 10-17.

Ross, Ronald G. 1976. "Placing the DBA." Journal of Systems Management 27 (May): 25-33.

Rubenstein, A. H.; Radnor, M.; Baker, N. R.; Heiman, D. R.; and McColly, J. B. 1967. "Some Organizational Factors Related to the Effectiveness of Management Science Groups in Industry." Management Science 13 (April): B508-18.

Rue, Joseph. 1976. "Power, Politics, and DP." Datamation 22 (December): 50-59.

Sackman, H. 1971. "Experimental Analysis of Human Behavior in Time Sharing and Batch Processing Information Systems." In Management Information Systems: Progress and Perspectives, edited by C. H. Kriebel, R. L. Van Horn, and T. J. Heames. Pittsburgh: Carnegie Press.

Sass, C. J. 1975. "MIS—Are You Missing the Plane?" Infosystems 22 (March): 50-51.

Scamell, Richard W., and Baugh, Eddie W. 1975. "Team Approach to System Analysis." Journal of Systems Management 26 (April): 32-35.

Schaffir, Kurt H. 1974. "Marketing Information Systems." Management Informatics 3 (February): 29-36.

Schatzoff, M.; Tsao, R.; and Wiig, R. 1967. "An Experimental Comparison of Time Sharing and Batch Processing." Communications of the ACM 10 (May): 261-65.

Schein, Edgar H. 1964. "The Mechanism of Change." In Interpersonal Dynamics, edited by Warren G. Bennis, Edgar H. Schein, David E. Berlew, and Fred I. Steele, pp. 362-78. Homewood, Ill.: Dorsey.

Schneidewind, Norman, Jr. 1967. "The Practice of Computer Selection." Datamation 13 (February): 22-25.

Schroeder, Roger G., and Benbasat, Izak. 1975. "An Experimental Evaluation of The Relationship of Uncertainty in The Environment to Information Used by Decision Makers." Decision Sciences 6 (July): 556-67.

Schulman, Edward L., and Weinberg, Gerald M. 1973. "Training Programmers for Diverse Goals." Data Base 5 (Winter): 16-21.

Schultz, Randall L., and Slevin, Dennis P., eds. 1975a. Implementing Operations Research/Management Science. New York: American Elsevier.

_____. 1975b. "Implementation and Organizational Validity: An Empirical Investigation." In Implementing Operations Research/ Management Science, edited by Randall L. Schultz and Dennis P. Slevin, pp. 153-82. New York: American Elsevier.

Schwartz, M. K. 1970. "MIS Planning." Datamation 16 (September): 28-31.

_____. 1969. "Computer Project Selection in the Business Enterprise." Datamation 15 (June): 47-52.

Seaberg, Ronald A., and Seaberg, Charlotte. 1973. "Computer Based Decision Systems in Xerox Corporate Planning." Management Science 20 (December): 575-84.

Seib, Richard. 1978. "DP Facilities Structure Should Look Like Your Organization." Journal of Systems Management 29 (October): 26-27.

Senn, James A., and Dickson, Gary W. 1974. "Information System Structure and Purchasing Decision Effectiveness." Journal of Purchasing 10 (August): 52-64.

Severance, Dennis G. (n.d.) "The Evaluation of Data Structures in Data Base System Design." Working paper, Cornell University.

Severino, Elizabeth. 1978. "Going Distributed? Integrate Data Bases to Avoid Failure." Data Management 16 (March): 12-16.

Shafto, Robert A. 1976. "Planning for Planning." In Proceedings of the Eighth Annual Conference, pp. 71-73. Chicago: Society for Management Information Systems.

Shaw, John. 1976. "Why do Systems Fail—Part I." In Proceedings of the Eighth Annual Conference, pp. 49-50. Chicago: Society for Management Information Systems.

Shidal, Jerry G. 1978. "Long-Range DP Plan." Journal of Systems Management 29 (April): 40-45.

Shio, Martin J. 1977. "New Look at MIS." Journal of Systems Management 28 (May): 38-40.

Shults, Eugene, C. and Bruun, Roy J. 1974. "The Hard Road to MIS Success." Infosystems 21 (May): 68-71 and (June): 46-48.

Sibley, Edgar H. 1977. "The Impact of Data Base Technology on Business Systems." In Information Processing 77, edited by Bruce Gilchrist, pp. 589-96. Amsterdam: North-Holland.

Sihler, William H. 1971. "Toward Better Management Control Systems." California Management Review 14 (Winter): 33-39.

Simon, Herbert A. 1977. The New Science of Management Decision, rev. ed. Englewood Cliffs, N.J.: Prentice-Hall.

_____. 1969. The Sciences of the Artificial. Cambridge, Mass.: M.I.T. Press.

Singer, J. Peter. 1969. "Computer-Based Hospital Information Systems." Datamation 15 (May): 38-45.

Smith, C. Peter. 1977. "Resolving User/System Differences." Journal of Systems Management 28 (July): 16-21.

Smith, Lyle B. 1967. "A Comparison of Batch Processing and Instant Turnaround." Communications of the ACM 10 (August): 495-500.

Smith, Walton E. 1977. "Centralization vs. Decentralization." Data Management 15 (January): 24-25.

Soden, V., and Tucker, Charles C. 1976. "Long-Range MIS Planning." Journal of Systems Management 27 (July): 28-33.

Solomon, Martin B. 1970. "Economies of Scale and Computer Personnel." Datamation 16 (March): 107-10.

Sorensen, Richard E., and Zand, Dale E. 1975. "Improving the Implementation of OR/MS Models by Applying the Lewin-Schein Theory of Change." In Implementing Operations Research/Management Science, edited by Randall L. Schultz and Dennis P. Slevin, pp. 217-36. New York: American Elsevier.

Souder, W. E.; Maher, P. M.; Baker, N. R.; Shumway, C. R.; and Rubenstein, A. H. 1975. "An Organizational Intervention

Approach to the Design and Implementation of R & D Project Selection Models." In Implementing Operations Research/ Management Science, edited by Randall L. Schultz and Dennis P. Slevin, pp. 133-52. New York: American Elsevier.

Spaniol, Roland, and Smith, Eugene. 1976. "The DP Professional and Education: Preliminary Survey Results." Data Management 14 (August): 30-31.

Sperry Rand Corp. 1958. "Administrative Planning for Business Data Automation."

Sprague, R. H., Jr., and Watson, H. J. 1975. "MIS Concepts." Journal of Systems Management 26 (January): 34-37 and (February): 35-40.

Srinivasan, C. A., and Dascher, Paul E. 1977. "Information System Design: User Psychology Considerations." MSU Business Topics 25 (Winter): 51-57.

Strassman, Paul A. 1976. "The Future Direction of Information Services to Impact the Bottom Line." In Proceedings of the Eighth Annual Conference, pp. 37-46. Chicago: Society for Management Information Systems.

Stuart, W. F., Jr. 1968. "An Experiment in Data Processing Management." Datamation 14 (June): 64-65.

Swanson, E. Burton. 1974. "Management Information Systems: Appreciation and Involvement." Management Science 21 (October): 178-88.

Thompson J. 1962. "Organizational and Output Transactions." American Journal of Sociology 68: 309-24.

Townsend, Robert. 1970. Up the Organization. New York: Alfred A. Knopf.

Turing, A. M. 1950. "Computing Machinery and Intelligence." Mind 59 (October): 433-60.

United States Bureau of Labor Statistics Bulletin 1276.

United States Department of Labor. 1959. "Occupations in Electronic Data Processing Systems." Washington, D.C.

Van Horn, R. L. 1973. "Empirical Studies of MIS." Data Base 5 (Winter): 172-80.

Vazsonyi, Andrew. 1973. "Information Systems in Management Science." Interfaces 3 (May): 30-33.

Vertinsky, Ilan; Barth, Richard J.; and Mitchell, Vance F. 1975. "A Study of OR/MS Implementation as a Social Change Process." In Implementing Operations Research/Management Science, edited by Randall L. Schultz and Dennis P. Slevin, pp. 253-72. New York: American Elsevier.

Walsh, Myles E. 1978. "MIS—Where Are We, How Did We Get Here and Where Are We Going." Journal of Systems Management 29 (November): 6-21.

Watson, Hugh J.; Sprague, Ralph H., Jr.; and Kroeber, Donald W. 1977. "Computer Technology and Information System Performance." MSU Business Topics 25 (Summer): 17-24.

West, G. M. 1975. "MIS in Small Companies." Journal of Systems Management 4 (April): 10-13.

Wetherbe, J. C., and Dock, V. T. 1976. "Breaking the Description Dilemma; Personnel Selection by Group Analysis." Data Management 14 (December): 16-19, 42.

Wetherbe, J. C., and Whitehead, C. J. 1977. "A Contingency View of Managing the Data Processing Organization." MIS Quarterly 1 (April): 19-25.

Whisler, Thomas L. 1970. The Impact of Computers on Organizations. New York: Praeger.

Willoughby, Theodore C. 1972. "Staffing the MIS Function." Computing Surveys 4 (December): 241-59.

Willoughby, Theodore C., and Pye, Richard A. 1977. "Top Management's Computer Role." Journal of Systems Management 28 (September): 10-13.

Wilson, W. R. 1976. "Requirements for the Survival of the Future Information Executive." In Proceedings of the Eighth Annual Conference, pp. 7-9. Chicago: Society for Management Information Systems.

Wimbrow, J. K. 1971. "A Large-Scale Interactive Administrative System." IBM Systems Journal 10: 260-82.

Wofsey, Marvin M. 1968. Management of Automatic Data Processing. Washington, D.C.: Thompson.

Wynne, Bayard E., and Dickson, Gary W. 1975. "Experienced Managers' Performance in Experimental Man-Machine Decision System Simulation." Academy of Management Journal 18 (March): 25-40.

Yasaki, E. E., Sr. 1977. "The Many Faces of the DBA." Datamation 23 (May): 75-79.

Young, Lawrence F. 1978. "In-Company User Training." Journal of Systems Management 29 (May): 28-31.

Zachman, John A. 1977. "Control and Planning of Information Systems." Journal of Systems Management 28 (July): 34-41.

Zani, William M. 1970. "Blueprint for MIS." Harvard Business Review 48 (November-December): 95-100.

# AUTHOR INDEX

# SUBJECT INDEX

# ABOUT THE AUTHORS

PHILLIP EIN-DOR is a senior lecturer and chairman, Information Systems Program in the Faculty of Management, Tel-Aviv University, Tel-Aviv, Israel. He received his Ph.D. and M.Sc. from Carnegie-Mellon University, and a B.A. from Hebrew University of Jerusalem. He has published extensively in the areas of management information systems and computer system management, and coauthored a textbook, Managing Management Information Systems.

ELI SEGEV is a senior lecturer in the Faculty of Management, Tel-Aviv University. He received the D.B.A. from Harvard Business School, M.B.A. from Tel-Aviv University, and B.Sc. from Technion, Israel Institute of Technology. He has coauthored Managing Management Information Systems, and published extensively on strategic decision making, management use of information, and management information systems.